THE
POULETTS
OF HINTON
ST GEORGE

THE
POULETTS
OF HINTON
ST GEORGE

The Story of a Somerset Village and its First Family

COLIN G. WINN

ALAN SUTTON PUBLISHING LIMITED

First published in the United Kingdom in 1995 by
Alan Sutton Publishing Ltd · Phoenix Mill · Far Thrupp · Stroud · Glos

British Library Cataloguing in Publication Data

A catalogue record for this book is available from the British Library.

ISBN 0–7509–1069–0

Typesetting and origination by
Alan Sutton Publishing Limited.
Printed in Great Britain by
WBC, Bridgend, Mid Glam.

Contents

List of Illustrations

To the Memory of
MY MOTHER, LUCIA WINN
who first brought me to Hinton St George

As o'er the hill with waving timber crown'd
In yonder drove, beneath an ash I lay;
Where bloom'd the hawthorn with its snow-white may;
And gilt-cups deck'd the grassy ground;
While merry hinds within the fields around,
A-singing, ended some enliv'ning lay;
I heard a waterfall, so far away
That stillness only brought its sullen sound;

And thought in silence, O thou peaceful place;
I would that summer weather could but last;
And, in this northern land, the lovely face
Of Nature could withstand the winter's blast;
And I, from all my worldly cares set free,
Could have, awhile, a happy home in thee.

'Rural Seclusion'
William Barnes

Acknowledgements

As in the previous edition I have many people to thank for their help and encouragement with this present work. I am greatly indebted to Keith Beers of Hinton House for all his help and encouragement. He has read and corrected the revised text at all stages and has allowed me access to the material he has collected in the Hinton House Museum.

I extend many grateful thanks to Jane and John Penoyre of the Somerset and South Avon Vernacular Building Research Group for allowing me access to their Architectural Study of Hinton House, and for their assistance with the description and history of the mansion. This enabled me to enlarge upon my own original account of the development of the house.

Thanks to Anton Bantock whose work on the Smyths of Ashton Court I have quoted from extensively, and with whom I had a long correspondence.

I acknowledge with thanks the help given by Mrs Marian Harding of the National Army Museum; Miss Jill Springhill of the National Portrait Gallery; and Mrs Elaine Hart of the *Illustrated London News* Picture Library.

Thanks to the Reverend John King for his help with aspects of the Poulett chapels; to Julian Litton who carried out the surveys of the Poulett vaults; to Colonel Charles Lane for information on the paintings of Harry Hall; to Andrew Ford of F.T. Enterprises for producing the Family Tree; and to Janet Blower for retyping much of my manuscript.

Thanks are due once more to Frederick James, who sadly is no longer with us. His wealth of memories of Hinton House and the Poulett family have enabled me to extend the story of the 8th Earl, his family and his former home.

Thanks are also due to the late Mrs Betty Cruse (nee Tozer) who gave me the copy of the Hinton children's 'Song of Welcome', printed here for the first time. It was Betty who as a child presented the new Countess with her bouquet in 1906! Also to the late Lady Bridgett Poulett-Robledo with whom I corresponded and from whose letters I quote.

Finally I extend my thanks to anyone whose name I have not mentioned who has helped in any way or shown interest and has thus encouraged me to bring my book to light again.

Photographic Credits

All photographs of the exterior and interior of Hinton House, the portrait of Sir Amias Paulet, the interior of the church and the Poulett monuments are reproduced by permission of the National Monuments Record under RCHME Crown copyright. The portrait of Sir Anthony Paulet by permission of the Societe Jersiaise, the 8th Earl by the National Portrait Gallery, and those of Lady Bridgett Poulett and Oriel Ross by the *Illustrated London News* Picture Library. The remainder of the illustrations are from the author's own collection.

Prologue to the Second Edition

'To save and recover somewhat from the deluge of Time'

Francis Bacon

It is almost twenty years since *The Pouletts of Hinton St George* was first written and published, soon after Hinton House was sold and vacated by the Poulett family. Since then much change has taken place. Hinton House has celebrated its 500th anniversary after much alteration and restoration by a caring group of private owners who now live in the mansion. An architectural survey and an archaeological study have enabled much of the development of the house to be documented and has pinpointed the historical fabric that remains. Happily the adaptation of Hinton House for multiple occupation has resulted in very little change to the exterior of the house and little to the interior of the State Rooms. Hinton House is now listed as a Grade IIa historic building, the highest rating it seems for a building in multiple ownership. With the present level of care and maintenance given by the owners to the grounds, the trees and the building itself, Hinton House is once again a mansion in which the village can take pride.

A museum with archives and artifacts of the history of the Pouletts, Hinton House and the village of Hinton St George has been established in the House, where scholars and the merely curious can study the Pouletts in the context of their former seat. Now too, with the grounds and Grand Saloon of the State Apartments being made available for the Village Fete, the Horticultural Show and the Gardens Open Weekend etc., and with frequent visits to the museum by villagers, students from local schools, and other visitors, the historic close relationship between House and village has been re-established. Hinton House is being featured in guide books and in books on great country houses, a recognition long denied by a strictly reclusive ownership and a steady deterioration of the fabric.

Because over the last two hundred years, the Pouletts have played little part in national affairs, it is easy for the reader and indeed for the author to lose sight of the importance of these Pouletts of Hinton St George. But in their time they were a very important family indeed.

In the fifteenth and sixteenth centuries members of the family served as Sheriffs of Somerset no less than eight times, and acted as magistrates and justices, while they virtually ruled the island of Jersey as Governors for fifty years. In the seventeenth century the first Baron Poulett became one of the only two peers in Somerset for his service to King Charles I. He also served in Parliament and acted as Sheriff, eventually becoming a Deputy Lord Lieutenant of the County, wielding power there on behalf of the King. In the eighteenth century, under Queen Anne, the 1st Earl Poulett became virtually Prime Minister of the country by his appointment as First Lord of the Treasury. Successive Earls served as Lords Lieutenant of Devon, Dorset and Somerset and held posts at Court as Lords of the Bedchamber while continuing to serve in Parliament and the House of Lords.

The Pouletts were hosts at Hinton House for their monarchs on several occasions, entertaining Charles I, Charles II and William III. They were on close terms with Queen Anne, George II and his family (also entertaining Prince Adolphus at Hinton House), George

IV and William IV. They were steadfast in their duty to country and Crown and skilled but honourable when it came to making difficult decisions conflicting with their duty and conscience. This is well illustrated by the stand made by Sir Amias Paulet when, in spite of his stern and often harsh treatment of Mary, Queen of Scots, he refused to carry out her secret execution although ordered to do so by Queen Elizabeth, and risked both his life and lands by his refusal.

In a society where not only power but survival often depended on friendship and relationships with other powerful families, the Pouletts forged ties through marriage with the Earl of Pembroke, the Lord Lieutenant of Somerset; and Baron Fairfax, the important Parliamentarian at the time of the Civil Wars. As well as links with the Marquess of Winchester and the Duke of Bolton, marriage also joined them with Baron Rycote and the Earl of Lindsey, and later with the Earl of Morley and the Duke of Beaufort.

The Pouletts can be regarded as trend-setters, at least in the West Country away from fashionable London. Sir Amias was greatly exposed to new ideas, first as Ambassador to France in the 1570s and later as Keeper of Mary, Queen of Scots at various locations. Visitors to Hinton were impressed by what they found. Cosmo III, Grand Duke of Tuscany, at Hinton in 1669 not only saw and marvelled at Hinton House with its rooms 'noble, fine and spacious', but also the grounds with the parterre, vast lawns and the fine park which would seem to have anticipated by almost a hundred years the informal 'naturalized landscapes' popularized later by William Kent and Lancelot 'Capability' Brown.

Hinton House has had work carried out by many well known architects including Sir John Soane, Matthew Brettingham, James Wyatt and Jeffrey Wyatville, while William Kent made plans and designs for the Park. Inigo Jones was not involved as has often been alleged, although the Palladian south front dating from the 1630s is in his style. In the nineteenth century the house was brought up to date again with the latest Georgian and neo-Gothic styles.

The Pouletts were feudal lords who at one time owned over 13,000 acres with fifty individual farms, and controlled the lives of everyone for several miles in every direction from Hinton St George. As Sheriffs and magistrates they had the responsibility for judgements and sentencing, including the time when the future Cardinal Wolsey was put in the stocks. Equally importantly, they had the power to survive the future consequences. This power to survive saw them through the rigours of the Civil War, until the Restoration and better times arrived. They also survived the financial crisis of the 1890s.

They were collectors and connoisseurs and created an art collection containing at one time nearly 600 paintings and drawings including works by Van Dyck, Rembrandt, Holbein, Murillo, Reubens, Watteau, Romney, Hogarth and others. There was furniture by Lock, Wyatt, Kent and Goodison; Brussels and Antwerp tapestries, and the famous Romanelli Cartoons.

In spite of continuing to exercise their feudal powers at home by closing their park or cutting off the water supply from Hinton St George at will, they were still considered 'fair and honest' by their tenants, whose lasting respect and affection had led them to harness themselves to his Lordship's car and draw it through the streets of the village at the 1908 celebrations of the wedding of the 7th Earl.

The interest in the Poulett family and their home continues and it is in this context, and with new information that time and additional research has disclosed, that I have been urged and encouraged to revise and extend the material for this second edition.

Colin G. Winn
Winchester 1995

Prologue to the First Edition

Hinton House is a dreary spot
Hinton House will be forgot
Here and there a shady tree
And Hinton House will cease to be.

Old saying from Hinton St George.

For the benefit of the stranger, Hinton St George is a village and parish in the extreme south of Somerset, some three miles north-west of the small town of Crewkerne which lies on the main A30 road. Hinton is a place of considerable charm and beauty, with a notable fifteenth-century church, a village cross, and a wide main street with stone and thatched houses of various periods. To the south-west stands the great mansion of the Earls Poulett, Hinton House and its extensive park.

I have commenced this prologue with the four lines of an old verse handed down from father to son at Hinton St George. It is precisely so that Hinton House shall not be 'forgot' that this book has been compiled. Indeed the verse very nearly did come true. The Poulett family that owned Hinton House for 500 years left it, and after the estate was sold, a great many trees in the park were ruthlessly cut down leaving just 'here and there a shady tree.' It was said at that time that the mansion itself was in very real danger of being demolished, but after some timely restoration work, this was happily averted.

What then of the family that lived there, these Pouletts of Hinton St George? What part did they play in the history of the country and in their village? In this book I have attempted to answer these questions and to fill a gap in the knowledge of local history. I first decided to delve into the story of the Poulett family at the time when the mansion was being sold, along with its historic contents, in 1968. I remember thinking that after 500 years, so much history and tradition were being dispersed, and that soon, all would be forgotten. I felt then that I wanted to find out what I could about the family that had lived in this huge house for so long, in the village where I myself had grown up.

This book then is the result. The Poulett family may not have played a great part in the history of the nation, and their story appears for the most part one of duty and responsibility fulfilled, and of continued allegiance to King and Country. As landlords they had been widely respected, and as far as Hinton St George was concerned, held in great affection. After the last war it is true to say that attitudes in this respect changed generally, as they did in Hinton also. There can be few great estates remaining today in England where the tenantry look to the Lord of the Manor for their livelihood, and where they do, they are indeed something of an anachronism in these days of affluence and independence. As the estate at Hinton dwindled so did the power and influence of the Poulett family. With this dwindling of power and influence, so too, declined the feelings and concern that Hinton had felt for the family. The *raison d'etre* for Hinton House had quite disappeared by the 1960s and this must have influenced Earl Poulett's decision to sell the remainder of his estate and his old home and retire to Jersey.

On 1 March 1973 the eighth and last Earl Poulett died, and a few days later he was laid to rest with his ancestors in the family vault in Hinton St George church. With his passing ended the 500-year-old link with the village. In the words of a much used cliché it was truly the end of an era. There was very little ceremony at his funeral and none of the pomp and pageantry that had attended the comings and goings of his predecessors.

Many of the older generation who lived during the heyday of the estate sigh for the 'good old days' and maintain they were happy and contented with their small lot, and in 'knowing their place'. A time so different when compared with today's hectic rat-race. Who can say if they are right or wrong? I think they are fortunate to have seen both sides of life.

In my own time I have seen Hinton St George change from a semi-feudal entity to what today seems fast becoming an expensive niche for retirement. Local employment has virtually gone, where once there were some six farms and the Hinton Estate all employing local labour. However, such alteration is not confined to this one village. It is part of the changing pattern of social life all over the country.

Since commencing this work I have found that there is a great deal of interest in the Poulett family and Hinton House, and I have received much help and encouragement during my researches.

Colin G. Winn
Winchester, 1976

Pedigree of the Earls Poulett

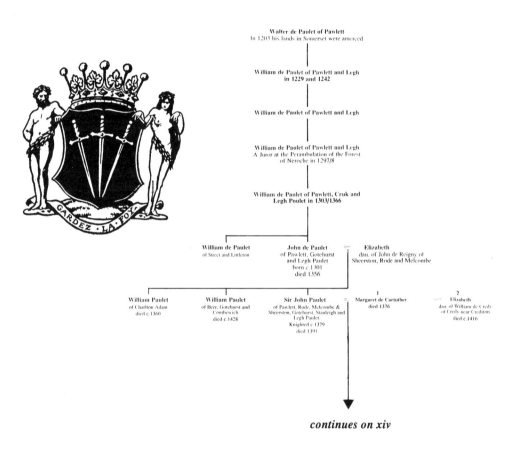

Walter de Paulet of Pawlett
In 1203 his lands in Somerset were amerced

William de Paulet of Pawlett and Legh
in 1229 and 1242

William de Paulet of Pawlett and Legh

William de Paulet of Pawlett and Legh
A Juror at the Perambulation of the Forest
of Neroche in 1297/8

**William de Paulet of Pawlett, Cruk and
Legh Poulet in 1303/1366**

William de Paulet
of Street and Littleton

John de Paulet
of Pawlett, Gotehurst
and Legh Paulet
born c.1301
died 1356

Elizabeth
dau. of John de Reigny of
Sheerston, Rode and Melcombe

William Paulet
of Charlton Adam
died c.1360

William Paulet
of Beer, Gotehurst and
Combewich
died c.1428

Sir John Paulet
of Pawlett, Rode, Melcombe &
Sheerston, Gotehurst, Stauleigh and
Legh Paulet.
Knighted c.1379
died 1391

1
Margaret de Cartuther
died 1376

2
Elizabeth
dau. of William de Credy
of Credy near Crediton
died c.1416

continues on xiv

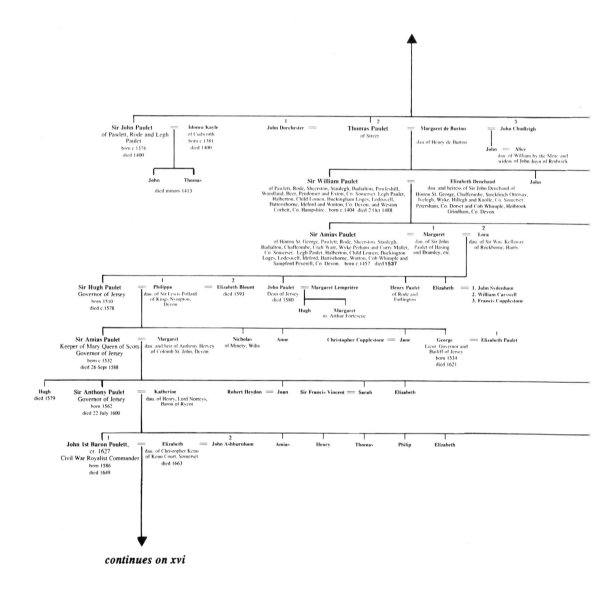

Sir John Paulet == Idonea Kayle
of Pawlett, Rode and Legh   of Cudworth
Paulet   born c.1381
born c.1376   died 1400
died 1400

1
John Dorchester ==

2
Thomas Paulet == Margaret de Burton
of Street   dau of Henry de Burton

3
John Chudleigh

John == Alice
dau. of William by the More and
widow of John Juyn of Rodwick

John   Thomas
died minors 1413

Sir William Paulet == Elizabeth Denebaud
of Pawlett, Rode, Sheerston, Stanlegh, Badialton, Powleshill,   dau. and heiress of Sir John Denebaud of
Woodland, Beer, Pendomer and Exton, Co. Somerset. Legh Paulet,   Hinton St. George, Chaffcombe, Stocklinch Ottersay,
Halberton, Child Lomen, Buckingham Loges, Lodiswell,   Ivelegh, Wyke, Hillegh and Knolle, Co. Somerset.
Battersthorne, Ideford and Wotton, Co. Devon, and Weston   Petersham, Co. Dorset and Cob Whimple, Holbrook
Corbett, Co. Hampshire. born c.1404 died 2 Oct 1488   Grindham, Co. Devon.

John

Sir Amias Paulet == Margaret   == Lora
of Hinton St. George, Pawlett, Rode, Sheerston, Stanlegh,   dau. of Sir John   dau. of Sir Wm. Kellaway
Badialton, Chaffcombe, Craft Warr, Wyke Perham and Curry Mallet,   Paulet of Basing   of Rockborne, Hants.
Co. Somerset. Legh Paulet, Halberton, Child Lomen, Buckington   and Bramley, etc.
Loges, Lodeswell, Ideford, Battisthorne, Wotton, Cob Whimple and
Sampford Peverell, Co. Devon. born c.1457 died 1537

1
Sir Hugh Paulet == Philippa   == Elizabeth Blount
Governor of Jersey   dau. of Sir Lewis Pollard   died 1593
born 1510   of Kings Nympton,
died c.1578   Devon.

2

John Paulet == Margaret Lemprière
Dean of Jersey
died 1580

Henry Paulet
of Rode and
Earlington

Elizabeth == 1. John Sydenham
            2. William Carswell
            3. Francis Copplestone

Hugh   Margaret
            m. Arthur Fortescue

Sir Amias Paulet == Margaret
Keeper of Mary Queen of Scots   dau. and heir of Anthony Hervey
Governor of Jersey   of Colomb St. John, Devon
born c.1532
died 26 Sept 1588

Nicholas
of Mincty, Wilts

Anne

Christopher Copplestone == Jane

George == Elizabeth Paulet
Lieut. Governor and
Bailiff of Jersey
born 1534
died 1621

1

Hugh
died 1579

Sir Anthony Paulet == Katherine
Governor of Jersey   dau. of Henry, Lord Norreys,
born 1562   Baron of Rycot
died 22 July 1600

Robert Heydon == Joan   Sir Francis Vincent == Sarah   Elizabeth

1
John 1st Baron Poulett, == Elizabeth   == John Ashburnham
cr. 1627   dau. of Christopher Kenn
Civil War Royalist Commander   of Kenn Court, Somerset
born 1586   died 1663
died 1649

2

Amias   Henry   Thomas   Philip   Elizabeth

continues on xvi

xiv

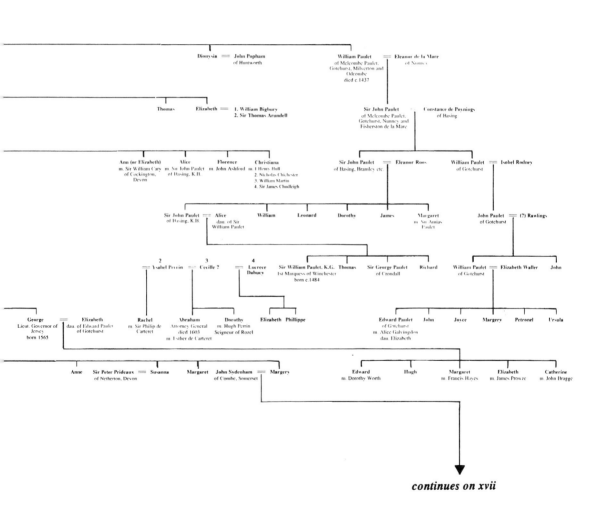

continues on xvii

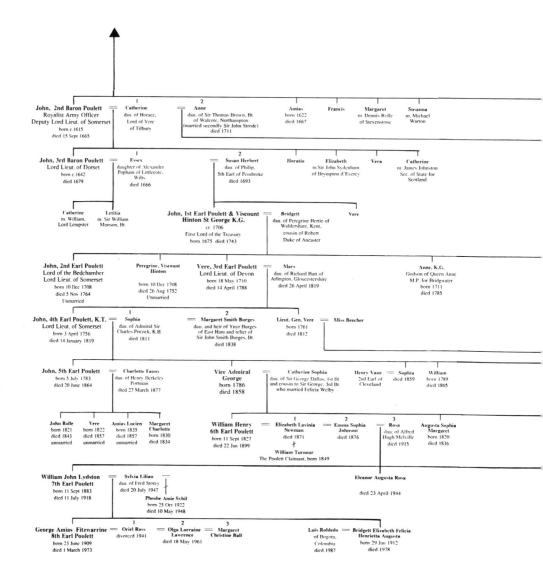

John, 2nd Baron Poulett = ¹ **Catherine** ‖ ² **Anne** | **Amias** | **Francis** | **Margaret** | **Susanna**
Royalist Army Officer | dau. of Horace, | dau. of Sir Thomas Brown, Bt. | born 1622 | | m. Dennis Rolle | m. Michael
Deputy Lord Lieut. of Somerset | Lord of Vere | of Walcote, Northampton | died 1667 | | of Stevenstone | Warton
born c.1615 | of Tilbury | (married secondly Sir John Strode)
died 15 Sept 1665 | | died 1711

John, 3rd Baron Poulett = ¹ **Essex** ‖ ² **Susan Herbert** | **Horatio** | **Elizabeth** | **Vere** | **Catherine**
Lord Lieut. of Dorset | daughter of Alexander | dau. of Philip, | | m Sir John Sydenham | | m. James Johnston
born c.1642 | Popham of Littlecote, | 5th Earl of Pembroke | | of Brympton d'Evercy | | Sec. of State for
died 1679 | Wilts. | died 1693 | | | | Scotland
| died 1666

Catherine | **Letitia** | **John, 1st Earl Poulett & Viscount** = **Bridgett** | **Vere**
m. William, | m. Sir William | **Hinton St George K.G.** | dau. of Peregrine Bertie of
Lord Lempster | Monson, Bt | cr. 1706 | Waldershare, Kent,
| | First Lord of the Treasury | cousin of Robert
| | born 1675 died 1743 | Duke of Ancaster

John, 2nd Earl Poulett | **Peregrine, Viscount** | **Vere, 3rd Earl Poulett** = **Mary** | **Anne, K.G.**
Lord of the Bedchamber | **Hinton** | Lord Lieut. of Devon | dau. of Richard Butt of | Godson of Queen Anne
Lord Lieut. of Somerset | | born 18 May 1710 | Arlington, Gloucestershire | M.P. for Bridgwater
born 10 Dec 1708 | born 10 Dec 1708 | died 14 April 1788 | died 26 April 1819 | born 1711
died 5 Nov 1764 | died 26 Aug 1752 | | | died 1785
Unmarried | Unmarried

John, 4th Earl Poulett, K.T. = ¹ **Sophia** | ² **Margaret Smith Burges** | **Lieut. Gen. Vere** = **Miss Beecher**
Lord Lieut. of Somerset | dau. of Admiral Sir | dau. and heir of Ynyr Burges | born 1761
born 3 April 1756 | Charles Pocock, K.B. | of East Ham and relict of | died 1812
died 14 January 1819 | died 1811 | Sir John Smith Burges, Bt.
| | died 1838

John, 5th Earl Poulett = **Charlotte Fanus** | **Vice Admiral** = **Catherine Sophia** | **Henry Vane** = **Sophia** | **William**
born 5 July 1783 | dau. of Henry Berkeley | **George** | dau. of Sir George Dallas, 1st Bt. | 2nd Earl of | died 1859 | born 1789
died 20 June 1864 | Portman | born 1786 | and cousin to Sir George, 3rd Bt. | Cleveland | | died 1805
| died 27 March 1877 | died 1858 | who married Felicia Welby

John Rolle | **Vere** | **Amias Lucien** | **Margaret** | **William Henry** | ¹ **Elizabeth Lavinia** | ² **Emma Sophia** | ³ **Rosa** | **Augusta Sophia**
born 1821 | born 1822 | born 1835 | **Charlotte** | **6th Earl Poulett** | **Newman** | **Johnson** | dau. of Alfred | **Margaret**
died 1843 | died 1857 | died 1857 | born 1830 | born 11 Sept 1827 | died 1871 | died 1876 | Hugh Melville | born 1820
unmarried | unmarried | unmarried | died 1834 | died 22 Jan 1899 | | | died 1915 | died 1836
| | | | | **William Turnour**
| | | | | The Poulett Claimant, born 1849

William John Lydston = **Sylvia Lilian** | **Eleanor Augusta Rosa**
7th Earl Poulett | dau. of Fred Storey
born 11 Sept 1883 | died 20 July 1947 | died 23 April 1944
died 11 July 1918 |
| **Phoebe Amie Sybil**
| born 25 Oct 1922
| died 10 May 1948

George Amias Fitzwarrine = ¹ **Oriel Ross** | ² **Olga Lorraine** = ³ **Margaret** | **Luis Robledo** = **Bridgett Elizabeth Felicia**
8th Earl Poulett | divorced 1941 | **Lawrence** | **Christine Ball** | of Bogota, | **Henrietta Augusta**
born 23 June 1909 | | died 18 May 1961 | | Colombia | born 29 Jan 1912
died 1 March 1973 | | | | died 1987 | died 1978

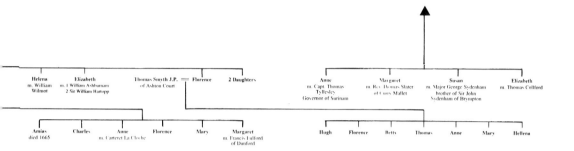

| Helena
m. William
Wilmot | Elizabeth
m. 1 William Ashburnam
2 Sir William Hartopp | Thomas Smyth J.P.
of Ashton Court | Florence | 2 Daughters | | Anne
m. Capt. Thomas
Tyllesley
Governor of Surinam | Margaret
m. Rev. Thomas Slater
of Currs Mallet | Susan
m. Major George Sydenham
brother of Sir John
Sydenham of Brympton | Elizabeth
m. Thomas Collford |

| Amias
died 1665 | Charles | Anne
m. Carteret La Cloche | Florence | Mary | Margaret
m. Francis Fulford
of Dunford | | Hugh | Florence | Betts | Thomas | Anne | Mary | Hellena |

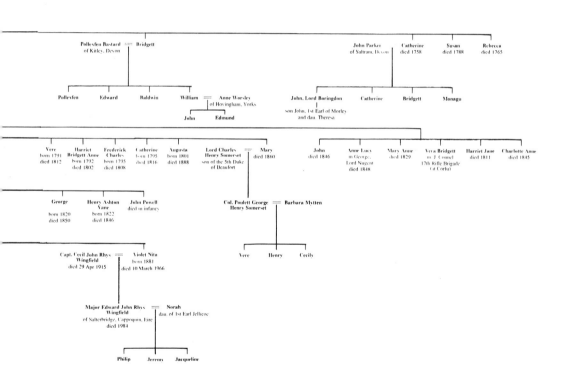

| Pollexfen Bastard
of Kitley, Devon | Bridgett | | John Parker
of Saltram, Devon | Catherine
died 1758 | Susan
died 1788 | Rebecca
died 1765 |

| Pollexfen | Edward | Baldwin | William | Anne Worsley
of Hovingham, Yorks | John, Lord Boringdon
son John, 1st Earl of Morley
and dau. Theresa | Catherine | Bridgett | Monagu |

John   Edmund

| Vere
born 1791
died 1812 | Harriet
Bridgett Anne
born 1792
died 1802 | Frederick
Charles
born 1795
died 1808 | Catherine
born 1795
died 1816 | Augusta
born 1801
died 1888 | Lord Charles
Henry Somerset
son of the 5th Duke
of Beaufort | Mary
died 1860 | John
died 1846 | Anne Lucy
m. George,
Lord Nugent
died 1848 | Mary Anne
died 1829 | Vera Bridgett
m. J. Connel
17th Rifle Brigade
(in Corfu) | Harriet Jane
died 1811 | Charlotte Anne
died 1845 |

| George
born 1820
died 1850 | Henry Ashton
Vane
born 1822
died 1846 | John Powell
died in infancy | Col. Poulett George
Henry Somerset | Barbara Mytten |

| Capt. Cecil John Rhys
Wingfield
died 29 Apr 1915 | Violet Nita
born 1881
died 10 March 1966 | Vere | Henry | Cecily |

| Major Edward John Rhys
Wingfield
of Salterbridge, Cappoquin, Eire
died 1984 | Norah
dau. of 1st Earl Jellicoe |

Philip   Jeremy   Jacqueline

The Line of Descent of the Pouletts of Hinton St George, 1430–1973

Sir William Paulet (1404–1488) m. 1430 Elizabeth Denebaud
   succeeded by his son
Sir Amias Paulet (1457–1537) m. (2nd) Lora Kellaway
   succeeded by his son
Sir Hugh Paulet (1510–1578) m. 1528 Philippa Pollard
   succeeded by his son
Sir Amias Paulet (1532–1588) m. 1557 Margaret Hervey
   succeeded by his son
Sir Anthony Paulet (1562–1600) m. 1583 Katherine Norris
   succeeded by his son
John, 1st Baron Poulett (1586–1649) m. 1613 Elizabeth Kenn
   succeeded by his son
John, 2nd Baron Poulett (1615–1665) m. 1640 Catherine Vere
   succeeded by his son
John, 3rd Baron Poulett (1642–1679) m. (2nd) 1667 Susan Herbert
   succeeded by his son
John, 1st Earl Poulett (1675–1743) m. 1702 Bridgett Bertie
   succeeded by his son
John, 2nd Earl Poulett (1708–1764) unmarried
   succeeded by his brother
Vere, 3rd Earl Poulett (1710–1788) m. 1755 Mary Butt
   succeeded by his son
John, 4th Earl Poulett (1756–1819) m. 1782 Sophia Pocock
   succeeded by his son
John, 5th Earl Poulett (1783–1864) m. 1820 Charlotte Portman
   succeeded by his nephew
William Henry, 6th Earl Poulett (1827–1899) m. (3rd) 1879 Rosa Melville
   succeeded by his son
William John Lydston, 7th Earl Poulett (1883–1918) m. 1908 Sylvia Storey
   succeeded by his son
George Amias Fitzwarrine, 8th Earl Poulett (1909–1973, without heirs) m. (3rd) Christine Ball

CHAPTER I

The Early Pouletts – The Years up to 1600

From Crokehorn by hilly ground but plentiful of
corne grasse and elme wood, scant a 2 miles to
George Henton village, so caullied bycause the
Paroch Chirch there is dedicate to S. George.

Leland

The early beginnings of the village of Hinton St George are lost in antiquity. The name Hinton, George Henton or Hantone as it was variously known formerly, is traced by the *Oxford Dictionary of English Place-Names* to the Old English or Saxon '*Hean Tune*' or '*Hea-tun*' meaning a tun or settlement on a high place or hill top. It was certainly an early English settlement chosen for protection. The Roman invaders would have known it, for a Roman villa was discovered nearby at Dinnington, which was last excavated in 1862. The old Roman road, the Fosseway, runs through the northern part of the parish, and Roman coins and tombstones have been discovered in the locality. Later the manor of Hinton came into Saxon hands. The first historic mention of Hinton is to be found in the Domesday Book (1086) which records that the owner then was one William de Eu (or Ow) who had succeeded a Saxon named Aelfstan of Boscombe in the lordship of a group of Somerset manors. William the Conqueror appropriated many of the estates of the defeated Saxons and distributed them among his principal followers. The Domesday reference to Hinton reads as follows:

William has one manor which is called Henton which Aelfstan held on the day on which King Edward [the Confessor] was alive and dead, and it rendered geld for 13 hides. These, 12 teams can plough. Thence William has 5 hides and 4 teams in demesne and the villeins 8 hides and 10 teams. There William has 16 villeins and 24 bordars and 5 serfs, and 36 animals and 44 swine and 190 sheep, and 2 mills which render 7s. 6d., and woodland one league in length and half [a league] in breadth and 60 acres of meadow, and it is worth £15, and when William received it, it was worth £12.[1]

These were unsettled times and in 1096 William de Eu joined a rebellion against King William Rufus, and was subsequently captured and executed for treason. There were several changes in ownership over the next 150 years. The Powtrell family was the prominent landowner until about 1216. There was a John Powtrell who was succeeded by George. George left the property to his daughter. Her marriage brought it into the Giffard family, through her husband John Giffard. Their daughter married into the Denebaud family, and

---

1. Extract from Folio 428 of the *Liber Exoniensis*.

they remained in ownership of the Hinton estates until about 1429 when the daughter – and sole heir – of the then Sir John Denebaud, Elizabeth, married Sir William Paulet. Thus the estate came into the hands of the Paulet family, whose descendants, the Pouletts, remained at Hinton St George until 1968. Since those days the Paulet family has spread far and wide, and the old surname is found today with a variety of spellings – Poulet, Powlett, Pawlet, Pollet, Paulette, to name but a few.

Who then were the Paulets? Where did they come from? Traditionally it is said that the family originated from France. One story states that about the year 1135 Geoffrey Plantagenet, Count of Anjou and third son of Henry II, landed in England. Among his followers came a knight of Picardy, one Hercules, Lord of Tournon. After the accession of Henry II the services of Hercules of Tournon were rewarded by a grant in Fee of the Lordship of the Manor of Pawlett, a village near Bridgwater in Somerset, where he took up residence and from which he assumed the surname of Poulet or Paulet. This story, however, cannot be traced back farther than the sixteenth century, and was probably the invention of the Elizabethan heralds.

Another source suggests the Paulets are descendants of the Aunou family, who owned Pawlett in the twelfth century. Henry I is said to have granted to Foulque d'Aunou, and his heirs, the manors of Grandson and Pawlett in North Petherton in Somerset. Foulque d'Aunou, who was living in 1124 was said to be descended from Baudri le Teuton, Signeur de Becqueville-en-Caux and Sire de Boquence. Baudri himself is said to have been an illegitimate son of Charles de Cambrai, Duke of Lorraine, the son of Louis IV of France, and was living in 1022. His grandson fought at the Battle of Hastings in 1066. However, there appears to be no documentary evidence to support either the descent of the Aunous from Baudri or Baudri's parentage. Nor is any relationship established between the Paulets and the Aunous. It is more than likely therefore, that the Paulets are an old Anglo Saxon family who lived and farmed in the area and who took their name from Pawlett village.

The first Paulet from whom there is conclusive proof of descent is

1. WILLIAM DE PAULET who held the manor of Legh in Hockworthy, Co. Devon, in 1229, and the same manor with Pawlett, Co. Somerset, each by the service of a ¼ Knight's fee in 1242/3. He may have been the son of Walter de Poulet whose lands were amerced (or fined) in 1203. William de Paulet was followed by his son

2. WILLIAM DE PAULET of Pawlett, Co. Somerset, and Legh, Co. Devon, who was the father of

3. WILLIAM DE PAULET of Pawlett and Legh. He was a juror at the Perambulation of the Forest of Neroche, Co. Somerset, about 1297/8. His son was

4. WILLIAM DE PAULET of Pawlett and Cruk in North Petherton, and Legh Poulet in Hockworthy, Co. Devon. He held Legh by the service of a Knight's fee in 1303, and a moiety of Pawlett in 1366. He had two sons, William Pawlett of Street and Littleton, Co. Somerset, who died without issue, and

5. JOHN DE PAULET of Pawlett, Gotehurst, Co. Somerset, and Legh Poulet, Co. Devon. He was born about 1301 and married Elizabeth, daughter and heir of Sir John de Reigny of Sheerston, Rode and Melcombe, in North Petherton, and Staulegh in Milverton. John and Elizabeth had three sons; two named William and

6. SIR JOHN PAULET of Pawlet, Rode, Melcombe and Sheerston in North Petherton, Gotehurst in Andersfield, and Stauleigh in Milverton, Co. Somerset; and Legh Poulet in Hockworthy, Co. Devon. He was knighted about 1379 for valour in the camp before St Omer, during the Hundred Years War whilst in the Earl of Buckingham's expedition aiding the Duke of Brittany against the French. He succeeded his two brothers who died without issue. Sir

John married twice. His first wife was Margaret de Cartuther who died before 1376. His second wife was Elizabeth, the daughter of William de Credy of Credy near Crediton, Co. Devon. Sir John died in 1391 leaving three sons and a daughter.

7. THOMAS PAULET of Street, Co. Somerset, his second son, became his father's heir. He served with the Earl of Somerset in Picardy in 1404. He married Margaret, daughter and heir of Henry de Burton, about 1404, and they had three sons and a daughter. Margaret de Burton later married John Chudleigh (see chapter 12). The eldest son of Thomas Paulet and Margaret de Burton was

8. SIR WILLIAM PAULET of Pawlett, Rode, Sheerston, Staulegh, Badialton, Powleshill, Woodland, Beer, Pendomer, and Exton, Co. Somerset; Legh Poulet, Halberton, Child Lomen, Buckington Loges, Lodiswell, Battisthorne, Ideford, and Wotton, Co. Devon; and Weston Corbett, Co. Southampton. He was born about 1404 and before 10 June 1429 married Elizabeth, the daughter and heir of Sir John Denebaud of Hinton St George, Chaffcombe, Stocklinch Ottersay, Ivelegh, Wyke, Hilleigh, and Knolle, Co. Somerset; Petersham, Co. Dorset; and Cob Whimple and Holbrook Grindham, Co. Devon. From Sir William and Elizabeth a continuous line of descent can be traced to the 8th Earl Poulett who died in 1973.

Another descendant of these early Paulets is the present Marquess of Winchester.[2] He has a common ancestor with the Pouletts in SIR JOHN PAULET (6) and Elizabeth de Credy. Their third son and the brother of THOMAS PAULET (7) was WILLIAM PAULET of Melcombe Paulet, Gotehurst, Milverton and Odcombe, Co. Somerset. He married Eleanor de la Mare of Nunney Castle near Frome, Somerset. He died about 1437. His son was

SIR JOHN PAULET of Melcombe Paulet, Gotehurst and Nunney. He married Constance, the daughter and co heir of Sir Hugh de Poynings, and heiress of Basing in Hampshire, in about 1428. Their eldest son was

SIR JOHN PAULET of Basing and Nunney Castle and other estates in Hampshire, Somerset, Sussex and Wiltshire. He married Eleanor, daughter and co heir of Sir Robert Roos, in 1458, and they had four sons and two daughters. Their eldest son was

SIR JOHN PAULET, K.B. He married his second cousin Alice, the daughter of SIR WILLIAM PAULET (8) and Elizabeth Denebaud, in about 1468. John and Alice had been espoused in their infancy, a common practice among the great families of those times. Their son was

SIR WILLIAM PAULET, K.G., (9) who was born about 1484 and who became the 1st Marquess of Winchester, and from whom descended the Dukes of Bolton and the present Marquess.

After his marriage to Elizabeth Denebaud, Sir William Paulet (8) seems to have settled at Hinton St George, and their only son, named Amias, may have been the first of the Paulet family to have been born there. Elizabeth knew the village well as it had been her family home for many years. At the time when Amias was born, about 1457, George Henton was a small, remote place. Not much has survived from those days with the notable exception of the preaching cross, which even then was over a hundred years old and was topped by a true cross. The house known today as The Priory was also here. It has a chapel dating from the fourteenth century showing it to have been a building of considerable importance. It may have been the original village manor house. It contains later-sixteenth-century features and was enlarged in the seventeenth and eighteenth centuries.

At this time also the present church was being built. The old Norman church which Elizabeth had attended had probably become too small or had fallen into decay. The

---

2. Paulet continues to be the family name of the Marquess of Winchester. The Hinton St George Paulets appear to have changed the name to Poulett after the creation of the Barony in 1627.

architects are unknown but there were craftsmen in the district who helped to build the beautiful structure which survives today.

There was a hermitage not far from Hinton, dedicated to St Ranus, on the main Crewkerne – Chard road. It was a place of pilgrimage and is mentioned by William of Worcester during his travels in 1415. The stretch of road is still known as St Rayne's Hill. The monks who lived here would have visited Hinton and preached from the cross.

Traditionally a mansion stood on nearby Castle Hill, said to have succeeded an earlier Croft Castle which had belonged to the Warres of Hestercombe. However, there is no definite record of a stone castle beyond a few bits of masonry found during an excavation earlier this century, but since names persist it is possible that there was a very early wooden palisade-type fortification there which left no recognizable stone foundations, metal fasteners nor earthworks that have yet been detected.

One mile south-west of Hinton from about 1280, there was a hamlet known as Craft or Hintonscraft, which was absorbed into Hinton Park in the mid-eighteenth century. It was held by the Carent family and later by the Warres, and was known as Craftwarre in 1499 when it was held by Sir Amias Paulet.

Many of the thatched buildings surviving in Hinton today were built during Amias's lifetime. The George Inn was new then, named in honour of the patron saint of the village and of England.

Little is known of Amias's early life. He would have learned the duties of a country squire and gentleman, and then, as was usual, he became a soldier. His family supported the ruling House of Lancaster and Amias naturally followed their lead. The Lancastrian party was virtually in exile when the Yorkist Edward IV died in 1483, and his young son Edward V, as one of the Princes in the Tower disappeared. Richard III came to the throne and the Duke of Buckingham attempted a rising against this unpopular king in order to put Henry Tudor on the throne, and to marry him to Elizabeth, the daughter of Edward IV. A number of Lancastrian sympathizers were involved in the plot which proved unsuccessful. Amias Paulet was evidently implicated for he was one of those attainted and suspected of treason. However, when Henry Tudor finally came to the throne in 1485 after Richard's death at the Battle of Bosworth Field, Amias was duly restored and cleared of any suspicion of treason by the new king. On 5 November that year he was appointed Sheriff for Somerset and Dorset and from then on was often in the Commission of the Peace. As Sheriff he was the immediate representative of the Crown in the two counties. It was his responsibility to provide hospitality for distinguished visitors from abroad, and for the periodic visit of the Justices of the Assize. He collected debts due to the Crown, and fines which were imposed by the Law Courts. He presided over the County Courts and proclaimed new laws and published any outlawries. Amias Paulet became well known for the active and conscientious way in which he carried out these tasks.

Ever mindful of his wider duties to King and Country, Amias was among those of the country noblemen who answered the call to arms in 1487 when rebellion threatened. An attempt on Henry VII's throne was made when a Yorkist army led by the Earl of Lincoln, the nephew of Richard III, invaded England from Ireland. Lincoln had lately returned to Ireland with an army of mercenaries from the Low Countries. A plot had been instigated whereby an impostor named Lambert Simnel, posing as the Earl of Warwick, was proclaimed King in Dublin. Lincoln brought his army, reinforced with a number of untrained Irishmen, and landed near Furness. King Henry, however, was ready, and had gathered a large loyal force led by the Earl of Oxford and the Duke of Bedford. Amias Paulet was among this force and took part in the Battle of Stoke on 10 June. Lincoln had about 8,000 men and attacked

Henry's army with great courage. His German mercenaries fought well, but the half-naked Irish were no match for the king's armed men and were slain, as an eyewitness reported, 'like dull and brute beasts'. The battle lasted for three hours, but the numbers of the royal army told in the end and most of the rebel leaders, including Lincoln, were killed. Amias Paulet acted in a noteworthy manner during the battle for he was knighted for valour the same day.

During the period when Sir Amias was Sheriff of Somerset, the future Cardinal Thomas Wolsey was curate of the nearby village of Limington. It was the occasion of the local fair and the youthful Wolsey attracted attention by his noisy behaviour there, brought about, it is said, by over-indulging in drink, and so enjoying himself all the more at the revels. When brought before the stern Sheriff Paulet, he was sentenced to the indignity of being placed in the stocks for 'disorderly conduct'. Amias obviously had no time for youthful high spirits! Wolsey was to make him regret the incident many years later.

Sir Amias married firstly, by Papal Dispensation, his cousin Margaret Paulet, daughter of John Paulet of Basing. She presumably died without issue. He married again after 1504, and his second wife was Lora, the daughter of Sir William Kellaway of Rockbourne in Hampshire. They had four children, Hugh, Henry, John and Elizabeth. John became rector of Hinton St George and Dean of Jersey.

Soon after the Battle of Stoke Sir Amias commenced to build himself a new house at Hinton St George, no doubt to enhance his elevation to the knighthood, and also to meet the needs of a growing family. So in about 1490 the building of Hinton House began. The work gave much-needed employment at Hinton. It is said that every external stone was fashioned in the shape of a nail's head, and that much of the stone was brought from Castle Hill from the by now ruined mansion. It is more likely to have been Hinton stone, quarried in the park. In addition to the work on the house, the labourers of Hinton were given the task of building a wall around the grounds. This was at a time of great poverty, following a particularly hard winter.

Henry VII's throne was threatened again in 1497 when another impostor gathered an army of rebels and attempted to reach London. This was Perkin Warbeck, who claimed to be Richard of York, the younger of the Princes in the Tower. In September he landed in Cornwall and with his army of rebels made his way up to Exeter. Warbeck had gathered some 8,000 men and tried to beseige the city. Exeter, however, proved too strong and the attackers were beaten off in spite of their desperate efforts. The rebels then made their way to Taunton, but by now Baron Daubeny was hurrying to meet them with the loyal levies from South Wales, Gloucester, Wiltshire, Hampshire, Somerset and Dorset. Behind these, the royal army was forming under Henry himself. Warbeck, realizing defeat was imminent, tried to escape with a few trusty followers. He fled into Hampshire and finally surrendered at Beaulieu. Henry dealt leniently with the rebels. He was content that Warbeck was proved to be an impostor. A few of the ring-leaders were executed at Exeter, but for the rest Henry was satisfied to impose fines on the rebels and on all those who had aided them. Sir Amias Paulet was one of those officials who was employed to collect these fines. The actual collection went on until 1507 and some £15,000 was paid in all.

In 1501 Sir Amias performed one of his more pleasant duties. Princess Catherine of Aragon arrived at Plymouth to commence her journey to London where she was to marry Prince Arthur, the heir to the throne of England. As Sheriff of Somerset Sir Amias met her at the border of the county and with other West Country gentlemen, personally welcomed her at Crewkerne on 17 October. Unhappily, Prince Arthur did not survive to become king and in 1509, when his father died, it was his brother who was crowned Henry VIII and who married the young widow Catherine.

Sir Amias now took up his military career again and in 1513 joined the new king in a successful foray into northern France, Sir Amias being in charge of twenty-five men.

A man of many interests, Sir Amias was later called to the Bar and in 1520 was a member and Treasurer of the Middle Temple in London. Cardinal Thomas Wolsey, now at the height of his power, had never forgotten nor forgiven Sir Amias for the episode at Limington. His opportunity for revenge came when Sir Amias was brought before him on a charge of heresy and encouraging Lutheran teachings. A copy of Tyndale's scriptures was found in his possession and he was accused of circulating it among the Temple law students. Wolsey forbade Sir Amias to leave London without permission, and he was forced to remain in the Temple for several years. During this time he had a new gateway built for the Temple, and to appease Wolsey, he placed the Cardinal's badges prominently over the doors. He was free to leave London by 1524, for in that year he was appointed a Commissioner to collect the subsidy in Somerset.

Sir Amias Paulet must have been a wealthy man although it is said that he was in debt to Henry VII and Henry VIII. This may well have been one of the reasons why he was excepted from the general pardon of 30 April 1509, although he was eventually pardoned on 28 August that year. He died on 10 of April 1537. The following is an extract from his will:

> I leave my soul to God Almighty, and my body to be buried in the Church at Chaffcombe. I leave to the Parish Church of Chaffcombe 3s. 4d., of Chard 3s. 4d., of Crokehorn 3s. 4d., of Ilminster 3s. 4d., of South Petherton 3s. 4d., of Dynington 3s. 4d., to the Abott and Convent of Ford 10s.

We can only wonder what the value of 3s. 4d. was in those days! His wish to be buried at Chaffcombe appears to have been ignored, for on the monument erected later by his son in Hinton church, it clearly states that he lies there in his home village.

Sir Amias's eldest son Hugh was born about 1510 and followed his father's example in taking an active part in the affairs of his county. From 1532 he was Justice of the Peace for Somerset and in 1536 became Sheriff for Somerset and Devon, a duty he undertook again in 1542 and 1547.

In 1537 he was summoned to attend on the king with 300 armed men when the Northern Rebellion broke out. Hugh found favour with Henry VIII for he was knighted on 18 October that year and two days later was invited to the baptism of Prince Edward, afterwards Edward VI.

When his father died Sir Hugh became heir and sole executor. To the Hinton estates he added the manor of Sampford Peverel in Devon which he purchased from the king for £1,000.

The muster lists of 1539 show that Sir Hugh provided from Hinton forty armed men, thirty billmen, twenty archers, five tenants and nine others.

When Glastonbury Abbey suffered the fate of countless other religious houses and monasteries at the time of the Dissolution, and the Abbot was executed, Sir Hugh was made Administrator of the Abbey Lands and a supervisor of the rents. For this he received a salary of £12 per annum. Twelve years later he settled a colony of Huguenot refugees in the ruins.

In 1540 Sir Hugh was one of the knights appointed to meet Anne of Cleeves on her arrival in England, and to escort her to the waiting Henry VIII.

His duties took him to France in 1543 with the king and he was treasurer to the English army at the siege of Boulogne. He took part in the fighting and distinguished himself at the capture of the Braye – part of the defensive fortifications – on 1 September 1544. The following year he captured and burned the town of Davourn, and a hill near Boulogne which changed hands several times during the fierce fighting later became known as Paulet Hill.

Edward VI came to the throne in 1547, and back in England again, Sir Hugh – a known supporter of the Protestant cause – was one of those charged by Henry VIII's executors on 11 February with the 'good order of the shires near unto them in the west'. It was then that his third term as Sheriff of the two counties commenced.

The Reformation was not accepted by all the king's subjects and in 1549 there were the rumbles of rebellion again in the West Country. Sir Hugh was made Knight-Marshal of an army raised by Lord Russell to put down the rising. He led the pursuit of the rebels and after a defeat at Sampford Courtenay, finally crushed them at King's Weston near Bristol.

In 1549 Sir Hugh was also given an appointment which commenced the connection of the Paulet family with the Channel Island of Jersey, which was to last for the next 400 years. There had been raids on the island by the French and complaints had been made about the island's Lieutenant Governor, Henry Cornish. So, on 5 November Paulet was sent to investigate. His warrant, signed by Members of the Council of State of Edward VI, reads as follows:

> After our hearty commendations whereas it has pleased the King's Majesty by our advice to send presently to that His Majesty's Isle of Jersey this bearer Sir Hugh Paulet instructed for the order of that Isle. This shall be to will and command you on His Majesty's behalf not only to credit him in these things he has to say but also to obey and follow that he shall prescribe unto you WITHOUT FAILING us you tender His Majesty's pleasure and will answer for the contrary at your peril. So fare you well from Westminster the 5th November 1549.

Sir Hugh landed in Jersey on Christmas Eve and quickly got down to work. He reviewed the island's Militia to test their strength and investigated the complaints against Cornish which resulted in the latter's dismissal by Paulet almost at once. Sir Hugh returned to England after three weeks and presented his report to the Council. On 20 March he was himself made Governor of Jersey for life in the place of Edward Seymour, Duke of Somerset, and returned to the island with his brother John and his own two sons, Amias aged 18 and George aged 16.

One of Sir Hugh's first concerns was the strengthening of the defences of the island and in particular the castle of Mont Orgueil which was his headquarters. He brought over some lead from the destroyed roof of Glastonbury Abbey for use at Mont Orgueil, completed the building of the great central tower begun by his predecessor and added to the walls and fortifications generally. The costs were considerable and he wrote in 1599 that he had spent £1,400 from his own pocket. He took the army in hand also, and, says the Jersey Chronicler: 'drilled the men hard, so that they would know how to man the bulwarks, for he had been all his life a Captain expert in war'.

He was also concerned with the religious practices on the island and was ordered to enquire into the liturgy and to see that Catholic practices were put down. He was thus empowered to destroy all statues and images in the churches and to demolish chapels and the wayside crosses and generally to 'extirpate, oust and abolish all idolatry, bigotry and superstition'. Somerset before him had removed much of such offensive material, however, and Sir Hugh could find little else left for him to dispose of except the church bells. So all the bells, except one in each parish, were sold. Their sale brought in £171 9s. towards the island's fortifications! On the whole there appears to have been little opposition to the

Reformation in Jersey and Paulet cannot be regarded as a persecutor of Catholics or indeed, he would not have remained in his post during the reign of Mary I. The Jersey Chronicler says of him and his rule: 'He was a great lover of justice, and while he was Governor, the island remained in perfect peace and tranquillity. He kept the people bound together in complete unity and concord.'

Sir Hugh still had other duties which often took him away from Jersey. In 1556 he received the thanks of the Council for 'travail taken this last summer in well ordering the West Partes'. In 1559 he was made Vice-President of the Welsh Marches under Lord Williams.

In 1562, when France was in turmoil with Huguenot troubles, Queen Elizabeth's ministers saw an opportunity to regain a foothold in France and obtain possession of the French Channel Ports. They plotted with the Huguenot leaders and agreed that in return for help in their cause by England, they would ultimately hand over Calais to Elizabeth. In the meantime Le Havre was to be surrendered and occupied by English troops and held as a pledge until Calais was surrendered. Queen Elizabeth commissioned Sir Hugh, being a man of 'wisdom and long experience' to act as adviser to the Earl of Warwick who was to take command of the garrison in Le Havre. However, England did not foresee the Peace of Amboise which was signed in March of the following year. The Huguenots obtained some measure of toleration and were reunited with their countrymen in a desire to be rid of the English invaders. The 5,000 men of the English garrison in Le Havre struggled all through that winter and the following spring to hold the attacking French forces at bay. They were badly provided with arms and ammunition and lacked food, drink and clothing. Besieging them also were the Catholic troops of the German Rheingrave. Originally helping the French against the Huguenots, they had now joined in aiding to drive the English out. Sir Hugh Paulet conferred unsuccessfully with the Rheingrave to agree terms in April 1563. In June he returned to England to obtain more help. But by this time a new enemy had appeared. Warwick noted in a communication that a strange disease had come amongst them 'whereof nine had died this morning and many more very suddenly'. By the third week in June the plague was carrying off two hundred men a week. Paulet returned in July with 800 hastily recruited men, but they were raw and untrained and sent without leaders. If they were lucky enough to escape the plague they only added to the troubles of the harassed commander. By 15 July the garrison was down to 1,200 while the surrounding French forces numbered some 20,000 men. On 24 July Warwick lost command of the harbour and his communications with England were cut. On the 26th he was forced to make the best terms he could with the enemy and intimated his willingness to parley. The flag was hauled down two days later and the remnants of the war-weary and plague-stricken garrison took to the ships to return to England. England's honour was intact and France was rid of the foreigner. Nevertheless it was a bitter blow to Elizabeth's pride, and in November Sir Hugh Paulet was appointed one of the Commissioners with the sorry task of settling debts incurred in the expedition.

When in his sixties, Sir Hugh was Knight of the Shire for Somerset in the Parliament which met on 8 May 1572. He took the musters for Somerset in June 1575, and in May 1578 a warrant was issued to pay him £100 a year for the repair of Taunton Castle. He died in December probably that same year although the exact date is not known. Sir Hugh was married twice, first in 1528 to Philippa the daughter of Sir Lewis Pollard of King's Nympton in Devon. They had three sons, Amias, Nicholas and George; and two daughters, Anne and Jane. In 1560 he married his second wife Elizabeth, the daughter of Walter Blount of Blount's Hall in Staffordshire. Elizabeth was the wealthy widow of Sir Thomas Pope, the founder of Trinity College, Oxford. After Hugh died she was generally regarded as being of Roman Catholic sympathy and was reported to have held Mass frequently at her house. State papers of the period refer to her as a recusant suspected of harbouring priests and Jesuits in her great house in Clerkenwell, inherited from her first husband. It is recorded that Sir Hugh visited Trinity College with Elizabeth on several occasions and in 1561 assisted the Fellows in a suit against Lord Rich. In 1566 he gave £20 towards a new garden wall for the college. Elizabeth died in 1593 and is buried in Trinity Chapel.

It was during Sir Hugh's lifetime, in about 1541, that Henry VIII's official antiquary John Leland made his tour of the country and wrote his itinerary. He visited Hinton and Hinton House and referred to Sir Hugh's 'goodly manor'.

Sir Hugh is buried at Hinton with his first wife Philippa, and their effigies may be seen on their tomb in the memorial chapel. He served under four monarchs and lived during the reigns of three kings and three queens, if we can count the short term of Lady Jane Grey.

Sir Hugh's brother John was a Roman Catholic and accompanied him to Jersey in 1549. He was appointed Rector of the parish of St Martin in Jersey and subsequently became Dean of the island. The rest of his family were strongly Protestant but Dean John appears to have been allowed his freedom of thought and action owing to a spirit of tolerance which then existed in religious matters on Jersey, and helped no doubt by the fact that his brother and nephew were Governor and Lieutenant Governor respectively. Huguenot refugees pouring into Jersey did not help the Catholic cause there, however, and in 1558 upon the death of Queen Mary, John's name disappeared from the Act Book of the Ecclesiastical Court, the rights of which he had tried hard to retain under his leadership. He was still performing clerical duties in 1568 for he is recorded as having been collecting dues from the parishes. Eventually, in 1576, John lost his authority as Dean when all the duties of that office were transferred to the Calvinistic Colloquoy. He was, however, always treated with respect and seems to have moderated his religious views under the pressure of events around him. He was still known as Dean until his death in 1580. He was at one time Bursar of two schools in Jersey. There is even a record of his marriage, late in life, to the daughter of the Seigneur of Trinity Parish. He had a son, Hugh, who became Attorney General of Jersey; and a daughter who married the Seigneur of Longueville. With regard to Dean John's death, one report says that he committed suicide: 'It is said that he opened a vein in his foot in a warm bath and thus ended his days.'

Sir Hugh's third son George arrived in Jersey in 1549. He was to remain there for the rest of his life and performed about sixty years of public service to the island, thirty-six of them as Bailiff and also acting many times as Lieutenant Governor. He concerned himself with the state of the fortifications and the Grammar Schools, and was also an elder of the Reformed Church. In 1609 he was one of the Commissioners appointed to review the laws of Jersey. He apparently married four times.[3] From his second marriage, a daughter Rachel married Sir Philip de Carteret of the prominent Jersey family. A letter dated 30 April 1614 from King James I to the then Governor of Jersey, Sir John Peyton, says:

> We are well pleased that our old servant George Paulet shall now retire to his private ease . . . and because you have displaced Paulet from his Lieutenancy after 50 years of service, it is our pleasure that you allow him £20 a year during his life.

George Paulet died in 1621 and was buried in the parish church of St Saviour in Jersey. He had earlier inherited the Seigneurie of the Fief St Germain; this title reverted to his daughter Rachel de Carteret, and the Seigneurie remains in the de Carteret family's hands to this day.

---

3. The *Biographical Dictionary of Jersey* records that George married Elizabeth Paulet, but there may be confusion with George, the son of Sir Amias Paulet who married his cousin Elizabeth Paulet of Gotehurst.

CHAPTER 2

Sir Amias Paulet, Keeper of Mary, Queen of Scots

Never shall cease to spread wise Paulet's fame
These shall speak, and men shall blush for shame
Without offence to speak what I do know,
Great is the debt England to him doth owe.
Memorial to Sir Amias Paulet

Sir Amias is without doubt the most famous of the Hinton St George Paulets. He was the eldest son of Sir Hugh Paulet and his first wife Philippa Pollard. Born in about 1532, during the reign of Henry VIII, he first took up public duties when at the age of 18 or so he accompanied his father, his uncle John and his brother George to Jersey in 1549, when Sir Hugh took up the post of Governor of that island. Sir Hugh was frequently absent from Jersey, and in 1556, Amias, then 24 years old, was sworn in as Lieutenant Governor. The following year he married Margaret Hervey, the daughter and heir of Anthony Hervey of Columb St John in Devonshire.

After 1559, Sir Hugh being so often away from Jersey, Amias acted more and more on his father's behalf. Huguenot refugees were pouring on to the island from France to escape persecution and found a champion in Amias Paulet. He supported them as much as possible, and even appointed a Huguenot minister from France to the town church in Jersey, and attended the first celebration of the Lord's Supper there, along with Helier de Carteret and many other notables. De Carteret was a great friend of his and a member of one of the leading families in Jersey.

Throughout his life Amias was a strong and high principled Puritan and his rule of Jersey was notable for his repression of the Catholic religion there, which contrasted strongly with his treatment of the Huguenot refugees. His puritanism showed not a little when he wrote to the Council in England, asking for an Order that the Jersey merchants should sell more tin and cloth etc., to France, before they should be allowed to bring in so much wine, for he said: 'It is lamentable that so much money passes from the island in such unprofitable wares.'

Amias was often called away from the island to fulfil other duties, leaving his brother George, and later his own son Anthony, to keep watch over the island's affairs. Both George and Anthony ruled the island with even greater rigour than Amias ever practised, their behaviour sometimes amounting almost to tyranny, so that Amias was forced more than once to issue a mild reproof. He undoubtedly loved Jersey and continued to watch the course of events there attentively until the time of his death.

He carried on with the strengthening and rebuilding of the island's defences begun by his father. In 1570 he reported that the fortifications were advanced 'to a good height'. Work was evidently progressing slowly, for in 1573 he asked for a grant of £400 to complete work started four or five years previously, and then a further grant of £400 the following year. Ten years later when rumours of invasion were rife, Amias emphasized the necessity of finishing the fortifications, and reported that part of Mont Orgueil Castle: 'Standeth yet upon his old ruynous and rotten walls.'

Amias was knighted in 1575 and in September 1576 was appointed Queen Elizabeth's Ambassador at the French Court. Amias remained in Paris with his wife and family until he was recalled in November 1579. His stay in France was not particularly eventful, nor it seems, a very happy time for him – in fact he often expressed his homesickness for Somerset and Jersey in the various letters he wrote at the time.

Among those who accompanied Sir Amias in his large entourage to Paris were the young Francis Bacon, and Arthur Throckmorton who became the brother-in-law of Sir Walter Raleigh. Arthur stayed in France until 1577 and from his own diary it is apparent he was something of a spendthrift, and of rather irresponsible character. He seems to have been a trial to Sir Amias for in that year Amias wrote thankfully that Arthur had learned French and was returning home:

Being hereunto required by his mother, who hath promised to him licence to travel into Italy, because having now gotten the French tongue in good perfection he cannot make any other profit by his abode in France. To be plain with you I think myself very happy that I am honestly delivered of him. He is a very young man, and hath his imperfections, which riper years and a good counsel may remove from him. He may not go into Italy without the company of some honest and wise man, and so I have told him, and in many other things have dealt very plainly with him. I hear he hath been chargeable to his mother, which must be imputed to his folly, having had his meat and drink with me for himself and his man, and I have not only from his first coming to Paris provided him of a horse, but also have found his horse at my charges. His mother prayeth that his coming over may seem to proceed of his own request, because the Queen shall not be offended with it.

Arthur did not forget his debts to Sir Amias, and later in his diary relates that whenever he obtained a sum of money, he was able to pay some back to Sir Amias.

Sir Amias obviously kept a fatherly eye on the young men under his care for he wrote to Sir Nicholas Bacon concerning his son, the young Francis, as follows:

This quiet time doth give me no occasion to trouble your Lordship with long letters, only I must tell you that I rejoice much to see that your son my companion, hath, by the grace of God, passed the brunt and peril of this journey; whereof I am the more glad, because in the beginning of these troubles it pleased your Lordship to refer his continuance with me to my consideration. I thank God these dangers are past, and your son is safe, sound and in good health, and worthy of your fatherly favour.

During this time, France was still embroiled in differences with the Huguenots, while the Netherlands were in a state of war with the occupying Spanish. Queen Elizabeth as always, had her eye on the main chance and was trying to use the situation on the Continent to the best advantage for herself and her country. She therefore reopened the question of her proposed marriage to Alençon, Duke of Anjou, the younger son of Queen Catherine de Medici of France. Alençon, although a Catholic, was a supporter of the Huguenots, and his army was already in the Netherlands aiding them against the Spanish. Elizabeth thought that such a marriage would have the effect of strengthening the Anglo-French alliance (as well as furthering the possibility of providing an heir!). Spain too, might be compelled to come to terms with the rebels in the Netherlands, thus dispelling the fears of a Spanish invasion,

Sir Amias Paulet 1532–1588 Keeper of Mary, Queen of Scots (by Zucchero)

should that country become too firmly entrenched just across the sea. Negotiations for the marriage commenced in the summer of 1578 and Sir Amias as Ambassador corresponded profusely on the subject, though it must be added not very enthusiastically. He had no wish to see a Catholic so near the throne of England. He must have been very relieved therefore when the proposals came to nothing.

Paulet's period as Ambassador to France paved the way for his later and more famous appointment as Keeper of Mary, Queen of Scots. His correspondence at that time throws light on the views and interests of the French and English Courts in the Low Countries, and particularly on the actions of the Queen Mother Catherine, who while busy scheming on behalf of Alençon, contrived, through Paulet (who was a not unwilling instrument), to arouse Elizabeth's fears and jealousy of Spain and Don Juan. For by this time Mary of Scotland, for long a prisoner of Elizabeth, had despaired of any help coming from France. Spain seemed her only hope of rescue. Don Juan, Governor of the Netherlands, was looking forward, after the settlement of the Provinces, to a raid upon England for the purpose of giving Mary her freedom, and then claiming her hand as his price. Mary for her part, was negotiating the removal of her young son from Scotland to France to be brought up by her kinsmen of the House of Lorraine. Sir Amias never ceased harping on these topics, and often seems to have written his letters with the express purpose of agitating Elizabeth's mind. However, his dispatches did their work. Queen Elizabeth was filled with fear and suspicion. The guard on Mary was rigorously tightened and intrigues were renewed for removing her from the Earl of Shrewsbury's guardianship into 'surer keeping'.

Paulet's period as Ambassador ended in November 1579 when he was succeeded by Sir Henry Cobham. Sir Amias wrote: 'I am Jack-out-of-office, and I thank God for it.' He returned to Jersey, now as Governor, having succeeded his father after Sir Hugh had died in 1578. In 1581 he was serving on a Commission in Guernsey making grants to churches from money raised by the sale of church property there.

He spent the winter of 1582 at his manor of Sampford Peverel, but was back in Jersey in 1583 when he was present in the Royal Court when his brother George was sworn in as Bailiff, and his son Anthony as Lieutenant Governor. In 1584, as a measure of the high regard in which he was held at Court, he was made a Privy Councillor.

The first mention of Sir Amias in connection with the Queen of Scots is in a letter dated 4 January 1585 in which Lord Burghley informs Sir Francis Walsingham that Lord St John of Bletso had refused to take charge of Mary in succession to Shrewsbury. Queen Elizabeth was much displeased and she commanded Burghley 'to write to Rycote for Sir Amias Paulet'. (Rycote, near Thame in Oxfordshire, was the home of Lord Norris, whose daughter Katherine was married to Amias's son Anthony and where presumably Sir Amias was staying.) The choice of Sir Amias Paulet aroused a good deal of speculation and surprise among his contemporaries. They asked why, when other men were available, the queen should go to the west of England 'to pick out Paulet?' Neither his rank nor fortune justified the choice and he was not even then in the best of health. Mr John Somers, the assistant to Sir Ralph Sadler, Mary's temporary keeper, wrote on 13 January (the day of Mary's removal from Wingfield to Tutbury Castle in Staffordshire), to propose the substitution of other fit persons instead of Paulet: 'Your good judgement of the weak state of his body, and the distance of his dwelling, I think, are to be allowed for a sufficient supersedeas in this matter' – although Somers was actually under the impression that Sir Amias would only be coming to assist Lord St John.

Other motives have been suggested for the change in Mary's guardian; that Elizabeth considered Shrewsbury had treated his prisoner with too much courtesy and indulgence, and that she purposely placed Mary under a man of inferior rank who would be likely to be extra vigilant and severe with his charge, with an eye on future favour or preferment.

However, the queen and Walsingham had made up their minds and so all objections were put aside. Sir Amias accepted the position and was due to take up his new duties on 1 March, but he did not arrive at Tutbury until nearly two months later. His instructions, dated 4 March, were apparently not explicit enough for him and he queried the queen's commands regarding the amount of liberty he was to allow his new charge.

As for Queen Mary herself, she viewed the prospect of Sir Amias as her guardian with some alarm, and appealed to Elizabeth saying that Paulet, while in France, had shown himself to be her enemy. The Queen undertook Paulet's defence in a letter to Mary, as follows:

> And as for Poulet, against whom you seem to take exception, in respect of his dealings (as you say) against you at such time as he had the charge of our Ambassade in France, the question is whether the cause grew from himself or from you and Ministers there. If he did not advertise us truly of such things as he heard were practised by yourself and them against us, therein he did but discharge his duty. And if you still hold the rule which you have heretofore professed, that you love and esteem best those who serve us most faithfully, then have you more cause to like than dislike him, for we repute him to be towards God religious, towards us most faithful, of calling honourable, by birth in respect of the antiquity of his house, most noble. And therefore, if we should see hereafter cause to use him in Sadler's place, you need not to doubt that a man that reverenceth God, loveth his Prince, and is no less by calling honourable than by birth noble, will never do anything unworthy of himself.

So Sir Amias arrived at Tutbury with his wife (who was expecting a child), his son George, and some forty servants and thirty soldiers. Sir Ralph Sadler was waiting there to welcome the new keeper and to introduce him to Queen Mary. Paulet was now quite clear in his own mind regarding his instructions for the treatment of his prisoner. From now on her life would be one of the strictest confinement. To his Puritan mind, the guardianship of Mary, and the task of making it impossible for her to do any more harm, seemed assigned to him by God. Mary's worst fears must have been realized when she met Sir Amias for the first time. He left her no illusions as to what his future conduct towards her would be. He wrote to Queen Elizabeth of this first meeting as follows:

> I told her that I was bound by duty of allegiance to serve your Majesty truly and faithfully and would not fail to employ all my endeavours to acquit myself of that duty, neither would be diverted from it by hope of gain, for fear of loss, or for any other respect whatsoever. Your Highness's commandment and service being first observed, I did assure her that your pleasure was that I should do her all the good offices, and show her all the courtesy that might seem convenient, wherein there should be no fault on my part. And to the intent that this course might have this continuance without let or interruption, to her satisfaction and to the better discharge of my duty, I prayed her to have care of my poor honesty and credit, a thing more precious unto me than living or life, and that nothing might be done directly or indirectly by her or her servants, that might procure me blame, or suspicion of blame at your Majesty's hands, having no worldly thing in so great reputation as your service and contentment.

His first action was to remove the Cloth of Estate which hung above her chair. Mary set great store by this symbol of her queenship, but Paulet would not tolerate it. He says:

> I found at my arrival here in the great chamber where Sir Ralph did usually dine and sup, a Cloth of Estate for this Queen, representing by letters the name of her father and mother, and furnished with the Arms of Scotland in the midst, and the same quartered with the Arms of Lorraine on every side. Sir Ralph Sadler told me at my first entering into the said chamber that this Cloth of Estate was set up at the first coming hither of

this Queen, upon a meaning that she should dine and sup ordinarily in that chamber, referring the standing or taking down of the same to my discretion.

So down it came, in spite of Mary's protestations! 'There is no other way to do good to this people than to begin roundly with them – whatsoever liberty or anything else is once granted unto them cannot be drawn back again without great exclamation,' he wrote to London. From then on Mary's life became more and more uncomfortable. Paulet began by strengthening the armed guard of the castle, and no strangers were allowed to enter the precincts. Mary's domestic staff were forbidden to go out except when accompanied by a soldier. Mary herself was stopped from giving alms to the poor in the neighbourhood, a charity which gave her much pleasure. Paulet justified this action by the comment that the laws of the realm had provided so carefully for the relief of the poor that no one could want for anything except 'through their own lewdness or the negligence of the officers of several parishes'. The true reason was that Paulet thought the recipients would be sympathetic towards Mary and might be more open to bribes or be willing to carry messages. Everything that went in or out of the castle was closely examined, so that it became impossible for any secret correspondence at all to be carried on. All Mary's private letters to her acquaintances at home and abroad were carefully checked. They were mostly in French and although Amias was familiar with the language it was very difficult for him at times to ensure that there were no hidden meanings. Mary had been used to riding out for exercise, accompanied always by a heavy guard, but eventually she was deprived of even that pleasure. Her coachman, Sharp, was not allowed out without permission or without a guard, and was deprived of the privilege of dining with Paulet's servants, as he had formerly done with Sadler's. The laundresses in particular caused great worry to Sir Amias. He suspected them of smuggling messages in and out with the bundles of washing, especially when he discovered that two of them were related to Sharp.

Sir Amias had his personal problems too. He suffered terribly with gout which frequently took him to his bed, and he felt the need for an assistant in his duties. A few months after his arrival at Tutbury he wrote:

Although I have increased in health daily sithence the first day of my arrival here (I thank God for it) and do now find myself able to go strongly and as speedily as at any time these two or three years last past, yet, being subject to the gout, and considering the nature of the disease, I must look for a fresh assault in the accustomed season, at which time the importance of this service will require the assistance of some honest and faithful gentleman, which no doubt may be easily found both in the Court and in this country.

As a result of this appeal Richard Bagot joined Amias as his assistant.

Housekeeping was another problem which worried Sir Amias. He frequently wrote for more money to run what were in fact two households, that of Mary and her servants, and his own. Food prices were high, and Amias wrote angrily that: 'This Queen's servants are always craving, and have no pity at all on English purses.' He seemed fairly satisfied however, when he wrote:

God is my witness that I have great and singular care of her Majesty's profit in this service, and have already cut off all fees of Court and a great number of other superfluous charges, reducing all things to such order as if I lived in my own house in Somersetshire; and even now making my profit of the straitness of this house, have reformed many disorders to her Majesty's benefit and to the surety of my charge, which could not have been done so cleanly before this time.

Tutbury, however, was far from being the ideal prison. The building was both cold and damp and not conducive to the good health of either the guardian or his charge. Mary repeatedly asked to be moved to more pleasant surroundings, pleading that her health of mind and body was breaking under the conditions she was forced to endure at Tutbury. Sir Amias, however, had no sympathy for his prisoner's ailments, regarding them rather as a rightful punishment for her sins. His attitude also to her religious convictions was at times both bigoted and cruel. On one occasion he tried to burn a package sent to Mary from her agent Charelles in London, because it contained various items connected with the Catholic religion. In his narrow-minded way he wrote of the incident thus:

> Charelles hath sent to this Queen by the carrier, by your permission, as he writeth, a box full of abominable trash, as beads of all sorts, pictures in silk of all sorts, with some Agnus Dei, etc. I was far more willing to have burnt it than to permit it to be delivered. I am a near neighbour to much damnable wickedness, trusting to live so long to see it plucked up by the roots.

By the autumn of 1585 Mary's health had not improved and conditions at the castle had worsened, helped by the great floods which had occurred during the year. Sir Amias commented:

> Her Majesty will be a great loser this year in the meadow grounds which were reserved for the use of this house by reason of the great floods which have done great hurt in these parts; but I trust this loss shall be recompensed with usury in the rents which I have increased upon the tithes, and some other things which I have set.

The middens were full and evil-smelling and the cold and damp increased. Representations from Paris to Elizabeth finally led to a search being started for a new prison for Mary. Various large houses in the district were suggested, including Tixall, the home of Sir Walter Aston. Sir Amias opposed this, saying that Aston was one of the few loyal men in 'this infected shire' and it would be better not to lose his affections. Finally the choice settled on Chartley Hall, the Elizabethan manor house owned by the young Earl of Essex. It seemed ideal, for there was a large moat around it to give added security against the possibility of the prisoner's escape. Sir Amias was delighted with the decision and wrote to Walsingham commenting on the moat thus:

> The water which environeth this house is of such depth as may stand in stead of a strong wall, saving that it is narrow in some places and therefore must be the better watched. One commodity sufficient in itself to recompense many incommodities, which is, that by reason of the abundance of water adjoining to this house, this Queen's laundresses may be lodged and do all their business within the gates, whereof I am the more glad, because, having done my best endeavour to procure some faithful women out of Somersetshire, I can find none that will be entreated to come so far.

Evidently no ladies from Hinton St George were willing to travel such a distance away from home!
Lord Essex himself was not so pleased and his protests managed to delay the move from

Tutbury until Christmas Eve. On her arrival Mary, considerably weakened by the journey, fell very ill. Even Sir Amias was concerned and found himself 'for charity's sake' bound to forward her complaints about her bed, which she had found 'stained and ill-flavoured'. She requested a down bed and Paulet added his own recommendation for this small comfort. On the whole Sir Amias showed very little sympathy towards his charge's ill-health or discomfort, seeing them merely as a lessening of his own worries as to her possible escape. He wrote that 'the indisposition of this Queen's body and the great infirmity of her legs, which is so desperate as herself doth not hope of any recovery, is no small advantage to her keeper, who shall not need to stand in great fear of her running away, if he can forsee that she be not taken from him by force'.

In view of these remarks our sympathies are not easily aroused for him when he goes on to say:

> I had some feeling of my gout at the very instant of my going to Chartley, so as I could not conveniently have repaired thither without the help of my coach, and therefore it may please you to procure that Mr Bagot's letter of assistance may be sent by the next.

Whilst being responsible for Mary, Sir Amias was ever mindful of Jersey, and in December 1585 he writes to London:

> It may please you to peruse this letter inclosed, which I have received this present day from Sir Thomas Leighton, who had written to the same effect to my son Anthony Poulet, as may also appear by this copy inclosed. My said son giving me farther to understand that the Count Briac [Charles de Cosse, afterwards marshal of France] prepareth certain ships at Newhaven, but to what end he cannot yet learn . . . Living here a prisoner, I cannot judge of the actions abroad, and therefore, do refer myself herein to your better knowledge of the state of foreign parts. But if you shall find that this attempt carrieth any apparent colour of truth, I shall most heartily pray your friendly mediation towards her Majesty for supply of men and munitions for the Isle of Jersey. Besides that it shall be very heedful that the inhabitants of Jersey be encouraged in all times of danger by the assistance of some English supply, it is also certain that the ordinary garrison maintained by the captain is less than sufficient to defend the castle of Jersey against the enemy. It may be that the castle is sufficiently furnished of munitions to pass over some little time of peace and quietness but in case of danger, it is of necessity that the same be furnished with a new store of powders, calivers, etc. Forbearing to set down the particulars of this supply until I shall hear from you how the same shall be needful, I have always been of opinion that in these like suspected times one or two of her Majesty's smaller vessels might be commanded to attend these isles, as well for their service upon all occasions occurring, as also to bring advertisement of their necessity, if any should happen.

But while Sir Amias was fighting the battles of Jersey on paper and in his mind, the realities of the present situation gave him little time for nostalgia. Life at Chartley continued much as it had been at Tutbury and Mary remained a complete prisoner, cut off from all outside contacts.

However, this situation was not to be allowed to continue indefinitely. Elizabeth's ministers, Cecil and Walsingham were not prepared to see the Scottish Queen's imprisonment prolonged. They wanted a guilty Mary Stuart, not an innocent captive. They looked forward to seeing her brought to trial, condemned and executed. It was therefore necessary for a plot to be instigated and the prisoner induced to take part in it – a conspiracy threatening the life of Queen Elizabeth herself. Following which, proof must be obtained that Mary was directly involved. A plot to kill Elizabeth, however, was already in existence. Philip of Spain had established an anti-English centre of conspiracy in France. Mary's confidential agent Morgan, who resided in Paris, was supplied with funds from Spain, his business being to carry on unceasing intrigues against England and Elizabeth. Links were maintained with the dissatisfied Catholic nobility in England through the mediation of the Spanish and French ambassadors. Walsingham, not to be outdone, had some of his own spies planted upon Morgan pretending to be devout Catholics, so that all the plans made on behalf of Mary were reported to England. Walsingham took no action at first, not being satisfied with the lives of a few conspirators – he wanted proof that Mary herself was involved. Therefore it became imperative that Mary should be allowed more freedom to involve herself with the plotters. Sir Amias was thus instructed not to maintain such a strict cordon of security around his prisoner, while Walsingham let Paulet know that it was necessary in order for Mary to become entangled in a plot.

Mary fell unsuspectingly into the trap. Since moving from Tutbury, her spirits had been considerably raised. Chartley was a little better than Tutbury and in its neighbourhood lived a number of friendly Catholic families. She felt sure that news from her friends would get through to her and perhaps even now she might still regain her freedom. Her amazement may be imagined when one day a ciphered letter came into her hands, the first she had seen for months. Mary was led to believe that a perfectly safe line of communication had been found between her and her friends. The method of deceiving Mary was comparatively simple. By the agency of a brewer who supplied Chartley with beer, and one Gilbert Clifford (a renegade Catholic who agreed to play the part of intermediary and confidence man) letters coming to Mary were put in a waterproof case inserted through the bung into a cask of ale, and carried into Chartley. Outgoing letters were smuggled from the castle in the same way in the returned empty barrel. Mary must have been full of joy. In spite of the hard Puritan Sir Amias and his close observation of her, she had at last outwitted him. She must have congratulated herself at the thought of the rage he would be in had he known that week after week she was ex-changing letters with Paris, Madrid and Rome. Sir Amias, for his part must have smiled to himself when week after week he saw the fresh supply of beer being brought in by the 'honest man' and noticed the haste with which Mary's butler went down to the cellar to fetch the precious letter. She was proving to him that she was every bit as deceitful as he had been pleased to think her. As for the brewer, he was more than satisfied. He was being paid twice over, by Mary and by Paulet. He was not slow to realize how valuable his part was in the proceedings and Sir Amias was outraged when the brewer demanded a raise in his payment. Amias disliked employing so many people, particularly those he called of such low worth, for he said: 'I had learned not to trust two where it sufficed to trust one.'

So the scene was set for the notorious 'Babington Plot', so-named after its young and ardent instigator, Sir Anthony Babington, by which Mary appeared to be implicated in its plan to assassinate Queen Elizabeth. When the fateful letter was discovered in which Mary gave her assent to the conspiracy, Walsingham and his henchmen were beside themselves with glee. At last they had all the proof necessary to remove Mary for good. Sir Amias, knowing that the execution of the Scottish Queen would soon free him from his gaolership, wrote: 'God has blessed my exertions, and I rejoice that He has thus rewarded my faithful services.'

Babington and his fellow conspirators were hunted down and arrested, and the bells of

London rang in triumph to celebrate the preservation of Elizabeth, the foiling of the conspiracy and the imminent end of the nefarious Mary Stuart.

Meanwhile, at Chartley Mary remained unaware that all was lost. She still hoped for deliverance and awaited the rescue she had been promised. At the beginning of August Sir Amias invited her to take part in a stag hunt arranged by Sir Walter Aston in his park at Tixall. Eight days later they rode out, Mary full of new energy and hope. However, near Tixall they were met by a troop of horsemen. To Mary's dismay, it was not the band of deliverers she had been expecting, but a force of Elizabeth's men led by Sir Thomas Gorge. Gorge told her plainly that Babington's conspiracy had been discovered and that her two secretaries would be arrested. Mary's feelings of horror increased, and when Sir Amias made no move to ride back to Chartley she saw the reason for the invitation to the hunt. She had been lured away so that her rooms could be thoroughly searched in her absence. She realized there and then that all her secrets must have been known all along to Paulet and to Walsingham, and that now all her hopes for the future were at an end. Mary was now forced to go on to Tixall House. She tried to resist and even sat on the ground and refused to move. Sir Amias then threatened to bring her coach and take her to Tixall by force if she would not ride on of her own accord. She finally agreed to go to Tixall where she was detained for seventeen days. She begged to be allowed to write to Elizabeth but Paulet refused to bring her any paper. Her physician Bourgoing was sent back to Chartley, but she was allowed two ladies and an equerry to attend her. Meanwhile her rooms and belongings at Chartley were thoroughly searched and all her letters and ciphers taken to London. With his usual eye for economy, Sir Amias took the opportunity to inventory her household, and made suggestions for cutting it down 'if this lady be restrained of her liberty'. The staff could be cut from thirty-eight to nineteen if such things as coachmen were removed, he suggested.

At last Mary returned to Chartley with Paulet. Outside Tixall a group of Staffordshire beggars were waiting to greet her in the hope of alms, her generosity in this respect being widely known. Much to Sir Amias's indignation she addressed the crowd in these words: 'Alas good people, I now have nothing to give you. For I am as much a beggar as you are yourselves.'

Back at her ransacked rooms at Chartley, Mary was almost immediately confined to bed. The strain of the past few days and the recurring illness in her legs were too much for her. One thing left to Mary after the search was her money which she discovered in a cupboard where she had left it. However, directions came from London that this too was to be seized. Mary depended on this money for her own necessities and for paying her servants. In order to take the money Amias arranged a small military operation. Armed men were at hand in an ante-room, and Sir Amias, accompanied by Richard Bagot, entered the apartment where Mary lay ill in bed. Her servants were sent from the room and Paulet demanded that the money be handed over. Mary at first absolutely refused to give up what was rightly her own property, but Paulet was adamant and eventually Mary instructed her servant Elizabeth Curle to open the cupboard. In a final effort to gain pity from Sir Amias, Mary got up from her bed and on her bare feet pleaded with him to leave her the money. She told him she had saved it for her funeral expenses, and for payment to her servants to enable them to reach their own country after her death. Paulet proved as hard as ever and the money was taken away. Mary told him then that all she had left were the two things which could never be taken away from her – her royal blood and her Catholic religion.

In London on 20 September, fourteen conspirators including Babington suffered the terrible fate of hanging, drawing and quartering at Tyburn. Queen Elizabeth was overjoyed at the turn of events and wrote to Sir Amias in most endearing terms:

Amias, my most faithful and careful servant, God reward thee treble-fold in three double for thy most troublesome charge so well discharged. If you knew, my Amias, how kindly, besides dutifully, my grateful heart accepteth and praiseth your spotless actions, your wise orders, and safe regards, performed in so dangerous and crafty a charge, it would ease your travails and rejoice your heart. In which I charge you carry this most just thought that I cannot balance in any weight of my judgement the value that I prize you at, and suppose no treasure to countervail such a faith; and shall condemn myself in that fault, which yet I never committed, if I reward not such deserts. Yea, let me lack when I most need, if I acknowledge not such a merit with a reward, *non omnibus datum*. Let your wicked murderess know how with hearty sorrow her vile deserts compelleth these orders; and bid her from me ask God forgiveness for her treacherous dealings towards the saver of her life many a year, to the intolerable peril of her own; and yet, not contented with so many forgivenesses, must fall again so horribly, for passing a woman's thought, much less a prince's; and instead of excusing (whereof not one can serve, it being so plainly confessed by the authors of my guiltless death), let repentence take place and let not the fiend possess her, so her better part be lost; which I pray, with hands lifted up to Him that may both save and spill. With my most loving adieu and prayers for thy long life, your most assured and loving sovereign, as thereto by good deserts induced. E.R.

Mary was now to leave Chartley for her last prison, and on 21 September, she left with Paulet for Fotheringay Castle in Northamptonshire. On the way the party stopped at the house of the Earl of Huntingdon at Lord's Place in Leicestershire. Here there was a demonstration by the local people in favour of Mary, and Paulet and his coach had to be guarded from the menacing crowds. They finally reached Fotheringay on 25 September.

Mary was now to stand trial and Paulet came to inform her of this on 1 October. Sir Amias saw it as his main task now to get Mary to confess to her crimes and to beg forgiveness for them. But Mary was in a calmer frame of mind and told Paulet he was like a grown-up with a little child, asking it to own up to its sins. More seriously she continued: 'As a sinner, I am truly conscious of having often offended my Creator, and I beg Him to forgive me, but as Queen and Sovereign, I am aware of no fault or offence for which I have to render account to anyone here below. . . . As therefore I could not offend, I do not wish for pardon, I do not seek, nor would I accept it from anyone living.'

Rather taken aback Paulet reported to London everything that had been said. Meanwhile, Mary's coachman was dismissed and rightly she saw this as a sign that her days of travelling were ended. Paulet no doubt saw it as another item of domestic economy successfully effected.

On 11 October the Commissioners began to arrive at Fotheringay and the next day a deputation of lords waited on Queen Mary, including Sir Walter Mildmay; Stallenge, the Usher of Parliament; Barker, Elizabeth's notary; and Paulet himself. The trial commenced on 14 October and throughout its duration Mary questioned Paulet about the various English gentlemen among the judges. Paulet reported to London of Mary's conduct during the trial which he found completely distasteful. He had always felt that Mary was at her worst when displaying what to him was her false charm of character. He wrote that her intention had been by 'long and artificial speeches' to arouse the sympathy of the judges and to throw all the blame on Elizabeth and her Council. He added that he was pleased to think that they had all been 'of one consent and mind to hear her cause with indifference'. In any event Mary was found guilty of the charge of treason. The sentence of death was not pronounced until later in

London and she was not immediately informed. Sir Amias meanwhile continued to carry out his instructions to secure a full confession. He went to see Mary in her apartments on 1 November, the Feast of All Saints. Mary had spent the day in prayer and reading the lives of the saints, and Sir Amias showed surprising courtesy in waiting until her prayers were over. They had a long talk, discussing history, and Mary enquired after some of the people at her trial who she thought had showed sympathy towards her, and asked their names so that she might remember them. Paulet brusquely replied: 'Not one of them was favourable to your cause'. He continued: 'Everyone else is astonished to see you so calm under the circumstances in which you find yourself. No living person has ever been accused of crimes so frightful and odious as yours.' However, Mary would not admit to any such crimes and merely repeated her claim that she stood witness for the truths of the Catholic religion, and argued with Paulet as to whether or not Elizabeth claimed to be supreme head of the Church. He maintained that Elizabeth was, on the contrary 'Head and Governor under God of things ecclesiastical and temporal in England'. To this Mary merely shrugged, and, with an expressive French phrase, *C'était manteau blanc ou blanc manteau*, dismissed the difference between the two titles. Paulet could only report to London his failure and disappointment. 'I see no change in her, from her former quietness and serenity certified in my letters,' he was obliged to write. These conversations with Mary (in which she frequently had the upper hand) became a source of embarrassment to Sir Amias and he wrote to Walsingham asking him for new instructions: 'Let me hear from you whether it is expected that I should see my charge often, which as I do not desire to do, so I do not see that any good can come from it.'

Mary received the news of her death sentence calmly. From then on Paulet treated Mary as any common condemned criminal. She had managed again to acquire a dais on which she sat, with a royal cloth of state above her chair, Paulet peremptorily ordered its removal, churlishly telling Mary that she was now 'only a dead woman'. Her own servants refused to carry out the order and Paulet's own men were forced to carry out this mean and petty task, and throw the canopy and dais down themselves. His behaviour towards his royal charge became more odious when he went so far as to sit down in her presence with his head covered. He went on to order the removal of the queen's billiard table, saying that it was now no time for her to be indulging in amusement. Paulet appears to have regretted somewhat his action in removing the canopy and dais as it seems to have been prompted by a rumour from London that Elizabeth disliked the idea of a dais, rather than by any definite instructions to remove it. In any event, the next day Sir Amias went to Mary and offered to do what he could to have the dais replaced. But once again Mary was to prove her superiority. She was able to point to the symbol of her faith – a crucifix – which she had already hung in place of the cloth of state. Writing later to Henry of Guise she said: 'I showed them the Cross of my Saviour in the place where my dais had been.'

Fears that Mary might yet escape had not diminished and Paulet requested that the garrison at Fotheringay be strengthened to seventy foot soldiers and fifty bowmen. Sir Amias was joined in his duties during November by Sir Drue Drury, and he wrote to Walsingham thanking him for sending him an assistant. His gout had been troubling him greatly during the past few months:

I can hardly express unto your lordship the great joy which I have conceived of your choice of Sir Drue Drury for my assistant in this charge, wherein, although I know that your lordship's chief and principal regard hath been to further her Majesty's service, yet because your lordship cannot be ignorant of the old acquaintance and good friendship between this gentleman and me, I take it for an especial favour that among so many others meet for this place, it hath pleased your lordship to make choice of one as was so likely to be welcome unto me, as indeed he shall be most heartily welcome. I am well recovered of my gout, I thank God, having felt no pain these three or four days, and now I doubt not but that these good news will set me on foot without delay.

During December Mary again attempted to communicate with Elizabeth. She wrote a letter and requested Paulet and Drury to despatch on her behalf what was to be a farewell to the English Queen. The two guardians, however, delayed in sending it, mainly because Paulet feared that Mary's words might soften Elizabeth's heart and delay or revoke the sentence of execution. Sir Amias wrote to Davison, Secretary of the Council that he would delay sending Mary's letter until the time of her execution was known, which they were hoping would be carried out before Christmas. The letter would then arrive after Mary was dead, when it would be too late for Elizabeth to exercise clemency. Paulet was fanatically convinced that Mary deserved to die. The return to her of her priest de Preau, with his strong Catholic influence, gave Paulet further cause to express his fears for Mary's immortal soul and he wrote to London on the subject thus:

This lady continueth in her former wilful and wicked disposition. No outward sign of repentence; no submission, no acknowledging of her fault, no craving of pardon, no desire of life; so it may be feared lest as she has lived, so she will die, and I pray God that this Popish ignorant priest be not admitted unto her by His just judgement to increase her punishment, being very likely that he will rather confirm her in her stubbornness towards her Majesty, and in all other errors in matters of religion, than seek to reclaim her to a better disposition.

When de Preau arrived, Paulet searched his papers and found two leaves of a diary among his philosophical papers. However, he dismissed de Preau from his mind, summing him up as being of weak and slender judgement. Mary's money taken from her at Chartley was at last returned to her.

Christmas came and went and no news of the impending execution arrived. Paulet was taken ill again with gout and was confined to his bed. In mid-January he wrote to Secretary Davison:

And now lately, by the space of fourteen days, I have been very sick of my gout and have not departed from my bed, where I remain as yet, not without great grief, I assure you, and do not look to be recovered in few days. These are the fruits of my long abode in Chartley House, a place environed with naughty and corrupt waters, which have increased so much my disease as I shall feel of it during the residue of my short days.

He now had a good excuse not to see Mary and could thus avoid those distressing conversations which he so much disliked. Mary for her part missed seeing Sir Amias, for although she detested him, he was at least her one contact with the outside world, and she begged him to pay her a visit when she heard he was up again from his sick bed. She wrote another long letter to Elizabeth requesting some decision to be made as to her future. Paulet adamantly refused to send this letter at all, saying that he was lying in bed with his arms bandaged, and that Mary must wait the answer to her earlier letter. Towards the end of January, the situation seemed to be continuing indefinitely, and Sir Amias did nothing to lighten Mary's burden by informing her steward Melville and the chaplain de Preau, that although they would continue in residence at Fotheringay, from then on they would be parted from their mistress. She would only be permitted to see her physician Bourgoing. This depressing news caused Mary to fear once again the possibility of a secret assassination and she said as much to Bourgoing who expressed these fears to Sir Amias. Paulet was outraged by the suggestion. He said that 'he was a man of honour and a gentleman, and would he wish so to dishonour himself as to wish to exercise such cruelty or to conduct himself like a Turk?' Nevertheless, his protestations of honour did not prevent him from imposing new humiliations on his prisoner. A few days later her butler was forbidden to carry the rod of office before her meat dishes. Mary protested strongly to Paulet, only to be coldly informed that her priest, her steward, her dais and her rod had all been taken from her because she was no longer a queen but 'an attainted convicted and condemned woman'.

In the absence of any definite news from Fotheringay, rumours circulated at the end of January that Queen Mary had in fact been rescued and had escaped. These rumours caused some consternation in London, and Paulet had to write reassuringly to Secretary Davison that the prisoner was quite safe:

> You may see by these letters inclosed, with mine answer to the same, that the report of the Scottish Queen's escape, or of her making away, as it is now termed, carrieth much credit in these parts, as it is followed with hue and cry. And although considering my later letters to like effect, I did not think it needful to advertise you thereof with speed, yet I would not hide it from you, and therefore do send it by one of my servants repairing to London about his own business, not doubting but that the same will come as speedily to your hands as if it had been sent by the post. These seditious rumours are not to be neglected, in my simple opinion, and indeed there is not a more ready way to levy forces to the achieving of that which these lewd reporters pretend to fear. I cannot let them flatter themselves with vain hope, but by the grace of God I will not lose this lady, my charge, without the loss of my life, neither shall it be possible for any force to take her out of my hands alive.

Perhaps these doubts and uncertainties about the safety of the prisoner brought matters finally to a head. After the weeks of procrastination on Elizabeth's part, she finally – although – unwillingly signed the death warrant at the end of January. She had misgivings until the last moment and wondered yet if there was not some other way to be relieved of the responsibility for Mary's death. She consulted with Davison about the terms of the Act of Association. Had not the Members of the Association sworn to kill anyone who should attempt her assassination? As Sir Amias Paulet and his companion, Sir Drue Drury were members of that Association, Elizabeth reasoned that it was their unquestioned duty to relieve her, their queen, of the unpleasant task of a public execution. Davison, she said, must tell Walsingham to write to the pair on those lines. Davison for his part, tried to persuade the queen differently, fearing yet another excuse for a delay to the execution, but she insisted, and the following letter, dated 1 February, was sent by Walsingham to Paulet:

> After our hearty commendations, we find by speech lately uttered by her Majesty that she doth note in you a lack of that care and zeal of her service that she looketh for at your hands, in that you have not in all this time of yourselves (without other provocation) found out some way to shorten the life of that Queen, considering the great peril she is subject to hourly, so long as the said Queen shall live. Wherein, besides a kind of lack of love towards her, she noteth greatly that you have not that care of your

own particular safeties, or rather of the preservation of religion and the public good and prosperity of your country that reason and policy commandeth, especially having so good a warrant and ground for the satisfaction of your consciences toward God and the discharge of your credit and reputations towards the world as the oath of association which you both have so solemnly taken and vowed, and especially the matter wherewith she standeth charged being so clearly and manifestly proved against her. And therefore she taketh it most unkindly towards her, that men professing that love towards her that you do, should in any kind of sort, for lack of the discharge of your duties, cast the burthen upon her, knowing as you do her indisposition to shed blood, especially of that sex and quality, and so near to her in blood as the said Queen is.

These respects do greatly trouble her Majesty, who, we assure you, has sundry times protested that if the regard of the danger of her good subjects and faithful servants did not more move her than her own peril, she would never be drawn to assent to the shedding of her blood. We thought it very well to acquaint you with these speeches lately passed from her Majesty, referring the same to your good judgements. And so we commit you to the protection of the Almighty.

This letter was received at Fotheringay on 2 February at five in the afternoon. With it was an enclosed note from Secretary Davison, which clearly reveals his desire to keep the matter a close secret. It reads as follows:

I pray let this and the inclosed be committed to the fire, which measure shall be likewise mete to your answer, after it hath been communicated to her Majesty for her satisfaction.

This was later followed by another letter from Davison again entreating Sir Amias to burn the earlier letter, and asking him to let Davison know that it had been so destroyed.

Sir Amias's reply to this royal command to commit secret murder has become famous in history. In spite of his unrelenting harshness towards his prisoner, his fanatical hatred of her, and his continued unswerving path of devotion to his duty and loyalty, he was not prepared to stoop so low, even for his queen, as to carry out cold-blooded murder. Here then, after all, was a man of integrity and courage, and courage was certainly needed to disobey what was after all the command of the sovereign. Sir Amias replied in a letter dated 2 February at six in the afternoon. Addressed to Walsingham it reads:

Your letters of yesterday coming to my hands this present day at five in the afternoon, I would not fail according to your directions to return my answer with all possible speed, which shall deliver unto you with great grief and bitterness of mind, in that I am so unhappy to have liven to see this unhappy day, in the which I am required by direction from my most gracious sovereign to do an act which God and the law forbiddeth. My good livings and life are at her Majesty's disposition and I am ready to lose them this next morrow if it shall so please her, acknowledging that I hold them as of her mere and most gracious favour, and do not desire them to enjoy them, but with her Highness' good liking. But God forbid that I should make so foul a shipwreck of my conscience or leave so great a blot to my poor posterity, to shed blood without law or warrant. Trusting that her Majesty, of her accustomed clemency, will take this my dutiful answer in good part (and the rather by your good mediation), as proceeding from one who will never be inferior to any Christian subject living in duty, honour, love and obedience towards his sovereign.

And thus I commit you to the mercy of the Almighty. From Fotheringay the 2nd of February, 1587. Your most assured poor friends

A. Poulet

D. Drury

Your letters coming in the plural number seem to be meant as to Sir Drue Drury as to myself, and yet because he is not named in them, neither the letter directed unto him, he forbeareth to make any particular answer, but subscribeth in heart to my opinion.

Sir Amias did not destroy the letters which had so aroused his indignation, for he left copies with his family so that it might be known that he had not agreed to the obnoxious proposals. A few days later he wrote:

If I should say that I have burned the papers you wot of, I cannot tell if everybody would believe me, and therefore I reserve them to be delivered to your hands at my coming to London. God bless you and prosper all your actions to His Glory. From Fotheringay, the 8th February, 1587.

Yours most assuredly to my small power

A. Poulet.

Meanwhile Elizabeth had signed the death warrant so that the matter was, for all intents and purposes, settled before she received the reply from Sir Amias. Nevertheless, the queen is reported to have been enraged at his refusal to carry out her wishes. Angrily she stamped up and down before Davison, shouting that she could not stomach those 'dainty and precise fellows' who would promise everything and perform nothing. She considered Paulet a perjurer. He had signed the Bond of Association undertaking to serve the queen at the risk of his own life. The matter must be ended, and she considered it a scandal to everyone concerned that she had not been freed from the 'burthen' of responsibility. However, whether the queen knew or not, the warrant and the executioner, on the orders of Burghley and the Privy Council, were already on their way to Fotheringay.

So at long last, on 8 February 1587, Mary, Queen of Scots, was beheaded. She behaved regally to the last. Paulet's men had the task of leading her to the scene of execution, her own servants having been denied to her. Sir Amias himself was present and watched her die. On the scaffold she turned to him and said, 'Thanks, Sir Amias, this will be the last trouble I shall give you.' She also asked him to intercede with Queen Elizabeth that her wishes in her Will should be carried out for the benefit of her servants. Eventually this was done and her estate was valued at 17,000 crowns. It is recorded that Sir Amias wrote later an account of Mary's trial and execution, and that a copy of his manuscript was at one time preserved at Hinton House.

Queen Elizabeth appears to have forgiven Paulet his shortcomings over ending Mary's life, for the following April, on the eve of St George, he was appointed Clerk to the Duchy of Lancaster and Chancellor of the Order of the Garter in succession to Walsingham, and remained in this office for a year. In the following January he attended the Privy Council and signed orders directing Catholic recusants to be dealt with stringently. In February he was lodging in Fleet Street in London and corresponded with Lord Admiral Nottingham respecting the 'right of tenths' in Jersey belonging to the Government. One of his last appointments was as a Commissioner sent to the Low Countries with three others to try to make peace with Spain. This was resented by Catholics and one wrote: 'Paulet is adjoined in Commission, that hard gaoler of the Holy Queen and Martyress. Man muses they are so shameless.' In April he was staying in Twickenham, and he died in London on 26 September age about 56, when the whole country was celebrating the defeat of the Spanish Armada.

He was buried in the church of St Martin-in-the-Fields, but later, when this church was rebuilt, his body was re-interred at Hinton St George in 1728. His monument with additions was re-erected in the Poulett memorial chapel.

It is interesting to note that to historians he is generally known as Sir Amias Paulet, whereas he always signed his name 'A. Poulet', and wrote his Christian name as 'Amice'.

By his first wife Margaret, whose father Anthony Hervey was surprisingly a Catholic, Sir Amias had six or more children. The first son, Hugh, was killed in a street fight in Paris when aged about 22, in 1579. Hugh had acted as his father's confidential messenger, and left behind a memorial of his study of French in a French romance entitled *'L'histoire de la Duchesse de Savoye traduitte d'Anglois en Francoys'*. It seems that another son or daughter died in this same accident, as both Queen Elizabeth and Walsingham wrote to condole with Sir Amias on the death of his 'children'.

The second son, Anthony, became his father's heir. The third son, George, married a distant cousin, Elizabeth Paulet, and so became the owner of the old family home at Gotehurst in Somerset. George also served as his brother's Lieutenant Governor and later as Bailiff in Jersey.

Of Sir Amias's daughters it is known that Joan married Robert Heydon of Bowwood in Devon. Sarah married Sir Francis Vincent of Stoke d'Abernon in Surrey, while the youngest, Elizabeth, died unmarried. Elizabeth was probably born at Tutbury, and is thought to be the god-daughter of Sir Francis Walsingham, referred to in a letter from Paulet to him as 'your Lordship's little god-daughter and my little jewel'.

Anthony was born in Jersey in 1562 and before he was 21 became a Captain in Queen Elizabeth's Guard. Like his father and grandfather before him he served as Governor of Jersey. He was sworn in as Lieutenant Governor on 17 August in 1583, to replace his uncle George, who had been appointed Bailiff. Anthony remained in sole charge for five years, for Sir Amias, after his appointment as Keeper to Mary, Queen of Scots in fact never returned to Jersey.

In 1583 also, Anthony was married and there is a record of his wedding to Katherine Norris (or Norreys) who was the only daughter of Sir Henry Norris, Baron of Rycote, who had been Queen Elizabeth's guardian during the reign of Mary. His wife had acted as governess to Elizabeth and was nicknamed by her 'her own dear black crow'. Katherine's grandfather was Henry Norris, who was executed in 1536 as an alleged lover of Queen Anne Boleyn.

One of the guests at the wedding ceremony was Arthur Throckmorton, who had been in Sir Amias Paulet's train to Paris. In his diary Arthur relates that in May 1583 he received £100, out of which he was able to pay Sir Amias £20 of his debt to him. He was also able to buy some new clothes, yards of velvet for a cloak, a fashionable beaver hat with a silver band, a girdle with silver lace and hangers, and a silvered rapier in a black velvet scabbard. Thus attired he went down to Rycote, Lord Norris's splendid house near Thame in Oxfordshire, where the Palatine (Count Laski) was visiting, attended by Lord Russell, Sir William Russel and Sir Philip Sidney. They were all present when Kate married Anthony on a Sunday in the exquisite chapel of St Michael and All Angels, founded by Richard and Sybilla Quartermain in 1449, and full of wonderful carving.

Sir Anthony finally succeeded to the Governorship in 1590, in spite of local opposition to his appointment. His rigorous control of the island's affairs during his Lieutenant Governorship had already drawn reproofs from his father and when full power came into his

Sir Anthony Paulet 1562–1600
(Attrib. M. Gheeraerts)

hands he continued his stern autocratic policies. In these he was encouraged by his uncle George, the island's Bailiff. Two cases in particular have earned Sir Anthony his reputation. The first became known as the de Carteret affair. This started with a court case held before the Bailiff, George Paulet, when one of the Jurats named Dumaresq insulted the Bailiff. Tempers flared and high words followed, and two more Jurats supported Dumaresq. Anthony, then Lieutenant Governor, eventually ordered the three Jurats to cool their tempers in Mont Orgueil Castle for a day. Constitutionally, this action was quite wrong, as only the Governor could order imprisonment and only for military reasons. One of the Jurats, Jean de Carteret never forgave Anthony this indignity, and during the years that followed he frequently made charges against Paulet. Finally, two Commissioners were sent to Jersey to make full investigation into the charges against Anthony and Bailiff George. Their findings, however, completely exonerated the Paulets from any blame. All this nevertheless, aroused such strong feelings in the island that when Sir Amias died a great effort was made to prevent Sir Anthony from becoming his successor. Jean de Carteret laid a fresh series of charges against him before the Council in London, and was promptly thrown into the Marshalsea Prison, which he had recently left, for these 'injurious and slanderous' attacks. He continued to stir up agitation in Jersey by letters he wrote from prison and feelings ran so high in Jersey that Sir Anthony was forced to keep his guard constantly around him. However, in 1590 he was duly appointed Governor, but at a price. It is recorded that he had to grant 'unto her Majesty a yearly rent of £300 charged upon divers manors of his in Devon, Somerset and Dorset, during such time as he shall enjoy the office of Jersey and all the profits thereof'. He was sworn in before the Court Royal on 4 July. De Carteret's accusations continued and he sent a list of charges to the Council, one of which accused Anthony of selling cannon from Mont Orgeuil for his own profit and that he had sold corn to Spain while the Armada was preparing. The Council again immediately sent investigators and once more their report was a complete vindication of Paulet. The cannon proved to be obsolete ones bought by his father as scrap iron. The disputed corn was a ton which had been on its way to Bayonne to be sold to buy jewellery there for Anthony's wife. A storm drove the ship carrying the corn into San Sebastian where the Spaniards forced it to unload. All the other charges were proved to be without foundation and De Carteret was forced by the Council to make a public apology, and promise that hereafter he would 'lay aside all malice and factions and behave himself as becomes a dutiful subject towards the Magistrates set in authority by the Queen'.

In 1593 Sir Anthony wrote to Lord Burghley expressing his fears of a new Spanish attack on the island, but the enemy made no move. Soon after came the second celebrated case in which Sir Anthony's high-handedness involved him in trouble. In the same letter to Burghley, Anthony had written:- 'One of our English soldiers was bruised by a very bad fellow of this isle that the poor man liveth not above nine days after; whereupon action is intended against the offender, who deserveth no favour in so vile and noctious an act. I hear he intendeth to be a suitor for a pardon from her Majesty. All honest men of the Isle desire greatly to see examplary punishment done upon this evil member.' The Council asked for further particulars about this evil-doer, a man named Michel Poingdestre. In reply Paulet wrote: 'He is hated generally throughout the Isles, for his cruel conversation and corrupt dealing even from his youth. Though he hath gone about to produce testimony of good behaviour, it is manifest that those who signed are bad and vile people. The man is of wealth, and the Lord having by virtue of his indictment put both lands and goods into her Majesty's hands, I hope she will advise to bestow this escheat rather upon the strengthening of this place than permit so evil a member to enjoy it.' However, the Council had had a different version of the incident, from the alleged culprit's wife. She had said that her husband had met the soldier by chance while he was out on the shore gathering seaweed. They had not understood one another and the soldier, named Robins, had grasped Poingdestre who was aged about 75. However, Robins's foot had slipped and he had fallen without any apparent injury. A few days later he had died from some unknown cause. Now the lady felt her husband was unjustly accused of his death. There was no secret feud as the two had never met before and it was unlikely that an old man would attack a younger, much stronger one. The queen herself was present at the Council and was 'in pity much moved by the old man's distress'. Sir Anthony was ordered to release Poingdestre immediately on bail. But the old man was kept in prison and the Council had to send a stern rebuke to Paulet saying: 'He is not such an evil man as you writ, being we are informed of long time employed by yourself as farmer of the tithes. We have cause to think this matter more hardly carried against him than is conscionable. We straitly command you not to proceed further in this cause, till we be better informed. You shall be directed from here. In the meantime set him at liberty on good bail, and suffer him to have possession of his lands and goods.' Sir Anthony could do nothing but comply and he wrote: 'I rather wish Poingdestre's conversion than his overthrow. I do not seek his blood, but shall be glad if the queen will pardon him, provided his wilfulness be bridled.' In spite of his seeming high-handedness and harshness, it may be said that Anthony was only doing what he could to suppress the licence and loose-living that was rife in Jersey at the time. It was unfortunate for Poingdestre that he had been made something of a scape-goat.

In 1594 Sir Anthony experienced failure in another direction. Hoping to increase field sports on the island, he brought a number of hares to Jersey from England and released them, hoping they would breed and increase in numbers. But alas, in spite of strict laws by the Island Court, the local sportsmen quickly exterminated the lot!

Sir Anthony continued the work on the fortifications of the island. He first of all carried on with the work at Mont Orgueil commenced by his father and grandfather, assisted by the military engineer Paul Ivy. One gateway to the castle still shows today the arms of Elizabeth and the Paulets. Ivy advised the Council that no more money should be spent on the castle because of its condition and its tactical position. Instead Paulet was ordered to concentrate on the building of a new castle. The Council wrote saying: 'We have been informed that the Castle is very ill-seated, and lieth subject to a mighty hill but 400 feet distant, and so overtopt by it, and no man possibly can show his face in defence of this side next the hill, which giveth us good cause to think Her Majesty's charges already employed to be to small purpose. We therefore require you to deal with Mr Ivy, and having his advice, to consider what were meet to be done, that neither Her Majesty nor the inhabitants be put to any idle expense.' In March 1594 work was suspended at Mont Orgueil and construction of a new building on an islet in St Helier harbour began, named in honour of the queen – Elizabeth Castle. The queen contributed £500 and the States of Jersey £400. Oak and lime were brought from mainland Hampshire. In spite of setbacks such as the flooding of the cellars, the work progressed over the years and was almost finished by the time of Sir Anthony's death. Extensions were made by later Governors. Paulet's arms, impaling those of his wife, are at the side of the main gate.

In 1595 Sir Anthony returned to England 'to give account of his two years service' and during this visit he was knighted. Although only thirty-three, his health began to fail and in March 1596 he had to write to Sir Robert Cecil that he was unable to keep an appointment with him 'by reason of some infirmity'. He returned to Jersey later in the year and then went home to Somerset where in November he wrote that he was 'unable from illness to undertake the journey' to London. In May the following year he again attempted the journey back to Jersey but wrote that his illness to which he had been subject for three years became so much worse that he was hardly able to return to Hinton. A month or so later Sir Anthony did return to Jersey but in August he wrote that 'having spent this summer upon my charge here, though with difficulty and impairment of health, and finding my health requires counsel of a physician, which this place does not afford, against my will I beg you to obtain my licence to return to England for some time'. In August 1599 he wrote that the Queen had ordered him to remain at home in Hinton until he had fully recovered, but on 22 July the following year he died, at the early age of 38. His widow Katherine did not survive him long and died a year or so later. They were both buried at Hinton St George and their elaborate tomb may be seen immediately to the left of the chancel in the church. Around the base of the memorial are the figures of their ten children: their sons, John the heir, Amias, Henry, Thomas, who died aged 20, and Philip; and their daughters, Elizabeth, Anne, Margery, who married John Sydenham of Combe, Somerset, Susanna, who married Sir Peter Prideaux of Netherton, Devon, and Margaret.

CHAPTER 3

The Three Barons

A very accomplisht gentleman of quick and clear parts,
a bountiful housekeeper.
Revd Dr Thomas Fuller describing the 1st Lord Poulett

John, the eldest son of Sir Anthony Paulet, was born about 1586, nearly at the end of the reign of Queen Elizabeth. He was almost certainly born in Jersey and spent his early years on the island. His father died when John was aged 14. He was fortunate that education for such as he had widened in scope during the Elizabethan era and he was able to attend University College at Oxford, and although he did not graduate, he matriculated on 21 June 1601. At this time the period spent at University was usually limited to a couple of years, and it is doubtful if a very great measure of higher learning was achieved. Training in good manners would be received by young John and his contemporaries, but there would have been little time for much study in other subjects. He spent a brief period in the army and received a colonelcy of cavalry from Edward Seymour, the Earl of Hertford, on 27 November 1608. Two years later John was admitted as a student at the Middle Temple in London. A period of about a year at such an establishment was another means in those days of broadening the outlook and education of the wealthy. Like his stay at University, John would have received little beyond a basic knowledge of the law, enough, however, to provide a useful background for his future life in Somerset. By all accounts the time spent by young gentlemen at these seats of learning was often boisterous and rowdy.

After these early years spent away from home, John returned to Somerset to take up his position as an important country gentleman and county magnate. By the royal service of his father and grandfather, John Paulet had much influence at Court and in his county. In October 1610, ten years after the death of Sir Anthony, he stood for a Somerset Parliamentary seat in a by-election, which he won. He held the seat also in the election of 1614 for the so-called 'Addled Parliament'. The contest for this seat saw the start of a bitter feud between John Paulet and another prominent Somerset gentleman, Sir Robert Phelips of nearby Montacute, which was to last until the latter's death in 1638. Sir Robert was a latecomer in the bid for this particular seat, but he had the backing of his influential father Sir Edward Phelips, who had been Speaker from 1604 until 1611, and he expected Paulet to stand down. This Paulet did not do. John was aided by his friend Sir Maurice Berkeley, and this alliance proved too much for the Phelipses. Sir Edward used all his influence and rallied to his son's support people like the Earls of Hertford and Rutland, Lord Arundell and the Bishop of Bath and Wells. Paulet wrote to a supporter 'I know we have to do with a wavering multitude', and the Phelipses 'muster a great troope of justices and sirs'. But in spite of their backers and also attempts at trickery by Phelips and his associates, Paulet was successful. It is fair to point out that Paulet and Berkeley were aided by a none too particular Sheriff at the hustings. Sir Robert was furious, particularly as Paulet had apparently promised to withdraw if Phelips himself decided to stand. Before this event Phelips and John Paulet had been fairly good friends, but from then on their relationship was tempered with extreme loathing for each other.

In 1613, as befitted a man in his position in the county, John Paulet was appointed a Justice of the Peace, a post he was to hold until 1640. This appointment was the first step on the road to ultimate supremacy in Somerset, a position to which all such men of similar birth and family background aspired. As a Justice he had the responsibility of administering the law and punishing wrongdoers in his particular area. In this year also, John Paulet married. His bride was the young Elizabeth Kenn, the daughter and heir of Christopher Kenn of Kenn Court, also in Somerset. A serious blow occurred to John's pride and reputation in 1615. King James I had always distrusted the Puritans, and suspicion fell on Paulet when the Rector of Hinton St George, Edmund Peacham (whom John's grandfather Sir Amias had installed, being patron of the living) was arrested on charges of treason. Peacham was first prosecuted for a libel on the Bishops, which he had pronounced from his own pulpit. While the prosecution was pending his house was searched and an incriminating manuscript was discovered which contained a personal attack on the king. This document was taken to point to the existence of an organized conspiracy of Somerset gentry against the Act of Benevolence. The unfortunate Peacham was put to the rack and cruelly examined 'in torture, between torture and after torture' to extract a confession. He was eventually found guilty and sentenced to death. He escaped the executioner, however, and died in Taunton gaol about seven months later. John Paulet was suspected of complicity in Peacham's treason. He was twice examined by the Council, in November 1614 and again in March 1615, but no charges were ever formulated against him.

In 1617, by now having regained favour, John Paulet served the obligatory year as Sheriff. Among the gentry this was not a popular appointment. A sheriff was tied to the county for a whole year and could only leave it with royal licence. As a justice Paulet was unable to exercise that office during his shrievalty. This office among all others, such people as Paulet were not keen to undertake and all were very happy to relinquish it when their year was up. In a letter to Secretary Carleton, Paulet wrote from Hinton St George with unusual bitterness, that he was tied to that 'dull and durty place' by the sherrwick. Sheriffs were literally picked with a pin by the king from a list of gentlemen selected by the Lord Keeper.

In 1619 John Paulet was appointed Keeper of Neroche Forest, a few miles to the west of Hinton. Apart from the other duties of this new position, John was able to indulge in his passionate love of hunting, for the forest abounded in wild deer and boar. In 1621 he was back in Parliament for a year as M.P. for Lyme Regis in Dorset, and in 1624 came yet another appointment. John Paulet became Deputy Lieutenant of Somerset. The county was administered by some fifteen deputies responsible to the Lord Lieutenant, who at this time was William Herbert, 3rd Earl of Pembroke.

In 1625 James I died and was succeeded by his son Charles I. It was a great year for John Paulet and Hinton St George. On a journey to view the fleet at Plymouth the king stayed at Hinton House where John and Elizabeth Paulet provided the best of hospitality possible for their royal guest. The results of this visit was another visitor, perhaps not quite so welcome. In October arrived the Duke of Soubise at Hinton House. He was the French Huguenot leader who had recently been defeated by the Duke de Montmorency. King Charles was attempting to act as a mediator between King Louis of France and the Huguenots, but relations between France and England at this time were once again at a low ebb. The presence at Court of the somewhat belligerent Frenchman was an embarrassment to the king. To send him to stay at Hinton was a welcome solution. The Duke stayed at Hinton House for a year, and unwelcome as he was, it gave John Paulet his first important contact with Secretary Buckingham and a direct link with the king. He was able to report regularly on the attitude and intentions of his guest. Hugh Pyne was able to write later that the king had 'committed Monsieur Soubise to

John, 1st Baron Poulett
1586–1649 (Artist unknown)

Mr Poulettes custodie, because hee knew him to bee a good gaoler'. However, the enforced task was not without its compensations and John Paulet's reward came in 1627 when he was elevated to the peerage with the title of Baron Poulett, by Letters Patent dated 23 June. This indeed was a great step forward on the road to supremacy in the county. He became at this time one of the only two titled families in Somerset, the other being that of the Earl of Marlborough, formerly Sir James Ley of Beckington.

Another happy event occurred that year when his eldest daughter Florence, at the early age of 15, was married to the 17-year-old Thomas Smyth, the son of Sir Hugh Smyth of Ashton Court near Bristol. So began a close and loving link between the two families, which is borne out from the mass of letters which survive among the Smyth family papers. Together with the letters of the numerous members and branches of the Smyth family, there are many letters written by Lord and Lady Poulett, daughter Florence and her brother Amias. The two families were in constant touch, journeying frequently between Hinton and Ashton, and staying at each other's houses for varying periods of time.

The wedding was arranged but Sir Hugh Smyth was taken ill and was not expected to live. The ceremony had to be rushed through because Tom was a minor and could have been made a ward of court and the estate passed to the Crown. In fact Sir Hugh died three days after the wedding and Lord Poulett became Tom's guardian. John was unable to attend the funeral as he had important business to attend to in London. Apologizing he wrote 'I had no thought when I went to bed last night that any accident would happen to hinder my intention therein, but at midnight came a messenger sent in post haste to me from London to have me there at Saturday next. I am a little distempered with the journeys I have had of late and had physick in my belly yesterday and today and for that cause I have sent to London to make my excuse until ye next weeke: and this must serve my excuse to you that I am not at ye funerall of your father.' The urgent business in London was the matter of John's elevation to the peerage as Baron Poulett of Hinton St George. In March the following year Lord Poulett duly took his seat in the House of Lords.

John was now in an even better position to cultivate his connections at Court. Among his influential friends, he counted Sir Edward Nicholas, secretary to the Duke of Buckingham; Lord Conway, whom he provided with Cheddar cheese when it was available, and to whom he promised a sight of 'some tricksey lasses' should Lord Conway visit Hinton at Christmas. Also Secretary Carleton, now Lord Dorchester, to whom he wrote thanking him for raising his esteem among his neighbours and friends 'by manifesting the interest I have in you'. He was able too, to further his sons' interests (by now he had two) and in 1629 they were in the train of the Earl of Danby on his embassy in France. The elder boy, John, was already joint Keeper of Neroche Forest with his father. Lord Poulett's influence with Buckingham also brought about the appointment of his uncle George as a Somerset J.P. Lord Poulett was now an immensely powerful man, appointments were handed out at his word and dismissals carried out at his bidding.

In London King Charles's troubles with Parliament increased and in 1629 he dispensed with Parliament altogether and so began the eleven years of what has become known as the King's Personal Rule. More than ever before the affairs of the counties became directly the responsibility of the local Lords Lieutenant and their Deputies and the various officers under them, answering only to the Privy Council and the king. In Somerset the Lord Lieutenantcy continued in the Herbert family by the appointment in 1630 of Philip, 4th Earl of Pembroke, whose seat was at Wilton in Wiltshire. Presumably the as yet untried John Poulett was too new a peer to be given the top position. He was, however, by now the Chief Deputy and as such had the Lord Lieutenant's ear. His old enemy Robert Phelips was also a Deputy and the two men continued their struggle for supremacy in Somerset at every opportunity. Both Poulett and Phelips wrote many letters at this time to persons in authority. Many of Poulett's are now among the State Papers in the Public Record Office, whilst Phelip's letters and papers are in the County Record Office at Taunton. Several bear out the hatred each man felt for the other and show that not an opportunity was missed for belittling each other in their superiors' eyes.

Nevertheless John Poulett was by now to all intents and purposes the most important man in Somerset and among the wealthiest. He spent little time away from the county and his family, and disliking London as he did, found plenty to occupy him in the neighbourhood. All wealthy county magnates vied with each other in their show of importance and riches. Their mansions had to dominate their neighbours' houses. Their herds of deer must be the largest. When they moved round the county attending sessions or assizes their retinue had to make a great impression with the richness of dress and equipment for their horses. All this proclaimed the importance of the Lord of the Manor to the ordinary man in the street. Not to be outdone by the splendours of Montacute House, Lord Poulett set about adding a magnificent suite of state rooms to Hinton House in the style of the contemporary architect Inigo Jones. At Ashton Court Tom Smyth, now a J.P., was also building an even grander new wing to his family home. The similarity between the two wings indicates that the same builder or architect was probably employed. While the work was going on the two families spent long periods in each other's houses. John Poulett wrote: 'I shall not be sorry to hear your building goes slowly on, that you may be drawne to make use of my house ye longer and that I may have your company till your own be finished, and here you are at home as at Ashton, and mine shall ever be as free to you whiles he is owner of it.' In 1637 John made an arrangement with his two sons-in-law, Tom Smyth and Dennis Rolle of Stevenstone, North Devon (the husband of his daughter Margaret), to divide the year equally between their three homes and to agree to pay all household expenses for the time they acted as host. This friendly and economical arrangement apparently worked well, until sadly, Dennis Rolle died in 1638 aged 24. His widow Margaret erected a marble monument in the church at the family estate at Bicton in South Devon.

When at home Poulett of course, like the other magnates, entertained lavishly at his mansion and enjoyed the pleasures of the hunt when the season allowed, to the point of excess. The hunt held a high place as the foremost diversion for the wealthy men of the day. His reputation was further enhanced by the size of his hunting party and the number of his dogs and servants. The Phelips family were also passionate huntsmen, so much so that the family motto *Pro aris et focis* was taken by the locals to mean 'For hares and foxes'!

The festive seasons were also occasions for entertainment at the great houses. The Charter for Hinton Fair was granted to Lord Poulett in 1633, the fair to take place annually on St George's Day, 23 April. Also in that year Thomas Gerrard wrote his account of Hinton in his *Particular Description of Somerset*. The year is also notable for it was then that the village Churchwardens' accounts begin, which throw much light on the life of Hinton St George over the ensuing years.

A friend of the Poulett family was the famous Dr Thomas Fuller who from 1634 to 1642 was the vicar of nearby Broadwindsor just over the border in Dorset. Fuller was later to become known for his book *The Worthies of England* which included a chapter about Sir Amias Paulet. He also wrote a *History of the Church* in which he dedicated some sections to Lady Poulett. Fuller described Lord Poulett as 'a very accomplisht gentleman of quick and clear parts, a bountiful housekeeper'.

The duties of Deputy Lieutenants were considerable. They were supported by the Sheriffs and constables. The Lord Lieutenant's time was taken up primarily with his duties on the Privy Council and so the actual county administration fell to the deputies. Lord Poulett as Chief Deputy took precedence over the others and it was upon him that the Lord Lieutenant relied. It was one of the main duties of the deputies to raise and train men for the army. Each deputy had his own district of administration and raised a regiment of men in his own area. In the summer there would be a muster of the various regiments and a Grand Review would be held in which the troops were inspected by the Chief Deputy to assess their state of readiness for a call to arms if it should come. These years were peaceful ones for England and in consequence the attendance at training and musters was not regarded with much enthusiasm by the local men so called upon, especially when they were expected to attend at harvest time. There were always absentees and defaulters at the Review and the whole affair must have had its comic side. The troops on parade were lucky if they had any arms, and they had to wait while these were brought from the various village arsenals by the constables. When all was ready Lord Poulett would arrive in his coach, checking men and arms haphazardly. If there was time, there might be a display of drill. All this would be repeated the second day, after the absentees had been brought in. It would end when Lord Poulett left the parade ground in order to get home to Hinton in time for dinner!

For some years the King's Personal Rule went well and his decision appeared to be justified. The country was prosperous and at peace, and after personal difficulties the king's marriage at last appeared harmonious. Charles depended on two men to carry out his policy of a benevolent dictatorship. They were Thomas Wentworth, the Earl of Strafford and William Laud, the Archbishop of Canterbury.

The year 1631 saw the publication of the Book of Orders, an important piece of legislation by the Council, designed to bring about the strict enforcement of the law, and introducing better means to enforce the law itself. It also made provision for the relief of the poor and work for the unemployed. Poor children were to be bound as apprentices and there was to be strict suppression of vagrancy. Just before the issue of the Book, Lord Poulett had proposed to the local sessions that he build another house of correction at Crewkerne to deal with the increased number of petty offenders, vagrants and masterless persons. At this time the country, especially Somerset, swarmed with Irish vagrants. Depression had forced many honest men on to the road. In Somerset their numbers were increased by unwanted immigrants from Ireland smuggled over and landed at places along the Bristol Channel by unscrupulous ships' masters, no doubt lured by tales of easy fortunes to be made in England. Some of these wandering Irishmen reached Hinton St George, and there are references to them in the Churchwardens' Accounts. One such man and his wife and six children were given 6d. by the parish to help them on their way!

The year 1634 saw another problem for the local governors and the country. This was the extension of the collection of Ship Money to inland places. In the past this tax had been levied on coastal towns for the maintenance of the Royal Navy. The Navy, however, had been allowed to run down, piracy was a threat to English merchant shipping and there was no money to re-equip the naval force. It is interesting to note that Somerset had the distinction of troubling the Council more than any other county over the rating of ship money. Many districts or hundreds, and towns in Somerset complained that they were being rated in excess of the rate for 'common payments'. This rate curiously enough meant the 'Hinton Rate', which was the 'most aunciente, generalle and usuale rates of the countye'. This rate determining the proportion which each hundred was to furnish, either of men or money, had been devised by nine commissioners for musters at Hinton St George in 1569 for levying 100 men for Irish service. The hundreds insisted that this rate, fixed over sixty years previously, should still hold good for their rating of ship money. The Hinton Churchwardens' Accounts contain the following entry for the year 1635: 'A Note of the Aunciente customes and manner of tythinge and paiments of all Tythes within the manner of Henton St George lyeth in the chest in the Vestri.'

Lord Poulett had a period away from country and county duties in 1634 when he took command of *The Constant Reformation* a ship of 742 tons, carrying 250 men and 40 guns, in a fleet commanded by the Earl of Lindsay to protect British commerce from the French and Dutch. He wrote frequently to 'Sonne Smyth' at Ashton while he was away. After one sailing he wrote: 'We have been out but once to the French coast, but I think ye French fleet and ours will not meete unless ye winds bring us together agaynst their will.' In another letter he says: 'I was yesterday ashore to see my sister and went back to the shippe at night, and 'twas so ill weather that I hope 'twill be one of the greatest dangers escaped that I shall meete with this journey . . . I hear now by a boat of mine which came this day from the shore, that a boat that came after me over sett and all in her were drowned, but what the boat is, or who ye men are I do not yet heare. They are none of our ship's, thank God.'

While out at sea he writes:

We have been neare ye French fleete and ye Dutch fleete since wee came out, but unto none of ye men of warre who have all kept ye narrow seas and gone to ye West. Ye

Admiral is advertised that they are now 52 saile of shippes and lye at ye Lizard whither we are going as fast as ye wind will blow us. . . . Once or twice ye Alarm hath been given to ye fleete by 60 ships on sight and to the wind of us, which served us to put all things in readiness though when we came up to them wee found ourselves all friends and so parted. If wee have any enemies I hope they will keep themselves out of our way for we threaten what wee will doe if wee meet with them, yet I wish they would be so curteous as to give us leave to make our service this yeare, and them another yeare, I will say and ye rest doe, let them come.

There was still time for courtesy and hospitality, and one of the officers on board with him recorded that: 'My Lady Poulett and other ladies and many gentlemen of great quality came aboard and were nobly feasted and entertained.'

After only three and a half months an attack of gout, from which he continually suffered, forced Lord Poulett to give up the command of his ship. Home at Hinton again he writes: 'Our horses and hounds mend every day and indeed wee have had very good sport. . . . Jack Arundell and Frank are constant huntsmen. I carried Ralph Hopton into the Arundell Cockpit, where we unstopped some of his bottles and topped his march beer and had a pretty bout after a chase.' Gout was soon forgotten! His time at sea was not without reward for he was knighted on board another ship, *The Mary Honour*, in September the same year.

Matters came to a head between Poulett and Phelips in 1636 (Phelips was also the uncle by marriage of Thomas Smyth). Sir Robert Phelips had spent a period in the Tower of London where he had been imprisoned for his show of animosity in Parliament and consequently had lost all his local offices. He was released in 1628 and was soon reinstated as a Deputy Lieutenant, and over the years his feud with Lord Poulett had continued. Various episodes kept the animosity on the boil. In 1633 Phelips had had occasion to take to task a Captain John Boyse, a company commander of Poulett's regiment who was resident in Phelip's division, for refusing to take an apprentice into his ranks. Phelips was able to secure Boyse's dismissal from his captaincy. This of course directly opposed Lord Poulett's wishes, which only added zest to Phelip's actions. Lord Poulett was forced to accept the dismissal of Boyse and had also to fill the vacancy with the son of a magistrate, Robert Harbyn, who was allied with Phelips himself. The affair no doubt caused untold harm to the morale and discipline of Boyse's company and possibly to the whole of Lord Poulett's regiment.

In 1636 Phelips complained to the Lord Lieutenant that Poulett had mustered his regiment in his (Phelip's) division without notifying him of the muster or requesting permission to do so. In retaliation Lord Poulett arrested a country rustic named Roman Spracklinge for not attending musters. This Spracklinge had joined Poulett's regiment in 1627 to avoid the pressmen, carrying arms voluntarily given to him by Phelips for the occasion. When pressing was over, Phelips had taken back the arms and Spracklinge had ceased attending the musters. In an earlier dispute between the two rivals, mention had been made of Phelips's reappropriation of Spracklinge's arms, but the Council's judgement had not mentioned it. Poulett thought now that by raising the question of Spracklinge's non-attendance at musters in 1636, Phelips's actions in 1628 would be questioned again. What Poulett did not know, however, was that Spracklinge *had* attended the muster in question. He had been improperly summoned but had appeared on the second day after Lord Poulett had left the field. Thus he was clapped in gaol on a charge so carelessly drafted that even the date of the muster was given incorrectly. Through this error he was able to secure his release. Then egged on by Phelips, Spracklinge petitioned the Lord Lieutenant to right the wrong done to him. Lord Pembroke then called on Poulett and his colleagues to answer the petition. After a long delay their reply charged Phelips with obstruction, and said that if a trained soldier was to be protected from their warrants, then none would obey them in future. Lord Pembroke in reply said he would suspend Phelips if Poulett could prove his case, and a date was set for the case to be heard in London. In May 1637 the case was duly aired before the Lord Lieutenant and two Councillors. The evidence produced was overwhelmingly in favour of Spracklinge and exonerated him completely. Lord Poulett was reprimanded by Lord Pembroke and he felt so incensed that on his return to Hinton he had Spracklinge gaoled again in direct contempt of the Lord Lieutenant's judgement. For this unprecedented action Poulett received a most severe rebuke from Lord Pembroke in which he said that having taken the case into his own hands 'others ought not to have laid theirs upon it . . . which I take not well'. Poulett was in dire public disgrace and in very real danger of being dismissed from his post as Deputy Lieutenant. It was not, however, the first time that Lord Poulett had almost brought about his own downfall. As Keeper of Neroche Forest, he naturally viewed the plans of King Charles for its disafforestation, and the consequent loss of his hunting ground, with great misgivings. The tenants in Neroche and all the smallholders there could see that the tiny tracts of land to be allocated to them would not compensate for the loss of the commons they had enjoyed under the king's forest laws which had prohibited enclosure. Lord Poulett had seen the plans mainly as the termination of his hunting there, and also, though of less importance, the end of a royal office which gave him some close contacts at court. He had been therefore, actively engaged in opposing the measures and he had written numerous letters complaining of the commissioners who 'turned me out of my pleasure'. In January 1629 there had been a meeting of displeased local inhabitants at Ashill, organized by Poulett's ranger, and arranged no doubt with Poulett's blessing. The Commissioners complained about his obstinacy and his collusion with the opposition had by 1631 almost brought about the end of his favour at Court. He was threatened with a fine and showed unusual firmness in writing to Dorchester refusing to pay. Nevertheless the plans for Neroche were carried out, for the king himself had more than a passing interest in the matter, while Attorney General Heath had acquired the manor of Broadway from Sir Robert Phelips in return for Muchelney from the Crown. Phelips had been appointed an assistant to the Neroche Commissioners and was thus delighted to be in a position to further embarrass Poulett. Memories of these earlier events had certainly been revived for Lord Pembroke and had prompted him to issue such a stern rebuke to his Chief Deputy. It was a very real set-back to Poulett's quest for county supremacy, and it may be said that Sir Robert Phelips had then won their contest on that score. He was not to enjoy his triumph for long, however, for he died in April 1638.

Meanwhile things were worsening in the country on a wider front. In 1639 a revolt broke out in Scotland, brought about by Laud's attempt to impose the English Prayer Book on 'The Covenanters' – the mainly Presbyterian folk of the region. An army was raised to crush the rebellion but the rebels were not intimidated by the reticent English army, and the uprising threatened to spread south of the border.

In September 1640 the King called a Great Council of Peers at York. Lord Poulett and two of his sons attended, albeit very reluctantly. John writes to Smyth:

Sonne, I was so harte-swollen at parting that I made my expressions to you more by signes and wordes, for which you will excuse me. Here, in York I found ye King accompanyed with some few Lords and servants, but without an army or standard displaide, ye assignment being transferred to Newcastel wither the King intends to remove as soon as he hath given orders for his affaires. I do not hear ye Covenanters offer any submission but that they possess ye strong places and fortify them, banish ye

Papists and confiscate the goods of those that will not enter into ye Covenant; upon which pretence many Scots have refuge to ye King dailye of which some I think are honest and others I believe are spies.

He goes on to say that news had arrived that the Earl of Strafford (the king's Lord Lieutenant in Ireland) had sent 500 soldiers to Carlisle to proceed to capture Berwick under the command of Sir Jacob Astley. . . . 'Ye Earl of Essex is within 25 miles of it [Berwick] with 2,000 foote and 300 horses . . . and 'tis hoped that he will go in and find the place empty.'

His next letter reports the capture of Berwick and the king's decision to refortify the town. Charles decided that he would take it well if gentlemen of worth would put themselves into Berwick, 'where unto your two brothers (in-law) were assigned; which I was not otherwise sorry for but that they went from me in a tyme when I was very sick with the dregges of my ague and ye goute'. His old ailments had recurred due to the stress of the long journey north. He was lodging with a physician who 'can see nothing in my urinall but that I may come home safely after a few months and perhaps kill some of ye bucks at Ashton yet before the season passes'.

However, things did not go as was hoped and the Covenanters defiantly fortified Edinburgh and crossed the border into England. Eventually the king was forced to surrender and Poulett writes of the confused scene around him before the king's submission. 'Here is nothing but noise of drums and gunns and trumpets and horses and ye streets full of Cavaliers and yet are there the fewest voluntiers that ever I saw in any army . . . if you saw our men with their feathers and buff cotes and bigg lookes you would say the Scotts are like to have but a bad bargayn in meddling with us. . . . For my part that am not yet come to my buff cote and feather I pray for peace and that ye shocke of our arms may not be tried.' His prayer was answered and there was peace, although humiliating for the king. He had to promise never to interfere in the religion of the Covenanters again. He also had to pay all their expenses. This he found impossible to do as he was by now bankrupt. There was nothing else for him to do but to summon a new Parliament.

Elections were held, and after eleven years with no representation, the new members were eager to press for their democratic rights, bringing petitions against the king's illegal taxes and subsidies. Somerset produced a mixed selection of representatives, mainly royalist at heart, some, however, would later side with the Parliamentary cause.

Lord Poulett and Tom Smyth (as elected member for Bridgwater) attended what has become known as the Long Parliament. We read that they travelled to London with Florence and took lodgings in Chandos Street in Covent Garden to be ready for the opening on 3 November 1640.

One of the main issues which concerned the new Parliament was the impeachment of the hated Earl of Strafford. He had been Charles's Lord Lieutenant in Ireland and had overseen a policy of brutal repression and cruelty that had all but destroyed the rule of law in that unhappy land. Charles had recalled Strafford to London to support him and promised that he 'should not suffer in his person, honour or fortune'. Upon his appearance in the House of Lords he was forbidden to speak and removed to the Tower of London. His trial for treason opened in Westminster Hall on 22 March 1641. Tom Smyth attended. 'I am in haste and wearied out dayly with attending my Lord Strafford's trial which has held since Monday seven-night and is not halfe-way ended,' he writes. The trial went on until 13 April but the charge of treason could not be proved. Strafford had come to symbolize absolute monarchy and in Parliament's eyes his death was a political necessity. A Bill of Attainder was introduced which, regardless of his guilt or not, simply declared it to be the will of Parliament that he should die. The Bill was passed with a large majority and the Lords were stampeded into agreeing also. Charles was forced to give his assent and on 12 May, Strafford was beheaded before a vast crowd on Tower Hill.

During the year the king's position grew weaker. The Catholic queen was unpopular and there were renewed troubles in Ireland, ending in the Irish Massacre.

Charles was presented with the Grand Remonstrance which was a Bill of Indictment, accusing Charles and his councillors among other things, of promoting a militant Catholic Party and trying to impose an arbitrary Government on the country.

The king then charged five members of the Commons with treason and ordered their arrest. This was refused and the king went in person to the House to confront the disobedient Commons. The five men had flown, and Charles realized he was powerless to compel the people to surrender them. Charles left London for York in January 1642, and his position with Parliament went from bad to worse. In June that year, he was presented with the Nineteen Propositions which in effect would have taken most of the power from his hands. They proposed that Parliament should say whom the king's children should marry and by whom be educated. Laws against Roman Catholics would be strictly enforced in all walks of life, and the king must sign the Militia Ordnance which would give the control of the army absolutely to Parliament. Charles refused all this and the resulting division of the country into Royalists and Parliamentarians led inevitably to the Civil War.

All over the country those faithful to Charles rallied to his cause and raised men and arms to aid him. Similarly the Parliamentary sympathizers did likewise. John, Lord Poulett, in spite of the Puritan traditions of his family was an ardent Royalist at heart, owing as he did his title and position to his king. On the passing of the Militia Ordnance in 1642, he withdrew from Parliament and signed the York Manifesto of 15 June which declared that the king had no intention of taking up arms against Parliament. His son-in-law Thomas Smyth also proclaimed for the king and was expelled from Parliament as a delinquent. On 11 July the King's Commissions of Array were published and the Marquess of Hertford had received his Extraordinary Commission at York, to raise forces in Somerset. As Bath was a solid Parliamentary stronghold, Wells was chosen as the Royalist rallying point. Here Lord Poulett and his sons, John and Francis, together with Tom Smyth, joined Hertford, bringing with them a substantial troop of men. Other notables joining Hertford in Wells were John Digby, son of the Earl of Bristol, Sir Francis Hawley, and Poulett's old friend Sir John Stawell. The young Sir John Poulett took part in one of the early skirmishes of the war in the west when with Sir John Stawell and three troops of horse and dragoons, he went to protect the road between Wells and Glastonbury from a suspected attack by Parliamentary forces. Riding towards Somerton they came to Marshalls Elm and discovered in a cornfield 2 miles away an enemy force of 600 men. Stawell decided to parley, and he, with Hawley and young Poulett, met at the Elm with the Parliamentary leader John Pyne of Curry Mallet, and tried to discourage him from advancing. A battle ensued in which seventeen Parliamentarians were killed and eighteen died later from wounds.

Wells soon became almost surrounded by Parliamentary forces and Hertford ordered a retreat which was given to Sir Ralph Hopton to carry out. The withdrawal was effected during 6/7 of August by way of Glastonbury and Somerton and the Royalist force made its way to the castle at Sherborne in Dorset. By all accounts Lord Poulett was very unpopular in Wells because of his harsh dealings with the people there and on one occasion he was nearly lynched by a hostile mob, being rescued in time by a troop of cavalry.

The force remained at Sherborne for a month and a half, being joined by Sir John

The Return of the Pouletts from the Wars (Artist unknown)

Berkeley, Colonel William Ashburnham and other officers. Lord Poulett and his son John had both been declared delinquents by Parliament and warrants were issued for their arrest. Lord Poulett was also impeached for high treason. Hopton and Hertford were declared delinquents and evidence of their treason was offered by a report from Sherborne made by one George Leddoze, a merchant of Dorchester, who said, on his examination by Justices of the Peace, that he had been taken for a spy and was examined at Sherborne Castle by Poulett, Hopton, Stawell and Sir John Berkeley. He was asked whether he were for king or Parliament and had replied 'for both'. Lord Poulett had said that all Parliamentarians who were for the militia being under their own control, were proclaimed traitors and 'crop-eared rogues', and that Sir Walter Erle, M.P. for Weymouth, was the wickedest rogue of them all and 'one of the Devil's limbs'. Hopton and the others had agreed and Sir Ralph had said further that God was plainly with the Cavaliers in protecting so small a number as they were, and those who took up arms for Parliament, were 'bloodsucking rogues'.

Hopton's enforced stay at Sherborne was prolonged because being so small a force they were cut off from any outside help. Eventually, however, Hertford decided to retreat to Wales, and the force left Sherborne Castle, calling briefly at Hinton House before making their way to the coast through hostile country. On reaching Minehead they found only two boats and Hertford took a force of volunteers including the Pouletts and Tom Smyth over to Wales, leaving the remainder under the command of Sir Ralph Hopton. Here Lord Poulett's devoted 'Sonne Smyth' died at the beginning of October, possibly from small-pox combined with the rigours of the past weeks. He was 32 years old. Poulett accompanied the body back to Ashton for burial before rejoining Hertford in Wales. But in a skirmish near Bridgnorth he was taken prisoner by Essex. When he regained his liberty Lord Poulett rejoined Hopton in Somerset.

In May the following year, with Sir John Stawell Lord Powett sent 1,500 men to assist in the siege of Exeter. On 10 July a Commission directed Edmund Windham, the High Sheriff of Somerset, John, Lord Poulett, Sir John Stawell and seven others, or any three of them, to inquire by oath or witnesses what persons in the past year had been in rebellion or aiding those in rebellion, and if they had any 'lande tenaments or other hereditaments, or any goode ready money plate cattell or chattelle reall or personell and any debts owing unto them by any person or persons within this County'. These magnates were authorized to 'dispose of such lands tenament and hereditaments' etc., as 'His Majesty from Tyme to Tyme under his Signe Manuall shall direct and not otherwise'. Later Poulett raised a brigade of 2,500 men in the neighbourhood of Oxford (his name appears among the signatures to the Scottish Privy Council issued from Oxford on the eve of the Scottish invasion).

In the winter Poulett led his men into Devon and on 18 January 1644 he attacked and burned Ashe House near Axminster. This was the home of Lady Eleanor Drake, the widow of Sir John Drake and a near neighbour of Poulett's. She had become alarmed by Royalist activities in the West Country and had asked for a Roundhead garrison to protect her house. She was of 'good affection' to Parliament and had aided them with money and provisions and had persuaded her tenants in seven adjoining parishes to follow her example. The Parliamentary troops had been sent, but before the place could be fortified Lord Poulett had marched upon it with his Irish troops. He drove out the Parliamentarians, burned the house and 'strippt the good lady, who almost naked and without shoe to her foot but what she afterwards begged, fled to Lyme for safety'. Her son John could not help her. At this time he was a prisoner of the Royalist Prince Maurice. Her sister, the Countess of Marlborough, stood high with the Royalists and appealed for his release. But the Parliamentary forces were now moving towards Axminster, and as young Drake had threatened that he would get Lord Poulett's house at Hinton burned in revenge, his liberation was not unnaturally refused. (Lady Drake's daughter Elizabeth was married to Winston Churchill of Wooton Clanville near Sherborne. After the wars they returned to the ruins of Ashe House which was not rebuilt for many years. They had twelve children, one of whom, John, became the great Duke of Marlborough and who challenged the descendant of Lord Poulett to a duel after he had insulted the Duke in the House of Lords. It can be conjectured whether the ill-feeling then had anything to do with the bitterness over the burning of Ashe House. (Four years after the incident Lady Drake was awarded £1,500 compensation to be paid out of Lord Poulett's estate for the burning of her house. In 1650 she complained that she was still owed £600 and it was six years before she obtained the full amount. Ashe House still stands today, rebuilt again after another fire in 1788 but with some of the old rooms and the chapel still intact.)

After the battle of Ashe House, Poulett engaged a party of Parliamentary troops under Sir William Waller at Hemyock Castle and defeated them, and in March he occupied the town of Wellington. From here he went on to join the prolonged siege of Lyme Regis. Lyme was one of the few remaining enemy strongholds in the west. Although it had a Royal charter it had succeeded in holding out against the Royalist army for several months. In April 1644 a particularly fierce onslaught was made by Prince Maurice and his troops. The townspeople and their defenders were outnumbered by about nine to one, but they succeeded in keeping the Royalists at bay. Lord Poulett with Prince Maurice and Sir John Berkeley took part in the various forays and on one occasion Lord Poulett lent his own armour to a Captain Southern during a very fierce attack. Sixty Royalists, including Captain Southern, were killed that day and because of the armour a rumour was started that Poulett had himself been slain. The town succeeded in its defiance of the king and was eventually relieved by the army of the Earl of Essex who arrived on 15 June having advanced from Weymouth. The Royalists were driven off and were forced to retreat to Exeter, being harassed all the way by Waller's forces, and lost many men. In a Parliamentary report Lord Poulett is said to have made an order 'to kill men, women and children without mercy' at Lyme Regis, but to 'reserve such ministers as they could take that were well wishers to Parliament for to be flayed alive and suchlike equisite torments!' Such highly coloured condemnations of their Royalist enemies were a feature of Parliamentary reports at this time. Poulett is further reported to have said that 'no yeoman should earn more than £10 a year' and 'when the power should be totally on their side [when the king wins] they shall be compelled to live at that low allowance, notwithstanding their estates are gotten with a great deal of labour and industry'.

In the comparative safety of Exeter were established the king and his Court. Queen Henrietta Maria had earlier left for France leaving behind her new-born baby daughter in the care of the Governor, Sir John Berkeley. The baptism of the little princess, Henrietta Anne, was held in the cathedral on 21 July 1644 with Berkeley, Lady Dalkeith and Lady Poulett as sponsors. The king did not stay long in Exeter but set out with Prince Maurice and Hopton in pursuit of Essex and on 1 September there was a great victory in Cornwall when a large Parliamentary force surrendered to the king.

On 17 September King Charles returned to Exeter and made arrangements for his daughter's household. Also in Exeter at this time was an old friend of the Pouletts, Dr Thomas Fuller, the one-time vicar of Broadwindsor, and he was appointed chaplain to the princess. This was King Charles's last visit to Exeter and on 23 September he left the west for the city of Oxford. Lord Poulett accompanied him to Chard and was his host once again at Hinton House on 30 September, where they were joined by Prince Rupert who reported to the king on the defeats his armies were suffering in other parts of the country.

In October 1645 Lord Poulett must have been saddened by the news of the end of the siege of Basing House in Hampshire, where his kinsman John Paulet, the Marquess of Winchester, had held out for two years against Parliamentary forces attempting to capture the mansion. A determined final attack with siege guns led by Cromwell himself successfully breached the walls. One hundred defenders were killed and the house was captured and completely destroyed by fire and pillage.

Lord Poulett returned to Exeter and later had a violent quarrel with Prince Maurice which led to a rift in their friendship. John was appointed a Commissioner for Exeter and remained there when the tide of war again flowed in that direction. The city was besieged throughout the winter of 1645 and in January 1646, General Lord Fairfax called for its surrender. Sir Ralph Hopton was made Commander in Chief of Exeter and the beleagured Royalists held out until March. A treaty of surrender was finally signed on 9 April. Lord Poulett was taken prisoner on 13 April and brought to London. He was by now in very bad health and was allowed to stay at his own house in Chiswick, after intercession by his son's wife's brother-in-law, Lord Fairfax.

On 22 March 1647 the Commons ordered that, after payment of £1,500 to Lady Drake, the rest of Poulett's rents should be applied to the use of the State, but the Lords amended this order to the effect that £200 per annum should be settled on Lyme Regis, £1,500 paid to Lady Drake and the balance of the rents could be retained by Lord Poulett. The Commons disagreed and on 7 August ordered that 2,000 oak trees were to be cut down on his lands and those of his son, although they had settled land worth £4,000 on Lyme Regis. Eventually, however, again through intercession by Fairfax, his fine was reduced to £2,742, plus the payments to Lady Drake and Lyme Regis as had been proposed by the Lords. Thus Lord

Poulett was dealt with fairly leniently and was allowed the benefit of the Exeter Articles (the terms agreed on the surrender of Exeter, April 1648) and avoided any further punishment.

Hinton St George appears to have escaped most of the fighting, although early in the war a band of Parliamentarians touring the area looking for arms and Royalist sympathizers, arrived at Hinton House. There were about fifty men guarding the mansion and they put up some resistance. They told the would-be invaders to 'begone otherwise they would let bullets fly among them'. The gates were forced and some arms and horses were seized and a man was killed in the struggle. Visits by both sides are recorded and Royalist troops are said to have been quartered in the village in 1644 and cavalry in the huge cellars of the mansion. Pikes made for the defence of the house were at one time preserved at Taunton Castle museum. The Parliamentarians had considerable influence in the area, however, for in 1644 the Rector of Hinton, Richard Gove, was expelled from the living for Royalist preachings and led a miserable and precarious existence until the restoration of Charles II when he was appointed to the living of nearby East Coker in 1661. During those twenty years there was no permanent rector at Hinton, no regular services or sacraments and even the registers were not kept up to date, although there is a reference to a new church clock, and the churchwardens continued their duties in spite of the uncertainties of the times.

John, 1st Baron Poulett died on 29 March 1649 and was buried at Hinton St George, having lived to see the king he served die on the executioner's block on 30 January of that year. There is an extraordinary monument to him in the Poulett memorial chapel, probably erected by his son. It is built of coloured plaster and depicts the soul chained to mortality, but rising on outspread wings towards immortality. An inscription states that Lord Poulett and his wife had three sons and seven daughters. His widow Elizabeth subsequently married his old ally John Ashburnham, himself a widower. As we know, his daughter Florence married Thomas Smyth of Ashton Court. They had at least nine children, several of whom did not survive childhood. Florence married a second time and her husband was Colonel Thomas Piggott. They had a further six children before his death in 1676. Another daughter, Margaret, married Dennis Rolle of Stevenstone, Devon. Lord Poulett's son Amias served with his father in the army and became a Colonel. He was at one time quartered at Ilminster where he was involved in a military skirmish. At the end of the war he was fined £260 in 1645. He had paid it off by 1649, but it left him penniless. Details about his later years are to be found among the Smyth letters. John's third son, Francis, who also served with his father, left the army and became a magistrate. We hear of him as an executor of Thomas Smyth's will. Of Lord Poulett's other daughters, Susanna married Michael Warton, Elizabeth married first William Ashburnam, and second William Hartopp. Helena appears to have remained unmarried, while the names of the other two daughters are not recorded.

In his will Lord Poulett decreed that: 'The 4 poore people placed in the Alms house at Hinton and had but five pence a piece for their livelihood, my will is that there shall be six poore people in the houses, there being two new lodgings built for that purpose and that they shall have twelve pence a week a piece given them.' He also said, 'I desire to be buried at Hinton, that a tombe may be set over my body for me and my wife the Lady Elizabeth Poulett'.

So passed a devout God-fearing man, who lived life to the full – a devoted husband, father and grandfather, and a king's man to the end.

His eldest son, John, the 2nd Baron Poulett, had been born about 1615. He too had a gentleman's education and matriculated from Exeter College, Oxford on 2 April 1632. He travelled abroad for in March 1634 his father applied for licence to send him and his brother Francis 'beyond the seas' for a few years. He commenced his military career soon afterwards

John, 2nd Baron Poulett
1615–1665 (by John Hayls)

and was knighted with his father on board the *Mary Honour* in 1635. In 1639 he served with the king's army in the north with his father and his brother Francis. He was returned to Parliament for Somerset on 12 October 1640 and was created M.D. at Oxford on 31 January 1642. However, he left Parliament that year on the passing of the Militia Ordinance and joined his father at Wells in Somerset under the Marquess of Hertford, and was active in this area early in the war. King Charles was looking to Ireland for help in his cause, but the situation there had deteriorated. Rebellion had spread, with Catholics and Protestants on opposite sides. Sir John Poulett served in Munster in command of a regiment of foot. An armistice was concluded on 15 September 1643 and the troops were free to return to England. Sir John was transferred to Bristol and from there he went to Winchester and formed part of the garrison in that city when the Castle was besieged, and finally surrendered to Cromwell on 5 October 1645.

Sir John then joined his father at Exeter and surrendered with him when the city was taken in 1646. Like his father he was dealt with leniently and eventually paid a fine which had been reduced to £3,760. He succeeded to the title of Baron Poulett on the death of his father in 1649. The Commonwealth was declared and Oliver Cromwell ruled the land. Among the documents originally preserved at Hinton House was an official pass issued to Lord Poulett permitting him to move freely about the country, and was also obtained by the efforts and influence of his wife's brother-in-law, Lord Fairfax. The pass was worded as follows:

Whereas the Rt. Hon. John Lord Pawlett hath made his composition with the Parliament, according to the articles of Exeter, and is to have the benefitt thereof, and is desirous to repaire into the county of Somerset and elsewhere. These are therefore to require you to permit and suffer the said John Lord Pawlett, with six servants, horses, trayling armes, and necessaries, to passe into that countie of Somersett and such other parts of the nation as he shall have occasion to goe into and to returne back againe to London, without offering any violence to his person or any of his attendants, or to take away their horses or other things. And you are not to fayle in the observation hereof as you will answer the contrary. Given under my hand and seale the 25 day of Aprill 1649. T. FAIRFAX.

With the death of Charles I and Parliament victorious, the country settled down to an uneasy peace. Cromwell dealt harshly with resistance in Ireland and elsewhere in the country. In July 1651 the late king's son Charles had gone to Scotland and was accepted there as king. He marched with a large army into England as far as Worcester. Here he was soundly beaten in the last battle of the war on English soil. Charles fled across England and finally managed to escape to France in October. In 1653 Oliver Cromwell was made Lord Protector.

Lord Poulett was suspected of being involved in a Royalist plot in 1654/5 and in April 1656 John and his two brothers Amias and Francis were arrested under suspicion. Amias writes: 'We are now under ye restraint of Civil Governors, which is no small satisfaction to our condition; how long our confine is to and for what I know not. No bayle is to be accepted, though I could have ye best, thanks to kind friends.' Amias was not imprisoned for long and returned to Walcot Manor in Northamptonshire, the home of Sir Thomas Browne who was the father of Lord Poulett's second wife, Anne. Lord Poulett himself, on his release, left the country in February 1657, to join the exiled King Charles II and his followers in France. He took his eldest son John with him, who was sent to school in Paris. In 1660 they returned to England at the king's restoration. The country went wild with joy at the king's return. At Hinton the bells rang and Amias writes to his great-nephew Hugh Smyth from there to tell him that: 'No less than seven and twenty bonfires could we see all afire at once on Thursday night last . . . such a ringing of bells all night, such shoutings of ye people with ye expression of 'Long Live King Charles ye 2nd' and 'God Bless ye Parliament and General that will bring him in' that I may truly say I never heard noyes at night or day like it.' There is an account of a great outdoor party on Warren Hill in Hinton Park which was attended by Lord and Lady Poulett and Amias and Francis. Much food and drink was consumed around a great bonfire. The Royal Arms were set up again in the churches, including Hinton, for as Amias wrote, 'tis now a very happy time in sending out for painters to sett up ye King's arms again; some are already up; others in haste to have it so'.

In the Poulett tradition his Lordship was appointed a Deputy Lieutenant for Somerset and became a Major in the Somersetshire Regiment of Militia Horse. Hyde wrote to him for an account of the rebellious families in Somerset, which was a sign of the high regard with which the family was held again by the government. His uncle Amias too, returned to favour and recovered his positions of colonel of horse and Collector General, and was responsible to the Sheriff for supplies voted by Parliament. In 1661 the Bishop of Bath and Wells appointed Lord Poulett and his eldest son John as chief stewards for all the bishop's hundreds, manors and estates. A visitor to Hinton that year, Colonel Edward Cooke, wrote that Lord Poulett 'abounds not only in generosity in plentiful housekeeping, but also in very beautiful hounds and horses'.

The 2nd Baron Poulett married twice. His first wife was Catherine, the widow of Oliver St John, and daughter of Horace, Baron Vere of Tilbury. It was her sister Anne who was married

Catherine Vere, wife of 2nd
Baron Poulett (by John Hayls)

to Thomas, Lord Fairfax, who was instrumental in getting the family's fines reduced. In 1657 Fairfax and his family stayed at the Poulett's house in Turnham Green. John and Catherine Poulett had two sons, John and Horatio; and three daughters: Vere; Elizabeth who married Sir John Sydenham of nearby Brympton d'Evercy and had no children; and Catherine who was married in 1656 at Salisbury to James Johnston, the Secretary of State for Scotland.

Among Lord Poulett's accounts is a record of the funeral of Lady Poulett. Items purchased included lead and solder 'to lay the body of my Lady in Lede and soe into the coffen'. There were ten standards with lights to stand around the hearse. Mourning clothes for the family and staff were provided, made of black broad-cloth serge and silk purchased from Mr Prike of Exeter. Baize was used for the coach and horses and hangings for the hearse and inside the house. There was a funeral feast, and capers, olives, sugar and spices were bought from Mr Greneway of Crewkerne. The horses in the grand procession were decorated with escutcheons and shields also bought in Exeter. The funeral cost Lord Poulett almost £300.

Lord Poulett's second wife, whom he married on 30 January 1653 at Hinton St George, was Anne, daughter of Sir Thomas Browne of Walcot in Northamptonshire. They had two sons, Amias and Charles, and four daughters, Anne, Florence, Mary and Margaret. It is recorded in the Churchwardens' accounts that Lady Anne Poulett presented the church with a silver chalice in 1668. Her daughter Margaret married Francis Fulford of Dunford in Devon.

In December 1661 Lord Poulett was granted a lease for three lives by the Bishop of Bath and Wells for the Manor and Borough of Chard. It had previously been held by one Colonel Nathaniel Whetham who had seen his freehold confiscated during the Commonwealth. A dispute arose with Colonel Whetham when he refused to accept the sum of £1,000 set aside by the bishop as compensation. It must be said that as well as accepting the £1,000, Lord Poulett and the bishop required Colonel Whetham to sign an agreement renouncing all claims to title of the estate which he and any sub-tenants might possess. Whetham believed that by signing the document he would make himself liable to repay some £2,500 in purchase money to those who had bought estates or leases from him in the past. Several attempts were made to persuade Whetham to change his mind and sign but to no avail. Nevertheless the constitution of the manor was maintained and periodic courts were held in which new tenants were admitted in place of old ones and given leases on the court rolls to hold as evidence of their title. Colonel Whetham was driven to announce publicly in the parish church during a Sunday service that his neighbours 'have given out that I have sealed a release of all my right to the Manor of Chard unto my Lord Poulett. But I do here declare before you all that I neither have, nor ever will, seal any such release.' He also said that he had refused the offer of the £1,000.

The dispute dragged on. The bishop was asked by Nathaniel's family to try to settle the matter. The bishop promised to do what he could, adding that the £1,000 was still available for Colonel Whetham 'for his good services done to his now Majestie'. However, the £1,000 was not paid by the time Lord Poulett died in 1665.

Colonel Whetham began Chancery proceedings against the new Lord of the Manor, the 3rd Baron Poulett. However, it seems that the case came to nothing before the death of Whetham himself, and the Manor of Chard remained in the hands of the Poulett family for the period of the lease.

Following his remarriage the 2nd Lord Poulett appears to have spent a great deal of time at his house, Court de Wyck at Yatton in north Somerset, leaving Hinton House in the occupation of his two brothers Francis and Amias. Also living at Hinton were several children of his sister Florence who had remarried after the death of her husband, Thomas Smyth.

A great many of the letters of Amias Poulett, son of the 1st Baron, survive among the Smyth papers. He remained a bachelor and his writings show him to have been a good-hearted generous man. He loved the good things in life and revelled in rumbustious company. He was never happier than when out hunting and celebrating with a drink with his friends afterwards. He writes of the good times and the bad. We hear of a serious outbreak of plague or fever at Hinton in 1665, the year of the Great Plague in London. It carried off a great many people at Hinton House, many servants, and Mary, the daughter of Thomas Smyth. Another victim was Amias, the little son of his nephew Lord Poulett. He writes amusingly of the mustering of the local militia after the Civil War. He had an eye for the ladies too, although his remarks on the subject of marriage were somewhat cynical, as he tells of his plans to 'peep about for a wife'. In 1666 the country was aghast at the news of the Great Fire of London and Amias writes to Hugh Smyth from Hinton:

'Ye neighbourhood of this parts were cock a hoop for London this next week, but that warme resolve is scorcht to a shrivell by ye late fiery element that has had to kill an influence thereto.'

John, 3rd Baron Poulett
1642–1679 (after Kneller)

Amias was 47 when he died in 1667. He was ailing for some time and had not been able to visit Ashton Court recently. His last letters to Hugh Smyth, the son of 'Sonne Tom' were particularly poignant. 'I am hugely obliged to my Shrove Tuesday's friends that they had room among their merry thoughts for mee; it was a day I most wanted good wishes on; it proving a most disorderly of pain since I fell into this disorder, out of which I am so slenderly recovered as to be able with much help and halting to crawle to ye parlour and back again to my rest.' Finally: 'I have a request to you that you will enjoine ye abell carrying on of ye worke of Misstresses picture [Hugh's wife Ann], its service I shall not enjoy long and then twill be yrs. Lett that make you more concerned; if you object you will have another for yourself, yett remember you can never have too much of ye best. I must dye in a short time and then you will be obliged with it.'

The 2nd Lord Poulett died on 15 September 1665 at Court de Wyck, and was buried at Hinton St George. His widow married again, to Sir John Strode of Chantmarle in Dorset, and died in 1711.

The eldest son of the 2nd Lord Poulett's first marriage succeeded as 3rd Baron. He was also named John and was born about 1642, growing to manhood during the last years of the Commonwealth, much of that time in exile in France. After the Restoration he became an M.P. for Somerset from 1662 to 1665. In 1663 he married his first wife. She was Essex, the 19-year-old daughter of Alexander Popham of Littlecote, Wiltshire, who had been a Colonel in the

Susan Herbert, second wife of 3rd Baron Poulett (attrib. Gibson)

Parliamentary army. There were two daughters of this marriage, Catherine and Letitia, who married Lord Lempster and Sir William Monson respectively. Essex died after only three or four years of marriage and Lord Poulett married again on 15 July 1667. His bride was Susan Herbert, daughter of Philip, the influential and powerful 5th Earl of Pembroke and 2nd Earl of Montgomery, of Wilton House near Salisbury. Of this marriage was born a son and heir named John, and a daughter named Vere. In that year the newly-weds entertained a distinguished visitor at Hinton House, Cosmo III, Grand Duke of Tuscany who was on his way to Dorchester. He has left us with his impressions of the mansion, and speaks of gardens, parterres and terraces. He tells of six hundred deer of two kinds in the park, and of the woods for pheasants. The year 1671 was particularly notable, for in July King Charles II himself paid Lord Poulett a visit at Hinton House.

Lord Poulett's positions and powers increased, for in 1672 he was one of the Commissioners proposed to be appointed under the Parratt and Three Rivers Bill, and in 1674 he was appointed Lord Lieutenant of Dorset, a post he held until his death. He died on or about 26 June 1679 and was buried at Hinton St George. His Will, proved later that year, showed his estate to be worth within £200 of £5,000 per annum. His widow survived him until about December 1693. There is a record that she sued the trustees of the estate under a settlement made by her late husband in 1679 for the £4,000 portion to be raised by them for her daughter Vere who had died.

CHAPTER 4
The First Earl

His monument is that Fame which he has left in the World
Memorial to the 1st Earl Poulett

Born on 26 April 1675, John, 4th Baron Poulett succeeded his father at the age of four. He was by all accounts a sickly boy. In 1678 Colonel Edward Cooke wrote of him that 'he hath been a very weak child till very lately' and in 1680 another writer says that 'he is so marvellous infirm of the King's Evil that his life is under great suspicion (unless his present ague helps to lengthen it)'. However, in that year the young Lord Poulett was witness to a famous historical event. Charles II was still on the throne and his heir was his brother James, the Catholic Duke of York. Charles's illegitimate son, James, Duke of Monmouth was seeking recognition for himself as prospective heir to the throne, and backed by the influential Earl of Shaftesbury, planned a tour of the West Country seeking support for his cause. In that summer of 1680 the tour took place, contrary to his father's wishes. The duke and his entourage stopped at Bath and then at Longleat House, whose owner Thomas Thynne was a friend and supporter of Monmouth. From Longleat, through Bruton, he went on to Ilchester, where he received a heart-warming welcome, as he did also at nearby South Petherton. The next stop was at Whitelackington near Ilminster, the home of the Speke family. Here the duke's host was George Speke, an old Royalist sympathizer, and strongly Protestant. It was from Whitelackington that a visit to Hinton St George and the youthful Lord Poulett was arranged. On 25 August the duke's party rode off through the country lanes of Allowenshay and Dinnington until they reached the White Lodge in Hinton Park. This is generally believed to be what is now known as North Lodge at the Park Gates near Dinnington, not far from the main Chard–Crewkerne road. Here there was a great gathering of well-wishers and a splendid demonstration of affection and loyalty took place. This 'junket' had been arranged by a relative of Lord Poulett, Sir John Sydenham of Brympton d'Evercy, and the invitation had been accepted, for the Pouletts were well known for their Protestant leanings. During the day an incident took place which was subsequently used by the duke's political sponsors as a strong argument for the claims to Monmouth's right to succession. Among the crowds in the park that day there was a girl from Crewkerne aged about 20 named Elizabeth Parcet, the daughter of a poor widow. She had suffered for a long while from the scrofula or 'King's Evil'. A known cure for this complaint was to be 'touched' by the king. The Parcets were too poor to go to London to see the real monarch, and so Elizabeth had come to Hinton to see Monmouth. For she reasoned that if he were truly the legitimate heir of Charles II then surely he too would possess the royal touch of healing. She managed to get close to Monmouth and pulling off her glove she touched his bare wrist. A special pamphlet was published soon after, claiming that in ten days Elizabeth had been cured of her complaint. A list of witnesses to the cure was appended which included the vicar of Crewkerne.

The story of the unfortunate James, Duke of Monmouth cannot be followed here. In 1685 his attempted rebellion took place, ending with his final defeat at Sedgemoor and his subsequent capture and execution.

Monmouth's army came from Lyme Regis and marched through Chard and Ilminster, gathering supporters as it went, and then proceeded to Taunton. Men from South Petherton, Ilchester, Donyatt, Ilminster, Chard and Crewkerne and many other places in Somerset joined the rebel army, but the majority of the gentry including the Pouletts supported King James. Notable among the exceptions were Lord Poulett's neighbours George Speke of Whitelackington, Azariah Pinney of Bettiscombe, and Edmund Prideaux of Forde Abbey, all of whom were punished for their part in the affair. Seven men from Hinton St George are recorded as having joined the rebel army. Their names were Ben and John Butcher, Amos Dunne, John Dunne junior and John Dunne senior, John Gough and Richard Hoare. Ben Butcher, the Dunnes and Gough escaped capture, but John Butcher was tried at Wells and hanged at Axbridge. Hoare, a husbandman, was tried at Wells and sentenced to transportation. However, he was reprieved and another sent in his place. Hoare's land was subsequently forfeit and offered up for sale. Perhaps these men had been present at that earlier and fervent welcome in Hinton Park. However, the church bells at Hinton rang at the news of Monmouth's capture and the village did its best to forget that the 'junket' had ever taken place. There is a reference in the Churchwardens' accounts of a 'a payment of 16s. paid to 16 poor people of the Parish in the wants in the time of the Rebellion' but who they were is not recorded.

In November 1688 it is recorded that the Prince of Orange, the future King William III, while on his way to London to secure the throne after his landing in Torbay from Holland, stayed for two nights at Hinton House and hunted in the park. He was thus assured of Lord Poulett's support against King James and in 1690 the church bells rang for William's victories in Ireland.

It was not until 1696, however, when James had been deposed and William and Mary were on the throne that Lord Poulett finally took his seat in the House of Lords, and then only after a threat of committal for non-attendance. At this time he was described as 'certainly one of the hopefullest Gentlemen in England; is very learned, virtuous, and a Man of Honour; much esteemed in the Country, for his generous way of living with the Gentry, and his Charity to the poorest sort. He makes but a mean figure in his Person; is of middle stature, fair complexion, not handsome.'

After Queen Anne came to the throne in 1702 Lord Poulett gained prestige in Parliament and the Court. He sided, of course, with the Tory cause in Parliament but has been described as 'only a lukewarm politician'.

In May 1702 John Poulett was appointed Lord Lieutenant and Custos Rotulorum of Devonshire, and in the following December became a member of the Privy Council. This year also he married. His bride was Bridgett, the only daughter of Peregrine Bertie of Waldershare in Kent, and a niece of the Earl of Lindsey.

Relations between Scotland and England had reached a point where the possibility of union between the two countries had at last been reached and in 1705, after much disagreement throughout the summer, it was finally agreed to appoint Commissioners. In 1706 the Scottish and English delegations were chosen and included on the English side were Lord Poulett, his great friend Robert Harley, and John Sharp, Archbishop of York. The meetings of the two sets of Commissioners took place at the Cockpit in London, although the participants stayed in separate rooms, and only communicated with each other through the exchange of minutes. Under the treaty finally agreed, the Scots lost their separate Parliament, and all affairs were to be regulated by a United Parliament in London under the rule of a single monarch, but Scotland would keep her own Church and native laws. A substantial sum of money was paid over to Scotland as an equivalent for the fact that she would assume the burden of the national debt contracted before the Union. The most controversial matter raised

John, 1st Earl Poulett
1675–1743 (attrib. Gibson)

was the number of Scottish representatives to sit in Parliament, but this was settled satisfactorily at a joint meeting of the Commissioners held under the eye of the Queen herself. It was agreed there should be forty-five commoners and sixteen Lords.

The treaty was finally signed and sealed by the Commissioners on 22 July and presented to Queen Anne at a ceremony in St James's Palace. The Commissioners filed into the royal presence in twos, led by William Cowper (later the 1st Earl Cowper). When he came to give his speech, however, he forgot his lines and had to search his pocket for his notes. The Scots regarded this as a typical piece of English inefficiency. All in all, the Union was a very satisfactory accomplishment and gave the queen great personal pleasure. To her it seemed that in the interests of peace and unity all petty jealousies and feuding could be forgotten in the common cause. The Union was marked with a great Thanksgiving Service held in St Paul's Cathedral. For Lord Poulett, his work on the Commission was well rewarded. In the following December the Queen created him Viscount Hinton St George[1] and Earl Poulett. An extract from the Letters Patent reads thus:

Whereas the illustrious family of the Pouletts has through many past ages by glorious deeds become renowned and by the spending of both blood and fortune has always

1. The title is usually said (wrongly) to be Viscount Hinton of Hinton St George.

Bridgett Bertie, 1st Countess
Poulett (by Godfrey Kneller)

defended the rights of the Crown and liberty of the people. And whereas our much beloved
and very faithful John Lord Poulett of Hinton St George the head of that most noble family
reckons the first magnates of England among the offshoots of his stock, is powerful
through ancestral wealth, follows the virtuous footsteps of his ancestors, and by his mental
endowments, prudence, good faith and patriotism, adorns the dignity received from his
ancestors. And the same John Lord Poulett by the same name, estate, title, rank, styles,
honour and dignity of Earl Poulett by the girding on of the sword, the placing on his head
of the cap of honour and the golden crown, we distinguish and invest and truly ennoble by
these presents. To have and to hold the aforesaid name, estate, rank, style, dignity and
honour of Earl Poulett with all and singular the privileges, appurtenances, precedences and
other such things to the estate of Earl Poulett in any way appertaining or belonging to the
aforesaid John Lord Poulett and the heirs male by his body lawfully begotten for ever.
Witness the Queen at Westminster
24 December, 1706

The whole of Queen Anne's reign was marked with the rivalry and the jostling for power
of the Whig and Tory parties. On her accession in 1702 the automatic general election

resulted in a House of Commons with about 200 members belonging to no recognizable groups who were generally accustomed to work together, but the remainder, more than two thirds of the whole, were in some sense leaders or followers. The Duke of Marlborough was in a position of great power, holding the office of Master General of Ordnance; he had received the Garter and held other high military offices. His wife Sarah had become the chief office-holder at Court. Lord Godolphin was the Lord Treasurer and these three, by their friendship with the queen, were able to influence her policies with regard to the holding of various high places in Parliament and at Court. The members of Parliament were prepared to follow any leaders who appeared to be working in their own particular interests. Marlborough and Godolphin for their parts were willing to work with anyone who supported their main cause, that of carrying on the war of the Spanish Succession. By 1709 the ministry was to all intents and purposes a Whig ministry, with Tories of all complexions out of office. The Whig ministry supported Marlborough and Godolphin. The war dragged on with a weary series of campaigns but with no immediate prospect of peace. This brought criticism of the war and eventually dissatisfaction with the war itself. The queen was weary of the war also, and was personally unhappy with the ministers forced on her by the Marlborough clique. At this point the queen also became estranged from the Duchess of Marlborough, formerly her greatest friend. The duchess was supplanted by her cousin Abigail Masham, who was also related to the Tory Robert Harley and who, with Mrs Masham's help, succeeded in winning the queen's trust and took the opportunity to bring together all the forces of those who were tired of the war and the Whig ministry. Harley had resigned from the Secretaryship of State in 1708 and his prospects had seemed poor at that time. From then on he lost no opportunity to undermine the ministry with increasing support from the Queen. He whipped up support from his moderate Tory supporters and detached lukewarm Whigs from the fringes of their party. Lord Poulett gave his wholehearted support, and wrote to him saying that: 'Whig folly and their own past mistakes had converted many churchmen to the ideal of moderation.' The ministry had made two bad mistakes: firstly, it had bound itself to the doomed cause of no ending to the war over Spain, and secondly, it impeached the Reverend Dr Henry Sacheverell. Sacheverell had supported the High Church cause for many years and had denounced Whigs, dissenters and Low Churchmen. In 1709 he had preached a particularly violent sermon and had declared the ministry and Godolphin as enemies of the Church. The outraged ministry had foolishly impeached him. The mobs in London went wild with rage and troops were called in. Only a small minority in the House of Lords voted for his conviction, which was as good as a victory for him and his supporters. Three weeks later Harley was able to take the first step towards the disintegration of the Whig ministry. He was able to push the Duke of Shrewsbury into office as Lord Chamberlain. His second chance came only a month later when the Earl of Sunderland was dismissed as Secretary of State. Lord Poulett had twice been offered this post but had refused it. But for the fact of his refusal Sunderland would have been dismissed earlier. Marlborough was much displeased but the queen's mind was made up. Lord Poulett himself suggested Lord Anglesey to fill the post but the choice finally fell on Lord Dartmouth, a moderate Tory.

In August 1710 Godolphin himself was dismissed as Lord Treasurer. Marlborough, however, in spite of the breach between his wife and the queen consented to remain in command of the army. The Treasury was put into Commission, and Harley spent the last days of July sounding out his friends and allies as to who would be willing to serve as Commissioners. Lord Poulett, as a faithful friend and follower, the Hon. Henry Paget, Sir Thomas Mansell and Robert Benson were all asked to join, and accepted. On 5 August Harley went to the queen and Godolphin was asked to resign.

The queen wanted Shrewsbury, as First Lord of the Treasury, to head the Commission but he refused. Shrewsbury advised that Harley himself should be put at the head of the Commission, but this place was eventually given to Lord Poulett. It may have been given to him as something of a sop after his refusal to take Sunderland's place, but it is more likely to have been awarded because of the queen's esteem of him, and because she saw it more fitting that an Earl should be placed in such a position above a commoner. So Harley became Second Lord and Chancellor of the Exchequer. An election followed and the new ministry gained a large majority, something like three to one. Although Lord Poulett headed the new ministry it was Harley who continued to use his influence and to make major decisions. The defeated Whigs were now prepared to sit back and watch the new Commission ruin the economy of the country and so bring about their own downfall. Under Godolphin the National Debt had risen astronomically and the new ministry were unable to look to the banks and city men, who promptly withdrew their support. However, Harley surprised all his critics by managing to raise a large loan, enough to finance the army, in spite of the city financiers, by seeking out city Tories and others who had a grudge against the banks' stranglehold. Thus the first difficulty of Poulett's Commission was overcome. There was heartening news on the war fronts with Stanhope's victories in Spain at Almenara and Saragossa. Now Harley hoped to negotiate with Spain from a position of strength. The Parliamentary Tories wanted Harley to create a thoroughly Tory government but Harley favoured a more balanced administration, knowing that a Tory majority in Parliament would be as bad if not worse than the Whig rule which had just ended. Harley's main concern was to bring the war to an end. The voice of Jacobitism, supporting the claim of Catholic James, the son of James II, to the throne was heard again, and Harley was suspected of favouring his cause. Among the newly elected Tories was Henry St John, who was fast becoming the champion of the ambitious Tories in the House and he quickly worked himself into a position of favour with the queen. Harley hoped that the Commission would be ended soon and he himself handed the white staff of the Lord Treasurer's office, but the queen remained cool towards him. He had hoped for support from the Duke of Marlborough but this was not forthcoming, especially when in January, his duchess finally broke with Queen Anne and was dismissed from her posts as Groom of the Stole, Mistress of the Robes and Keeper of the Privy Purse. St John meanwhile continued his lead of the Parliamentary Tories and tried to push his own schemes through. The queen continued to regard him with favour and in spite of Harley's opposition supported St John's plan to send an expedition to Quebec. St John now took every opportunity to humiliate Harley in the House, and finally decided to become a serious rival for the Lord Treasurer's post against Harley. By the end of February things seemed desperate. Harley had risked all in an attempt to set up a government run by Court moderates, helping the queen to rule in a partnership with the predominant party. A scheme for a state lottery to save the country's economy was wrecked by the Whig opposition. An end to the war seemed as far off as ever with a series of set-backs to the allies in Spain. It seemed inevitable that Harley would have to resign in favour of St John, for if he stayed in office, he would have to lend his name to measures which ran counter to all he believed in.

Early in March, however, an event occurred which changed the fortune of the Commission and of Harley in particular. Harley had intercepted treacherous letters to the Jacobites in France which indicated that St John himself might be implicated. The messenger was a Frenchman who went by the name of the Marquis de Guiscard. He was an ex-priest who had been expelled from France for misconduct. He had been accepted in England with a view to his carrying out a plan to foment unrest in France, and was given the rank of colonel, and was thus in very close contact with St John, who was then Secretary of War. This plan came to nothing and Guiscard was retired on what he considered an inadequate pension. When he applied for an increase, Harley, disliking him intensely, had actually reduced the allowance. So Guiscard turned once more to the country which had once expelled him. He was able to convey messages to France in the diplomatic bag of Lord Portmore because of his friendship with that gentleman's wife. Lord Portmore had grown suspicious and opened one of the packages and the treachery was exposed. Two more packages addressed to British officers in Flanders revealed secrets only known to the Cabinet Council members and these seemed to indicate St John's involvement. Guiscard was arrested on 8 March. Lord Poulett and Harley hastily summoned the members of the Council to a meeting at the Cockpit that afternoon. The whole council attended, and the prisoner was brought in. Although he had been searched, somehow he had managed to hide a penknife in his pocket, unknown to his warders. He was questioned and shown the incriminating packages but denied the writing on them was his. The President of the Council, Lord Rochester, decided to end the proceedings and summoned the guards to remove the prisoner. Guiscard, after a little hesitation, suddenly sprang at Harley and stabbed him with the penknife. Luckily Harley was wearing several layers of clothing, which saved him from all but a superficial wound. The room was in an uproar. The Council members rushed around with drawn swords and Guiscard was finally overcome, but not before he was severely wounded by the enraged Lords. Footmen and messengers were called in and they finally tied him up by the neck and heels and he was carried off to Newgate prison. Lord Poulett, meanwhile, had kept his head and went for medical aid. He returned with a doctor named Bousier and reassured the wounded Harley by telling him, 'I have brought you the best surgeon in England'. The blade of the knife was found still stuck in Harley's clothing and he calmly wrapped it and the handle which he recovered from the floor, in Poulett's handkerchief. After treatment from the doctor, Harley was taken home in a hackney chair, with his faithful friend Poulett walking at his side. In fact Lord Poulett showed great concern and tenderness throughout the whole episode.

Harley took a little time to recover although the wound was not serious. Queen Anne, who was very upset when she heard the news of the attack, realized how much she depended upon Harley. Guiscard died in custody, which must have been a relief to St John who had thus avoided the possibility of being accused of complicity in treason. Harley returned to public life again on 26 April. His popularity had been restored and the leaderless House of Commons welcomed him with a speech and general ovation.

On 17 May Harley presented his scheme for trade in the South Seas with the idea of consolidating the National Debt. The lottery too was now proving a success. Although the balance of the parties had not changed while Harley had been absent from the House, the Guiscard affair and the Jacobite scare had done little to aid the High Tory aspirations. Harley received a letter from Lord Poulett in which he said: 'At last the Ministry could free itself from the taint of old courtiers.' The Duke of Buckingham was the only Jacobite of the old school left and Lord Poulett considered he could 'never be dangerous and will in many ways be useful'. There was a change of heart among the High Tories and many who had been unwilling to accept Harley as First Minister were now prepared to acknowledge his lead. At last, on 29 May, Queen Anne gave Harley the white staff of the Lord Treasurer and he was created Earl of Oxford and Mortimer. So Lord Poulett's period as head of the Treasury Commission ended.

With the decline of the popularity of the Duke of Marlborough, the Tories seized every opportunity to blacken the Whig conduct of the wars in Spain. One such occasion in January 1711 there was 'an examination' in the House of Lords into 'the late ill success in Spain'. Lord Poulett moved the question as to the occasion of the reverse at Almanza, which had occurred some four years previously.

On 12 June 1711 Lord Poulett became Lord Steward of the Household. The campaign against Marlborough continued and in May 1712 the House of Lords again debated the conduct of the wars. The courage of the Duke of Ormonde was in question, when Lord Poulett attacked the Duke of Marlborough in the following words: 'Nobody could doubt of the Duke of Ormonde's courage and bravery; but he was not like a certain General, who led troops to the slaughter to cause a great number of officers to be knocked on the head in a battle, or against stone walls, in order to fill his pockets by disposing of their commissions.'

Marlborough heard these words in silence but as soon as the House rose he sent Lord Mohun to Poulett with an invitation, quaintly worded in the style of the times, 'to take the air in the country'. Poulett, who had not been expecting such a comeback asked 'Is this a challenge?' Mohun informed him that the message spoke for itself and was indeed a challenge to a duel and added, 'I shall accompany the Duke of Marlborough and your Lordship will do well to provide a second'. Gentlemen usually kept these sort of affairs a secret from their wives but John was unable to hide his agitation from his wife Bridgett. Lady Poulett as a dutiful and no doubt anxious spouse, wrote immediately to Lord Dartmouth, the Secretary of State, informing him of the facts of the case. In all she wrote five letters to him. In the first she begged Lord Dartmouth 'to order the guards to be ready upon the two noblemen's falling out, I will listen when Lord Mohun comes, and will send a more speedy and exact account'. In her second note she says 'I listend and itt is my Lord Mallbouro that has challinge my Lord by Lord Mohun. Pray lett him be secured immedatly.' In her third letter Bridgett again urged Dartmouth to send the guards, adding 'The Treasurer must take it up with Halifax . . . that noe more quarille happen on this occasion which I hope you and the Queen will prevent for the present. Pray burn my letters and send the very next guard att hand to secure my Lord and Lord Mohun.'

Lord Dartmouth could no longer ignore the impending duel. He at once went to Marlborough and requested him 'not to stir abroad'. Furthermore, two sentries were placed outside the Poulett's house. Queen Anne herself was informed and sent a royal command to Marlborough that 'this might go no further' and she required his word to that effect. So the matter was concluded although Lord Poulett had eventually to make some sort of apology. Bearing in mind that the subject of selling commissions by Marlborough was actually under official investigation, it is no wonder that the duke was so provoked by Poulett's outcry. Duelling was, of course, the recognized way of settling an insult. Among the Blenheim manuscripts is a note referring to the incident:

It seems the Earle Pawlet was pleas'd to take the occasion to reflect very grossly upon my Lord Duke as if his Grace had fought so many battles and expos'd so many men's lives against stone walls with no other view than the disposal of Commissions. This is the substance of wt I have heard, but 'tis reported to have been much worse and utter'd in the most brutal manner. What grounds there could be for anything of this kind you are as good judge as anybody. His Grace thought his honr so farr concerned that the next morning he sent Lord Mohun to tell Lord Pawlet his Grace expected satisfaction, but the two Lords could not see each other till Saturday morning, when 'tis said Lord Mohun us'd pretty plain language. By this time it had got Wind. Sentries were posted att Ld. Pawlet's and Ld. Mohun's tho' the latter was not at home. Ld. Dartmouth was sent att the same time to his Grace. Thus by Her Majestys interposing Her authority I think all is put up again, but it is reported Lord Pawlet is order'd to make some apology the first time they meet in the House.

On 26 October 1712 Lord Poulett and six other peers were elected as Knights Companion of the Most Noble Order of the Garter and were installed at Windsor on 4 August the following year. At this time John, Earl Poulett was described by Prince Eugene as 'A man of very good estate, but never much bred to business, especially affairs of State, of a good easy and modest temper, much bigoted to the Church of England, and a true patriot in the opinion of the Tory party'.

When Queen Anne lay dying and the Hanoverian succession had been decided upon, the Whigs and Tories were still jostling for positions of power for the coming new reign. It was felt by the Privy Council that Lord Shrewsbury should be the next Lord Treasurer as he was most acceptable both to Hanover and England. This appointment had to be accomplished before the queen died, and thus a deputation from the Council presented itself to the almost unconscious queen. Anne's seven doctors had first assured them that 'Her Majesty was in a condition to be spoke to'. So with Lord Bolingbroke, Lord Harcourt as Chancellor, Lord Dartmouth as Privy Seal and Lord Poulett as Lord Steward, the deputation was received by Her Majesty. The official record states that: 'The Queen about one o'clock gave the Treasurer's staff to the Duke of Shrewsbury, My Lord Chancellor holding her hand to direct it to the Duke.' There is doubt if the queen was able to understand what she was doing, but if she had, it is concluded that she would have agreed with the Council's recommendation. Thus, the Council was able to prepare the country for the arrival of the new king from Germany, and the Protestant succession was assured.

On Sunday, 1 August 1714, Queen Anne, the last of the Stuart monarchs, died. With her death the power of the Tories declined. Jacobite hopes were dashed with the arrival of George I from Hanover. Marlborough returned from exile and the Whigs triumphed. John, Lord Poulett, with his Tory sympathies and because he showed no particular enthusiasm towards the House of Brunswick, lost his places at Court and in Parliament and retired to Somerset to live the life of a country gentleman. During the reign of George I he hardly spoke in Parliament although he did oppose the Septennial Bill in April 1716 which sought to increase the life of the present Parliament to seven years. It was passed, however, and Tory hopes of seeing their grievances righted by a general election were disappointed. During the reign of George II he was rarely heard; however, he did rally to the Court party by the gift of a place as Lord of the Bedchamber to his eldest son John in 1731. In December 1742 he spoke in support of the proposal to take Hanoverian troops into British pay.

At the height of his career at Court and Parliament between 1711 and 1714 Lord Poulett furnished Hinton House with a collection of Chinese lacquer furniture, and English japanned furniture in the Chinese manner. He favoured carved walnut furniture, and tables and stands in the baroque style made by the cabinet makers Coxted and Woster. Lord Poulett prepared a suite of rooms at his home for Queen Anne. The bedroom contained a magnificent state bed hung with crimson and gold while the walls of the rooms were hung with tapestries. Tradition says that the queen was invited to visit Hinton House on the occasion of the baptism of Earl Poulett's fourth son who was named Anne in the queen's honour, and for whom she stood as sponsor. Such a visit in those days, however, was most unlikely, and it was probably more for prestige that a set of rooms was thus prepared.

Earl Poulett had the odd nickname 'Swallow', by which he was known to his friends at Parliament. He died on 28 May 1743 and was buried at Hinton St George. A fine memorial bust and tablet by the sculptor Rysbrack stands to his memory in the Poulett private pew in the church.

CHAPTER 5

The Family of the First Earl and the Second and Third Earls

Distinguished by a peculiar urbanity of manners,
a transcendent courtesy and affability and a prompt
disposition to acts of kindness and benevolence.

Memorial to 3rd Earl Poulett

John, 1st Earl Poulett and his wife Bridgett had eight children. First there were twin boys, John and Peregrine. Then two more sons, Vere and Anne; and four daughters: Bridgett, Catherine, Susan and Rebecca. They all appear to have had a normal happy childhood. Their portraits as children were painted by Thomas Gibson, the fashionable society artist of the day, who depicted them at play or with their various pets: John with his spaniel, Peregrine with a deer, Vere feeding his parrot, Susan has a squirrel while Bridgett has a lamb. Anne is shown by a fountain.

John and his twin were born in London on 12 December 1708. No details of his education are known, but he was certainly introduced to Court life by his father at an early age. At 23 he was appointed Lord of the Bedchamber at the Court of King George II in 1731. In 1733 he first took his seat in the House of Lords having been summoned as Lord Hinton (or Baron Poulett of Hinton St George) on 16 January. He was of course styled Viscount Hinton until his father's death in 1743 when he succeeded to the title of Earl Poulett and inherited the estate. He took an active part in the life of the County of Somerset and held the post of Lord Lieutenant from 1744 until 1764. He was a Colonel of the 1st Somerset Regiment of Militia and a Recorder of Bridgwater. The 2nd Earl did much to improve the interior of his family home. He commissioned Matthias Lock, the famous London carver and designer, to supply new suites of furniture for Hinton House.

John did not marry and in his later years suffered much from ill health. In 1759 he wrote to General Townshend saying that after being a cripple for more than two years he began to feel some benefit from a remedy. He died on 5 November 1764 and was buried at Hinton St George. Walpole, writing to George II, said of him: 'He did not want sense but that sense wanted every common requisite.' In his Will John, 2nd Earl Poulett did not forget those who served him, for he left his foreign servant's son, Anthony Le Bastide, £4,000. To his brother Vere he left 'All messuages, manors, lands and covenants, all Real and Personal Estate'.

Not a great deal is recorded of John's twin brother Peregrine. He was M.P. for Bridgwater for some years until he died in 1752. He was styled Viscount Hinton from 1743.

The third son, Vere, succeeded his brother John in 1764 as 3rd Earl Poulett. He was born on 18 May 1710. He completed his education at Christ Church, Oxford, where he matriculated on 19 May 1729. Like his two elder brothers he was closely associated with Bridgwater and served as M.P. for that town from 1741 until 1747. On 4 March 1755 he married Mary, the younger daughter and co-heir of Richard Butt of Overton, Gloucestershire.

The Hon. Peregrine Poulett 1708–1752 (attrib. Gibson)

John, 2nd Earl Poulett 1708–1764, as a boy (attrib. Gibson)

Twin sons of 1st Earl Poulett

They were wed at the house of her uncle Nathaniel Lloyd in Lincoln's Inn Fields, where Mary had spent most of her childhood. They had two sons, John and Vere, who were born in 1756 and 1761 respectively. The 3rd Earl was granted the Freedom of the City of Bristol in 1765 by the Master, Wardens, Assistants and Commonalty of the Society of Merchant Venturers within the City of Bristol. In 1771 he was appointed Lord Lieutenant of Devonshire, a post he held until his death. Vere followed his ancestors in improving the family home and estate. In 1766 he greatly enlarged the pleasure grounds and gardens of Hinton House by closing the old main road through Hinton St George to Dinnington at West Street, and building a new road to the north of the church. This also enabled a pathway to be made linking the mansion directly with the church. Vere did not take much part in politics after he took his seat in the House of Lords. He sided with the Court party of George III, and did not vote on Fox's India Bill in 1783. He much preferred life in the country, and an amusing anecdote is told by Lord Egremont of an occasion when he was out shooting with bow and arrows, with Lord Poulett among his party. When asked how many geese he had slain, Lord Poulett answered: 'None killed, not one, but I put them all in the utmost consternation!'

In 1761 Vere purchased a house with a fine frontage to the River Thames at Twickenham, which became known as 'Poulett Lodge'. His younger son Vere was baptised in Twickenham parish church, and the rector there described the Earl and Countess as 'very affable good natured people'. Like his brother John, in his last years Vere suffered a long and painful illness 'under which he expressed no murmour' and he died on 14 April 1788 at the age of 78. Mary, his widow, lived on at Twickenham for some time after her husband's death and died on 26 April 1819 in St James's Place, London, after having lived to see her two sons present her with sixteen grandchildren. Vere and Mary are buried in the family vault at Hinton church, and there is a handsome memorial plaque to them designed by Sir Richard Westmacott, R.A.

The fourth son of the 1st Earl was the Honourable Anne Poulett. He is distinguished by being named after his sovereign, for Queen Anne is said to have graciously consented to be his sponsor. Anne was born on 11 July 1711 and received his education at Christ Church, Oxford. It was not until late in his life that Anne entered politics. The long reign of George III had begun and in 1768, when he was 58 years of age, Anne contested the parliamentary seat at Bridgwater, which had been the seat of his late brother Peregrine for several years. Surprisingly he was defeated at this first attempt but all was apparently not right with the election for upon petition, Anne was given the seat. The people of Bridgwater evidently regarded Anne as their champion against injustice for they presented him with the following address:

Thanks to Honble Anne Poulett – Mar 24th 1769 – from Electors of Bridgwater
The electors of this Borough would deservedly lie under the Imputation of your ingratitude were they not to acknowledge in the most respectfull manner the essential services you have lately done them. It is to your generous and noble support they are indebted for the Preservation of their Right to choose their Representatives in Parliament. You have gloriously defeated the execrable attempt to deprive them of that invaluable privilege and have effectually secured the enjoyment of it to them and their Posterity. They therefore desire your acceptance of their sincere thanks by subscribing their names and assuring you that they shall ever retain a most grateful sense of the signal regard you have shown them in strenuously asserting and maintaining the liberties of this town.

In Parliament Anne voted and spoke regularly in support of the Government and in 1744 his re-election to the Bridgwater seat was unopposed. In 1780 at the next election Anne's popularity was once more in no doubt, and he topped the poll. In all he served in four Parliaments for the Bridgwater seat. In Bridgwater parish church is a large painting depicting 'The Descent from the Cross' which is said to have been presented to the town by the Honourable Anne Poulett. Anne, like his father, was installed as a Knight of the Garter. He died on 10 July 1785 aged 74, at his London home in Albemarle Street, Westminster. In his Will he made several bequests to his family. To his sister Susan he left £4,000: to his nephew, John Poulett, £50 to buy a ring; to his nephew William Bastard, £400; while to his brother Vere, the 3rd Earl, he bequeathed 'two pictures of mine which he may choose!'

Two of the daughters of the 1st Earl married. Lady Bridgett was wed to Pollexfen Bastard of Kitley in Devon. Her sister Lady Catherine was married in 1725 to John Parker of Boringdon, also in Devon. John and Catherine later moved to Saltram House near Plymouth, the magnificent mansion which is now owned by the National Trust. Described as a 'proud and wilful woman', it is Catherine and to a lesser extent her husband who are recognized as the early builders of the present Saltram House, when they enlarged the existing small, mainly Tudor building by adding the south and east wings and altering and enlarging the west wing. An account written later says that Lady Catherine 'transferred the family residence from Boringdon to Saltram where she enlarged a small dwelling and made several improvements with a view to preserving it as a jointure-house. The superior beauty of this situation perhaps attracted the lady's attention, and induced her, and the subsequent occupiers, to continue the building and embellishment of the house and grounds.' It is clear from this account that Lady Catherine took the most active part in the venture, as her husband's name is seldom mentioned. The famous portrait painter Sir Joshua Reynolds was born at nearby Plympton in 1723, where his father was Master of the Grammar School. There is a story that Lady Catherine presented the children there, including the young Joshua, with their first pencils to encourage them to draw. Sir Joshua remained on very friendly terms with the Parker family for the rest of his life, and in particular with Catherine's son John and his wife Theresa, whose portraits he later painted and which still hang at Saltram today. Also at Saltram are portraits of the Poulett family which Catherine must have brought with her from Hinton House. They are of her mother and father, her sister Lady Susan and her great aunt, Lady Catherine Johnston. There are also two portraits of Catherine herself, one by the artist Thomas Hudson which hangs in the staircase hall. John and Catherine had two sons and two daughters; John, Montague Edmund, Catherine and Bridgett. Lady Catherine died in 1758, and her eldest son John, who later became Lord Boringdon, carried on the work of enlarging and improving his family home. He more than any other member of the family was responsible for Saltram as it is today for he purchased by far the greater part of the present contents of eighteenth-century furnishings and paintings. His son, also John, the 2nd Lord Boringdon, was made the 1st Earl of Morley in 1815, the descendant of whom is the present 6th Earl of Morley.

The two younger daughters of the 1st Earl Poulett, Susan and Rebecca, remained unmarried. Rebecca died in 1765 and a copy of her will is among the Poulett manuscripts at Taunton. To her sister Bridgett she bequeathed £40 – 'To be laid out in things which I require she wear in remembrance of me'. Her brother Anne received £800; her nephews, William, Edmund and Pollexfen, Bridgett's children received £30 each. Her nephew, John Poulett, the son of her brother Vere, was to receive 'my large amethyst, but not till after the death of my sister Susan Poulett as I give her the use of it for life'. (Susan died twenty-three years later!). £150 was 'to be laid out in a monument for my dearly beloved mother, in memory of the best of mothers'. Then there was £50 'to bind out the eldest son of Samuel and Margaret Allen of

Petherton to some trade that shall be judged proper by my executors and £50 more when he is out of his time to set him up in trade. Every servant that shall have lived with me 4 years and be living with me at my decease two full years wages. Those who have served 2 years, one years wages. Susan my dearly loved sister to be executrix of my Will.'

Susan erected a handsome monument to her sister in the nave of Hinton Church and later, another next to it, to her brother Anne. Susan outlived all her immediate family and died soon after the last of her brothers, Vere the 3rd Earl in 1788. Strangely, one of the ghosts said to haunt Hinton House is that of Susan, who is said to manifest her presence by the rustling of skirts on the Grand Staircase and in certain bedrooms.

The children of the 1st Earl Poulett were great friends of George Bubb Dodington, the politician, and in his diary covering the years from 1749 until 1761, we read that all the brothers and the two unmarried sisters were frequently in London, together with their young nephew William Bastard. John, who was by then the 2nd Earl Poulett, and his brother Peregrine were busy with Parliamentary affairs, but the family all met in the evenings for dinners with their friends and paid visits to Covent Garden and the pleasure grounds at Ranelagh. They often visited Dodington's riverside villa at Hammersmith, named 'La Trappe', as well as his house in Pall Mall.

Dodington had been Lord Lieutenant of Somerset for twenty years but had surrendered the post to Lord Poulett as part of the price of John's support for him as M.P. for Bridgwater, which town he had shared with Vere until 1747, and then subsequently with Peregrine. In 1752 we learn of a quarrel between the four brothers, John and Peregrine having fallen out with Anne and Vere. However, on 2 August Peregrine had died, and the seat at Bridgwater became vacant once more. Dodington wanted Vere to succeed to the seat and tried to arrange a reconciliation in the family as a result of Peregrine's death. Dodington took the matter up with Henry Pelham, the First Lord of the Treasury, but Pelham had already heard from Earl Poulett who remained disinclined to recommend Vere to the vacancy. Pelham himself disliked Vere. Dodington says 'He [Pelham] would not enter into it. Vere had left them unhandsomely, had treated him ill, personally, wherever he might be heard.' Pelham was all for healing the breach in the family but would have nothing to do with Vere. However, while they were all making up their minds, Robert Balch was declared candidate, and the matter was settled. Subsequently, in 1754 John gave his support to the candidate Lord Egmont, much to Dodington's disappointment and so he lost his seat there. Anne became the next member of the Poulett family to sit for Bridgwater in 1769.

On the death of Vere, the 3rd Earl, on 14 April 1788, the title passed to his eldest son John. His second son, Vere, married a Miss Beecher and they had a son and five daughters.

TABLE BY MATTHIAS LOCK FOR HINTON HOUSE

CHAPTER 6

The Fourth and Fifth Earls

In the despatch of the duties of his public station
He acted with the strictest Honour and Fidelity
Monument to the 4th Earl Poulett

Born at Hinton St George in the reign of George II on 3 April 1756, the future 4th Earl Poulett was baptised John in the church of St Giles-in-the-Fields in London. He had a modest education at Mr Cleaver's school at Twyford in Buckinghamshire. John took up an army career and became a colonel in the East Devon Militia in 1778. He married in 1782, his bride being Sophia, daughter and heir of Admiral Sir Charles Pocock, K.B. The Duchess of Devonshire, wife of the 5th Duke, said of Sophia Poulett: 'Lady Hinton is the oddest little woman I ever saw – very young and so childish and vulgar that one is amazed every now and then to hear her come out with very clever things. She was a great fortune, she has a comical ugly face, and her waist is longer than her legs.'

John succeeded to the title on the death of his father in 1788. In 1794 he was appointed Lord Lieutenant of Somerset, and also in that year was installed as a Knight of the Thistle. He was given a post as Lord of the Bedchamber at the court of King George III in 1795 which he held for the rest of his life.

The 4th Earl Poulett was responsible for a great deal of alteration to Hinton House. He grew tired of the rambling old house with its ornate west front, and the great three-storey wings which had outlived their usefulness. Between the years 1789 and 1793 he had much of the old house demolished and rebuilt, first in the current Georgian style, while the land was raised around the house to reduce the height to two storeys. In 1794 Lord Poulett appointed Sir John Soane as his architect to redesign the interior, and over the next four years Soane produced various plans and drawings and submitted them to the earl for his approval. Soane proposed alterations in a classic style with pillared porticos and a new front on the old south wing. The state rooms were to be given elaborate new interiors. In May 1797 Lord Poulett agreed that Soane's plans should be carried out, and then at the last moment he changed his mind. Soane was dismissed and James Wyatt was appointed in his place. The Gothic style was in favour and Wyatt was the acknowledged master in that field. So the remaining alterations and the remodelling of the interior were carried out in the Gothic style. Perhaps fortunately, the south wing and the state rooms remained unaltered after all. Lord Poulett kept Soane waiting for over a year before he settled his final account, despite three reminders.

The alterations to the mansion eventually changed the entrance from the west to the north side. In 1800 Lord Poulett purchased the gatehouse, designed by Inigo Jones, from nearby Clifton Maybank which was being demolished. It is assumed to have been re-erected at Hinton House and may have formed the entrance porch to the new Grand Entrance Hall which now made an impressive approach to the new reception rooms and the state rooms beyond. However, in 1814, after the sudden death of Wyatt, his nephew Jeffrey Wyatville added the present heavy Gothic porch and clock-tower on the north side, and what happened to the Clifton Maybank porch, and whether it was ever actually installed, remains a mystery.

The 4th Earl also carried out alterations to the parish church, employing Wyatt and later Wyatville as his architects. The north transept was remodelled to form the Poulett family pew, thus the family could attend the services with more dignity, comfort and privacy than before. The memorial chapel was also rebuilt and a new vestry added next to it for the rector, replacing the old one at the east end of the church, while underneath it all, the family vault was rebuilt and enlarged.

As Lord of the Bedchamber, the 4th Earl was very close to the king and his Court. Close enough indeed for the king himself to stand as godfather for the Earl's fifth son, Frederick Charles, and a christening gift of a handsome silver porringer was made to the infant. The earl also became a personal friend of George, the Prince of Wales and his brothers. Lord and Lady Poulett frequently visited Weymouth when the king and queen were there with the princes and princesses. Queen Charlotte wrote from Weymouth to the Prince of Wales in September 1792: 'We have a perfect compound of weather; wind, rain and sunshine succeed each other without interruption. We sailed yesterday as far as Lullworth in the finest sunshine possible, and at our return the rain came on so heavily that we were wet through, and so it continued all evening. Our company do not increase. The place itself is very full but all unknown to our society. Lord and Lady Paulet are expected today and Lord and Lady Digby intend coming for a fortnight and this addition will make a little variety. The Play House is a great resource to us and we go frequently. The actors are tolerable and some parts very well done.'

Several years later, in 1809, the Princess Amelia was sent to Weymouth in the hope that she might gain some relief from the serious illness with which she was suffering. With her was her sister Princess Mary. They stayed in Weymouth some four months and during their stay they had many visitors from the local gentry and aristocracy. Their brothers, Prince William, the Duke of Clarence, and Prince Adolphus, the Duke of Cambridge, were also visitors to Weymouth during this period. Prince Adolphus, or 'Dolly' as he was known to his sisters, came down in September and during his stay accepted invitations from several of the great houses in the neighbourhood, including Lord Ilchester, and Major-General Garth at Puddletown. While at Lord Ilchester's the prince met Lord Poulett, and Princess Amelia wrote to her father: 'Adolphus returned yesterday from Lord Ilchester's; he met the Pouletts there; not Lady Poulett for she is ill, and I understand the end of Octr. they go to town for Lady Sophia is to be married early in November.' This referred to the forthcoming wedding of the 4th Earl Poulett's daughter, Lady Sophia, to Henry, Viscount Barnard, later Duke of Cleveland, who were married on 18 November. Three days after this letter Princes Mary tells her father that they expected the Pouletts in Weymouth 'but they are not arrived yet'. However, on 2 October Amelia informs her father that Adolphus was off that day to visit Lord Poulett. So Hinton House saw another royal visitor in the personage of His Royal Highness Prince Adolphus, Duke of Cambridge. Writing of this visit Princess Mary told her father that: 'He passed one day at Lord Poulett's which he says is a very fine house and comfortable, at the same time nothing ever was so kind as both Lord and Lady Poulett had been to him.' The roads, the prince reported 'were dreadful!'

In 1801 Lord Poulett again became possessed of the Lordship of the Manor of Chard. Chard had been the property of the Bishopric of Bath and Wells previously, but it was alienated to Lord Poulett for the redemption of the land tax.

John and Sophia had a large family, five sons and five daughters. The boys were named John, George, William, Vere and Frederick; and the girls were Sophia, Mary, Harriet, Catherine and Augusta. Sophia, as already mentioned, married the 2nd Duke of Cleveland. She died on 9 January 1859 without issue. Lady Mary married Lord Charles Henry Somerset,

John, 4th Earl Poulett
1756–1819 (by James
Northcote)

the second son of the Duke of Beaufort. She died in 1860 and was buried in Brompton cemetery. There is a memorial tablet to her memory in Hinton Church, placed there by her only son, Colonel Poulett George Henry Somerset, who was born in 1822. The inscription reads that Lady Mary was much attached to Hinton St George.

The earl's second son, George, who was born on 10 May 1786, entered the navy on 2 August 1797, and became a Captain R.N. on 31 July 1806. He was naval aide-de-camp to King William IV and Queen Victoria during the period from 1830 to 1841. He was Receiver-General of the land and assessed taxes in Somerset in 1840. On 21 June 1850 he became a Vice-Admiral. He married Catherine Sophia, the daughter of Sir George Dallas, 1st Baronet, and they had five children; their third son William becoming eventually the 6th Earl Poulett. Vice-Admiral George died suddenly while out hunting near West Marden, Sussex, on 10 February 1858.

The rest of the 4th Earl's children, with the exception of John, Viscount Hinton, and Lady Augusta, died while very young, the three boys, William, Vere and Frederick were aged 16, 21 and 14 respectively, and the girls, Harriet and Catherine were 10 and 21 years old. Lady Augusta lived to a great age and her name appears on a plaque commemorating the building of the almshouses in Hinton in 1872. It is recorded that as a child Lady Augusta received lessons on the harp from a Miss Webb. Augusta died on 11 December 1888 aged 88.

*Master George Poulett 1786–1858
– as a midshipman. Second son of
4th Earl Poulett and father of 6th
Earl Poulett (by James Northcote)*

Sophia, Countess Poulett died at Hinton on 24 January 1811, and after five years John married again, taking as his second wife, Margaret, the beautiful and wealthy widow of Sir John Smith Burges, Bt., a successful merchant in the East India Company. The Duke of Clarence, later King William IV, a personal friend of both bride and groom, gave her away at the wedding which took place at St George's Church, Hanover Square. His wedding present to Margaret was a beautiful silver and cut-glass inkstand made by Paul Storr, with an inscription reading: 'The Gift of his Royal Highness the Duke of Clarence, to Lady Smith Burges, on her Marriage with Earl Poulett, July the 23rd, 1816.' At her wedding Lady Smith Burges brought with her a considerable fortune and a substantial yearly income. With her to Hinton came also the famous Smith Burges jewels, a collection of magnificent emeralds. The Poulett family were not a little piqued when later, after the death of the 4th Earl, Margaret returned the jewellery to the family of her first husband.

In 1818 she donated £20 towards the cost of a new oak pulpit for the church at Hinton. In her youth her portrait was painted by the great artist George Romney. The picture was brought to Hinton House and remained there for many years.

In 1815 John built new almshouses in Hinton for ten old people, south of the church, and

*Margaret Smith Burges, second
wife of 4th Earl Poulett
(by George Romney)*

provided bread, meat and clothing for them. He also provided a school house and a salary of £10 per annum for a Master to educate ten poor boys. Times were hard for the ordinary people in the parish. In 1801 there was great poverty and the Overseers' accounts record the payment of £9 18s. 6d. for rice for the poor. Again, from 1818 to 1820 the Overseers' expenses were heavy due to much poverty in the parish and in 1820 poor relief amounted to £466. Smallpox was a scourge at this time. There had been a severe outbreak in Hinton in 1772 when eighty-five children were involved and 8 guineas was paid for inoculations. There was another outbreak nine years later in 1781 and again in 1828.

John, 4th Earl Poulett, died on 18 January 1819 of apoplexy, aged 63, 'universally and deservedly esteemed and lamented.' A large mural monument was erected to his memory in the nave of Hinton Church by his widow who herself died on 18 May 1838 at Brighton, Sussex. She was buried at East Ham, Essex.

The heir, also named John, was born on 5 July 1783, at Charles Street, Berkeley Square, in Mayfair. As Viscount Hinton he was educated at Harrow and went on to Oxford University from where he matriculated at Brasenose College on 12 June 1801. The same year he entered the army and became a captain in the 1st Somerset Militia. He served in the 2nd Somerset Militia as a colonel from 1804 until 1819 when he returned to the 1st Regiment. That year his father died and John became the 5th Earl Poulett. While serving in France the following year he married Charlotte Fanny Portman, the only daughter of Henry Berkeley Portman of

Bryanston House, in Dorset. The wedding took place at the British Embassy in Paris on 28 August 1820. The next year, on 8 June their first son was born in Paris and baptised John Rolle at the Embassy. (He appears to have been named after John Rolle of Bicton, Devon, who became Baron Rolle of Stevenstone in 1796. His ancestor married the 1st Baron Poulett's daughter in the seventeenth century. Lord Rolle voted with Lord Poulett against Earl Grey's Reform Bill.)

In 1822 John and Charlotte returned to England and their second son Vere was born on 20 August at Hinton St George. The couple's happiness must have seemed complete when in 1830 Charlotte gave birth to a daughter who was named Margaret Charlotte; but this happiness was short-lived as the delicate little girl only survived for three years nine months, and she died on 31 May 1834. Consolation for their loss was found in February the following year when their youngest son, Amias, was born.

The 5th Earl carried out his duties as owner of a large estate conscientiously and found time for his military commitments and for periodic visits to take his place in the House of Lords. He was one of the twenty-two 'stalwarts' who voted against the third reading of the Reform Bill on 4 June 1832.

Hinton was particularly prosperous at the time. In 1840 two inns and eight shops are recorded, including a bookseller and stationer. Several villas were built in the village and there were two private schools. The earl employed some twenty indoor staff and ten more in the gardens.

His family was growing up and his three sons all took up military careers. The eldest, John Rolle, Viscount Hinton, had been educated at Eton, and when he was nineteen he entered the Grenadier Guards with a commission.

The second son, Vere, was educated at Harrow and Christ Church, Oxford. When he was 20 he joined the army and became an officer in the 68th Light Infantry. The following year in 1843, tragedy struck the family again for on 29 August John Rolle died in London, aged only 22.

Great changes were taking place in England at this time as a result of the Industrial Revolution. The new railways were spreading across the countryside. In Somerset in 1845 there were no less than twenty-eight companies interested in opening lines across the county. One such company, named the Bristol and English Channel Connection Railway, planned a route from the Dorset coast to the North Somerset coast which would pass through the parish of Hinton St George itself. The 5th Earl appears to have been sympathetic to some of these plans as he held shares in several of the companies. However, no railway came to Hinton, the nearest being the main Salisbury–Exeter line at Crewkerne. In 1856 Lord and Lady Poulett attended a ceremony at Crewkerne, where Charlotte cut the first turf at the start of the construction of that railway. A special little wheelbarrow and spade were made for the occasion by Giles Hayward of Crewkerne. Made of oak, carved with oak leaves and bearing the Poulett arms, they were presented to Lady Poulett afterwards, and were displayed in the Grand Entrance Hall at Hinton House.

In 1853, John became concerned over the affairs of his nephew, William Henry. William's wife had produced a son whom William refused to recognize as his own. After John's own two sons, still as yet unmarried, William Henry was the heir to the title and estates, there being no other living male in the direct line. In order to prevent the estates passing to the unfortunate infant in the future, John and his son Vere resettled them by deed of entail. Under this deed, if William inherited the estates, they would pass at his death to his legitimate heir, and should this heir die before the age of 21 they would revert to the heirs of John's other nephew, Colonel Poulett George Henry Somerset, the son of John's sister Mary.

William Henry did become the next heir, and much sooner than could have been expected, for greater sorrows were to visit John and Charlotte in 1857. They had proudly seen their youngest son, Amias, follow his brothers into the army. He chose the Grenadier Guards and became a captain. The Crimean War was now raging and Amias served with his regiment there, taking part in the siege and capture of Sevastopol. He returned home on leave and was taken ill and died at Hinton on 20 February 1857, aged 22 years. It was a terrible year for John and Charlotte for in the following year, on 20 August, Vere, their remaining son, now a Colonel in the 1st Somerset Militia, died while staying at their London home in Dover Street, Piccadilly. He was aged 35. So the grief-stricken couple were left childless. In time two memorials to their four children were placed in the Poulett chapel in the parish church. One is the large stained-glass window, and the other a marble monument depicting a weeping woman by an urn.

Both John and Charlotte lived to a great old age. In his later years the 5th Earl was a familiar sight in the countryside around Hinton. He is described as a man of simple habits, fond of the country and country pursuits. He spent a great deal of his time on the estate, and always wore breeches and leather gaiters. He carried his snuff in his waistcoat pocket, which was lined with leather, the better to preserve the precious powder. He spoke the Somerset dialect and was much attached to his beloved estate. He very rarely left it for he disliked London intensely. A favourite ride of his was along the road between Crewkerne and Windwhistle, and he often remarked that the air there was worth a guinea a mouthful. He lived to be 81 years old and died at Hinton House on 20 June 1864. A newspaper report of the time describes the funeral in the following words:

Many hundreds assembled to witness the funeral of the 5th Earl. Nearly the whole distance from the mansion to the church at Hinton was a mass of moving human beings. The coffin was made by Alfred Clark, foreman of the carpenters and joiners belonging to the establishment. The inner lead coffin was executed by Mr Norman, plumber of Hinton St George, the whole was covered with the richest Genoa velvet and superior furniture which gave the whole a rich and neat appearance. The procession moved off at 2 o'clock, 150 tenants and others leading. Then came mutes, followed by clergymen and others. The chief mourners were Earl Poulett and Col. Poulett Somerset, M.P., after whom followed the household.

The 5th Earl's Will proved to be under £120,000. Charlotte survived her husband by thirteen years and died at 20 Hanover Square, London on 27 March, 1877.

CHAPTER 7

The Sporting Sixth Earl

'A thorough man of Business'
A tenant of the 6th Earl Poulett

The title and the estate passed from the 5th Earl Poulett to his nephew William Henry, who was the son of Vice-Admiral George Poulett and his wife Catherine Sophia Dallas. At the time of his birth on 22 September 1827 there were two cousins and his two elder brothers standing between him and the family title and estates, and it is unlikely that in his early years William Henry ever expected to succeed to them. Named after his godfather King William IV, he was educated at the Royal Military Academy at Woolwich, and in 1845, when he was 18, commenced an army career by joining the 54th Regiment of Foot, and served in Gibraltar. His young life was a chapter of sad bereavements. By the time he was 23 he had lost his mother, three brothers, George, Henry and John, and his sister Augusta. His cousin John Rolle, Viscount Hinton, died also in 1843.

In 1846 he entered the 2nd Queen's Royal Regiment with whom he was to serve until 1852. In 1849 he contracted his first and, as it proved, most unfortunate marriage. The youthful William Henry was by all accounts, a wild and romantic character, and there are several stories regarding his first romance. One is that he made a wager with a brother officer while at sea in June 1848, that he would marry the first single woman he met on landing in England. Another version says that the bet was not made at sea, but while stationed at Portsmouth with his regiment, and was that he would wed the first girl he should see from the windows of the officers' mess. A third story says that he was smitten with an actress, and that he bet a thousand pounds that he would marry her within a month after first seeing her. The truth of the matter is perhaps not quite so romantic. In June 1848 21-year-old Lieutenant Poulett went with his regiment to Ireland. Whilst attending the fashionable Phoenix Park race course in Dublin he was introduced to a Miss Elizabeth Lavinia Newman, the daughter of a pilot from Landport, Portsmouth. A year later back at Portsmouth he accidentally met Miss Newman again, and although he had heard that she had been living with a Captain William Turnour Granville in Ireland, he nevertheless asked her to go away with him. Whether any wagering was made on these facts is not related. However, the lady was not prepared for William's company without marriage, and so the couple were in fact married on 23 June 1849. The union was doomed from the start. Less than two months later Elizabeth confessed that she was pregnant, and a son was born on 15 December. William was later to testify that she had admitted that the father was Captain Turnour Granville. However, as far as William was concerned then, the marriage was over. He left Elizabeth on 8 August and never lived with her again. The boy was subsequently baptised William Turnour Thomas!

William Henry continued his army career, and in 1852 he exchanged into the 22nd Regiment of Foot and joined them in the Punjab. He was at the storming of the Boree Pass in 1854 under Brigadier-General Boileau, and received a medal and clasp. William was passionately fond of horses and was a skilled rider. Racing was his greatest love. He is reported to have ridden in fifty-seven races while in the North-West Provinces in India and to

William Henry, 6th Earl Poulett
1827–1899

have won forty-three of them in one year. He remained in India until August 1855 when he returned to England to continue service with his regiment until 1857, when he sold out with the rank of captain on 23 October.

In that year William Henry must have forseen the possibility of his succession to the Poulett Earldom, for in February and August, his cousins Vere and Amias, the sons of the 5th Earl, both died, leaving him the only surviving male heir after his father. His father, Vice-Admiral George Poulett, however, died on 10 February 1858, and six years later William Henry became the 6th Earl Poulett on the death of his uncle John at Hinton St George on 28 June 1864.

On leaving the army William Henry had made his home in Hampshire at a house called Grenville Hall high up on the downs near the village of Droxford, about 12 miles from Portsmouth. Here he was able to devote his time to his passion for horses and horse-racing. Grenville Hall, which still stands today, was developed as a training establishment for his racing stud, with stables and staff-quarters, and the nearby open downland was ideal for gallops. Captain Poulett, of course, soon found favour with the local sporting gentry and from 1859 until 1868 was Master of the Hambledon Hunt, and was a familiar figure on hunt days, on his favourite mare Irish Molly. Reminiscing on those days a writer of 1864 says that since Captain Poulett 'became Master of the Hambledon Hounds, at no period since their existence have they been so liberally managed, or have they had better sport'.

In 1864 came the news from Hinton St George, that John, the 5th Earl Poulett, had died and that William Henry had inherited the estate and the title of 6th Earl. He did not take up immediate residence at Hinton House, and the mansion was let to various tenants on and off for a number of years. As the new Earl Poulett, William's immediate life was practically undisturbed and he pursued his interests at Grenville Hall with continued vigour. He was helped by his great friend, the famous rider and sportsman, George Ede, who lived with him. Ede had helped to found the Hampshire Cricket Club. He rode some 300 winners in fourteen years under the name of 'Mr Edwards' and had beaten the famous professional jockey Fordham in a race at Manchester, and the next day went on to score a century for the Hampshire Cricket Club.

Lord Poulett's racing interests took him all round the country and to the Continent. He became a well known figure in sporting circles, for his hunting and racing, and as a keen yachtsman. He owned many famous horses, among them Benazet and Endsleigh, but the most famous of all was the little grey named The Lamb, which won the Grand National twice. The story of The Lamb began in Ireland in 1862 where a farmer by the name of Henchy bred a grey foal from a mare who was supposed to have been sired by Arthur, the horse who had come second in the 1840 National. The sire of the foal was a great jumper named Zouave. The foal was thin and undersized and did not show much future promise. Henchy's son, a delicate boy, took to the foal and became inseparable from it, and because of his pet's temperament and colour, gave it the name of The Lamb. The boy, however, died and The Lamb was sold for thirty sovereigns as a three-year-old. His racing career started when he won some unimportant flat events. He was still extremely small, standing not more than 14 or 15 hands, and when offered for sale again, this time for only twenty-five sovereigns, there were no offers. One dealer refused him on the grounds that 'he was not strong enough to carry a man's boots.' However, he was eventually sold to a Dublin veterinary surgeon named Joe Doyle, and after running unplaced to Lord Poulett's Benazet in a 3 mile Handicap Chase at Liverpool, and also unsuccessfully at Leamington in the Grand Annual, where he was beaten by Chimney Sweep, he was leased to his Lordship, who had been impressed by the little horse's performance. George Ede was greatly taken with The Lamb, and after some training gallops realized that his great ambition to win the Grand National was a possibility after all. He had ridden in the National on six occasions before, with little luck, except for finishing second on Weathercock in 1858.

The Lamb's first runs for Lord Poulett were not particularly startling. He met Chimney Sweep again in the Grand Metropolitan Handicap at Croydon in 1868, which won the race and was thus made favourite for the National. Shortly before the Liverpool meeting Ede suffered a severe fall in a hurdle race, and when he was brought in from the course, was so covered with blood that a rapid recovery in time for the National seemed impossible. But recover he did, and his appearance on The Lamb at Aintree carrying Lord Poulett's colours for the meeting was the sign for a great ovation from the crowds. The Lamb looked magnificent – 'The picture of perfection'. The Grand National was by this time the leading event in the steeplechasing calendar and one of the top sporting and social occasions of the year. In 1868 the crowds were great as usual but the fields were not up to their normal standard, and the first day's races did not present much excitement. The only horse to make a showing was Pearl Diver, one of the favourites for the big race the next day. Other fancies included Chimney Sweep, The Lamb, and Moose. On the great day the crowds were at their maximum. The weather was wild and windy, and when the race commenced at 3.30 p.m. it was almost blowing a gale. The Lamb, backed at ten to one, quickly went into the lead. His rival, Chimney Sweep did not finish the race, for he struck a stone as he crossed the Melling Road, smashed a leg and had to be shot. The Lamb led Pearl Diver for the first circuit and was then overtaken by Alcibiade, the 1865 winner, with Pearl Diver, Moose and Colonel Crabtree close behind. A mile from home Alcibiade fell back and The Lamb and Pearl Diver went on. Racegoers still thought Pearl Diver would win, but The Lamb forged ahead to win from Pearl Diver by two lengths, with Alcibiade ten lengths away, third. Only three other horses finished the course. Great excitement greeted horse and jockey and they were led in to much cheering and shouting. The gale had continued at the height of the congratulations and when the wind blew down one of the big marquees, the police had to deal with some rowdies who, taking advantage of the confusion, were soon intent upon plundering the wreckage. All in all it was a memorable Grand National that year. Lord Poulett's trainer of The Lamb at that time was Ben Land, who had virtually transformed his appearance from the little over-delicate grey into the impressive and faultless horse that had fulfilled owner's, jockey's and trainer's ambitions to win the great race. Land gave up steeplechasing after this race, however, and tragically committed suicide some four years later.

It was to be another three years before The Lamb ran in the National again. In the interim he ran in various races but without much success. In 1869 he was entered in the 2¾ mile Sefton Chase, and started as an outsider among Lord Poulett's three entrants in the race. They finished consecutively, being beaten by Roving Maid, with the Earl's Benazet second, his Endsleigh third and The Lamb fourth. For two years The Lamb was out of the racing scene suffering from a wasting disease from which many feared he could not recover, but he was placed in the care of Mr Mannington who treated him by blistering his quarters and prescribing a long rest from racing of all kinds.

When the 1871 National came round The Lamb was in good shape once more, and more than ready for the challenge. His training was supervised by Lord Poulett himself, aided by Christopher Green, who trained most of his Lordship's horses at this time. Another newcomer was a fresh jockey – George Ede had ridden his last race in 1870, the Sefton Chase at Liverpool. He was riding Chippenham when they had a bad fall. Chippenham rolled on his jockey and dragged him along the ground for some way as his foot was caught in a stirrup. 'Mr Edwards' never recovered from his injuries and died a few days afterwards.

The Lamb's new jockey was to be Tommy Pickernell, the veteran jockey who rode under the name of Mr Thomas. The choice of Pickernell came about in a strange way, but truly in the tradition of the sporting 6th Earl Poulett. Shortly before Christmas, on the night of 14 December, William Henry had two dreams, and the next day he wrote to Tommy Pickernell as follows:

My Dear Tommy,
Let me know for certain whether you can ride for me at Liverpool on The Lamb. I dreamt twice last night I saw the race run. The first dream he was last and finished among the carriages. The second dream, I should think an hour afterwards, I saw The Lamb run. He won four lengths and you rode him, and I stood close to the winning post at the turn. I saw the cerise and blue sleeves and you, as plain as I write this. Now let me know as soon as you can, and say nothing to anyone.
Yours sincerely, Poulett.

Pickernell readily agreed to ride for Lord Poulett, but as far as saying nothing went, he need not have worried, for Lord Poulett himself was so certain of victory that he even sent out signed circulars to his friends to this effect. Large bets were wagered on The Lamb and although he made no appearance before the race, reports of his training and condition were widely circulated and his price continued to shorten. The race aroused much interest. There was a field of twenty-five runners, all considered top of their class, and included such horses as The Colonel and Alcibiade, both National winners in previous years. Also there was The Doctor, second in the race last year, and Pearl Diver, second to The Lamb in 1868.

Grand National Day arrived fine and bright. It was also a public holiday to celebrate the wedding of Princess Louise and the Marquess of Lorne so the crowds were out in force and were estimated at 45,000 at Aintree. Meanwhile The Lamb's position was rising to that of favourite for the race owing to various happenings. One of Lord Poulett's other horses, Broadlea, a rank outsider, won the Molyneux Chase on the first day; then it was rumoured that Pearl Diver would not run. More excitement was caused when a live lamb escaped in full view of many racegoers – some said at Liverpool station, where it ran down the platform; others reported seeing it on the actual race course. At all events it was an omen and caused a fresh flurry of bets. At last The Lamb arrived on the course to a tumult of cheers. He had benefited from his enforced rest and had even grown larger, standing a full 15.2 hands. His body had broadened and his grey coat shone like satin. The weather this time was glorious, and the race started at 3.45 p.m. (especially put back to enable Manchester business men to reach the course after work). From the 'Off' it was a tremendous race. Rufus led at the start with The Lamb close behind. There was a moment of horror when the leading runners were confronted by a crowd of enthusiasts actually on the course and the field charged through them 'knocking them down like ninepins, with severe injury to some.' At the end of the first circuit the first fifteen runners remained bunched together. Two notable horses had gone: The Doctor and Lord Raglan had both fallen. At a heavy stretch of rough land before Beechers, The Lamb faltered and lost his place, and was behind as they approached the Canal Turn. Two more horses fell here, right in front of The Lamb, but he sprang over them both and went on gamely. Towards the end the result was clearly between him and Despatch, and on the run-in The Lamb forged ahead to win by two lengths.

There was a tremendous reception for horse, rider and owner, all three were practically carried into the unsaddling enclosure. The Lamb lost most of his tail to souvenir hunters, while Lord Poulett lost his watch (afterwards recovered). Hardly before had there been such a popular win, or a more popular owner, carrying as he had the hopes and the money of the racing fraternity that day.

Soon afterwards The Lamb was sold for £1,200 to Baron Oppenheim and had a number of unspectacular races in this country before being taken to Germany. Here at Baden-Baden The Lamb sadly met his end. In the Grand Steeplechase he was in the lead when he slipped in mud barely 100 yards from the post; his foreleg was broken and he was at once destroyed. Paintings of The Lamb and Benazet with jockey George Ede up, wearing the colours of Lord Poulett, were at one time among the art collection at Hinton House. They bore the signature of the artist Harry Hall and were dated 1868.

The same year as The Lamb's last great victory, news reached William Henry in August that his estranged wife Elizabeth had died. A few weeks later, on 20 September, he re-married, his bride this time being Emma Sophia Johnson. After his wedding the earl spent more time at Hinton St George. (Some of the staff from Grenville Hall accompanied the earl to Hinton. Among these were members of the Aldridge family whose descendants still live in the village today.) It was to be a short marriage but apparently a happy one. Emma died only five years later, on 16 September 1876. Her monument in Hinton Church describes her as 'a gentle, affectionate and truly loved wife'. There were no children from this union. On 1

March 1879, at the age of 52, William Henry married for the third time. His bride on this occasion was Rosa, the daughter of Alfred Hugh Melville.

His Lordship's greatest wish was fulfilled on 11 September 1883 when his son and heir was born. The birth of William John Lydston was greeted by the ringing of the church bells at Hinton, and some 2,000 people were entertained on the estate by the proud father. There was also a dinner on a magnificent scale for some 300 of his tenants. One of the speakers at this dinner described the earl as a 'thorough man of business who saw in a moment what his tenants wanted and why they wanted it. He never said "no" to their desires if he could possibly help it, and if he was obliged to say "no", he did it in such a pleasant way that the denial was given without the tenant feeling it.' Another speaker, one of the tenants, enthused: 'I cannot say enough in praise of his Lordship. There is no man I respect more. To me he has always shown such kind condescension and regard, and I am sure all present can say the same.' The celebrations met with approval and it was said that festivities on this scale had not been known in Hinton for half a century.

The sixth earl and his wife also had two daughters, Lady Eleanor Augusta, born in 1879; and Lady Violet Nita, born in 1881. Lady Violet was married in 1904 to Lieutenant Cecil John Talbot Rhys Wingfield, of the 4th Battalion the King's Royal Rifle Corps, and a great-great-grandson of the 4th Viscount Powerscourt. Their son, Major Edward Rhys Wingfield married Lady Norah, the daughter of the 1st Earl Jellicoe, and they made their home in the Republic of Ireland.

Over the years William Henry took a considerable interest in the Hinton Estates and in particular the village of Hinton St George. After his third marriage he spent three or four months every year at Hinton House, where his hospitality was widely known. Great improvements to the estate were made in various ways. As early as 1865 a gas supply was introduced in the village, with the gas works at the bottom of Abbey Street. Gas lamps were situated at various points around the village, and Hinton House was illuminated by gas also. In 1872 new almshouses were erected in Gas Lane by the 6th Earl and his aunt Lady Augusta Poulett, the surviving daughter of the 4th Earl. They replaced the old almshouses off West Street. The water supply to the village was vastly improved in 1875. At considerable cost the water from a spring at the Lady's Bath in Hinton Park near Dinnington was diverted by pump into a new reservoir and from there by gravitation to the village. Elsewhere on the estate, at Maiden Beech a brickyard was established, and butter factories were built at Chard and Dinnington. The village school was built at Hinton in 1850 and William Henry always showed great interest in the welfare of the children. Every Christmas he provided a tea for them, and a giant tree from the estate was set up in the schoolroom laden with presents.

However, things changed. The 1880s and the 'Gay Nineties' were far from gay for agriculture. There was a severe period of depression when land values fell. The rent roll of the Hinton Estates, comprising nearly 11,000 acres, was at one time estimated at between nearly £20,000 and £30,000 a year, but by the end of the century had fallen to between £13,000 and £16,000. Things were so bad that the tenant farmers petitioned his Lordship to reduce their rents. With a reduction in prices for all farm produce, they were finding it increasingly difficult to meet their monetary responsibilities.

By 1895 the Earl found himself in grave financial difficulties, due partly to the depression and partly to the fact that he had practically disposed of his life interest in the estate by the sums of money which he had borrowed. In 1896 proceedings for bankruptcy were taken against him. In the course of these proceedings William Henry said that at the time of his succession the gross rental was only £13,000. This had risen subsequently to £16,000 but at the moment had fallen to £12,000. In 1892 the mortgagees had taken possession of the estate and since then Lord Poulett had been without any income from the property. Before this had happened he said his income was not more than £1,500 to £2,000. His Lordship ascribed his bankruptcy to the liabilities incurred by him as trustee to the estate of the late Lord Aylesford, and he had had to make good sums amounting with interest to £137,160. It may be true to say that the 6th Earl was not entirely to blame for these sorry circumstances, the fall in values for which he became legally responsible being wholly due to the terrible depreciation of agricultural values.

The Hinton Estate at this time comprised some 10,960 acres. It stretched about 9 miles from Crewkerne in the east to 2½ miles south-east of Chard. As well as Hinton St George, the estate comprised land in the parishes of Dinnington, Lopen, Kingstone, Seavington St Mary, Seavington St Michael, Chillington, Cudworth, Knowle St Giles, Crewkerne, Dowlish Wake, Chard, Tatworth, Chaffcombe, Merriott, Wayford and Misterton. There were fifty individual farms with tenant farmers. The largest of these was Coombe Farm at 691 acres. Other principal farms included Henley (627 acres), and Woolminstone and Fords Croft; all in West Crewkerne parish; Allowenshay and Ludney Farms in Kingstone parish; Hill and Sheephouse farms in Chillington parish; Chaffcombe Gate and West Farms in Cudworth parish; and Lopen Farm. Chard parish and Tatworth had eighteen farms including Walscombe, Tudbeer, Mounthindrance, Lordsleaze, Crimchard, Forton Manor, Tatworth Manor, Downings and Chard Common.

The whole estate was offered for sale for £600,000 in 1895 and a receiver administered the business affairs for several years. The agents for the sale were Messrs. Dowsett, Knight and Co., of Lincolns Inn Fields. To advertise the sale they used up most of their monthly publication *The Land Roll* for two successive issues with pages of descriptions and eulogies of the Estate, Hinton House, its contents and the Poulett family. The columns of this paper were full of enticing entreaties to men of wealth to purchase. One such read:

A great man without a great estate seems an anomaly . . . and although in adverse periods more estates than usual come into the market, it is difficult to secure one which is accompanied by nearly a thousand years of authentic honourable descent. We can offer such an one in the county home of the noble family of Poulett. A noble client in another county said to us recently, that if he sold his estate, which he and his ancestors have held from the Saxon period, he would require a million sterling for it, and its territorial area was less than the domain of Hinton St George to which we now draw attention.

It seems that the problems of pollution are not new to our day, for the estate agent of 1895 comments as follows:

If health is a primary condition with a man of wealth, he will reflect upon the differences of town and country life. Experiments in Paris proved that there were found 79,000 microbes in a litre of air at the Hotel de Dieu, 3,910 in the Rue de Rivoli, 455 at the Park at Montsouris, and 200 at the summit of the Pantheon. But on high mountains and out at sea there would only be one microbe in a litre of air; and the proportions between residing on such an estate as Hinton St George, near to the western sea, and that of any town in the kingdom, would vary in a remarkable degree in favour of Hinton, and the larger the town, the more unhealthy its climate. Experiments have proved that in by no means the worst part of Manchester there were carried down in three days nearly six hundredweight of sulphuric acid per square mile, besides thirteen hundredweight of blacks. . . . Those who value health will judge between town and country life.

Many other advantages and delights to be found on the Hinton Estate were listed:

Hinton possesses a great deal of fir timber . . . the sanative influence of fir forests is most remarkable. Where they prevail there is no epidemic visitation; the plague and the pestilence disappear, the polluted air is deodorized, and with an effect as magical as that of the tree which sweetened the bitter Marah of the wilderness, the presence of this tree purifies the most deadly atmosphere. The country has always charms, not less in winter than in summer. The uninterrupted sunshine, the green meadows, the waving corn fields, the melody of birds, the habits of animals, the robust walks, the always accessible ride or drive, the grandeur of the timber, the beauty of the flowers, the simple-heartedness of the rustics, the pursuits of botany, mineralogy, geology, natural history, horticulture, floriculture, and many other cultures combine to add instruction into recreation, while its pure air strengthens the brain and body power for the serious conflicts of life which an existence in towns cannot give in equal measure. Fishing is liberally provided on the Hinton St George Estate, and what is more fascinating than the art of angling? It has restored the worn out energies of many public men. Whether in the punt, on the bank, or wading upstream, the pleasurable excitement causing complete diversion of mind from any anxiety which may oppress it, ensures a beneficial result which proves its value. Shooting is a more favourite diversion even than fishing. It necessitates more exertion and gives more change. Walking the turnips and stubble, trying the hedgerows, driving the woods and plantations, decoying and securing wild duck and other birds on the lakes, the exhilaration of constant motion in the brisk autumn air, or in the keen sharpness of frosty winter, gives an appetite which defies indigestion, and sends a healthy thrill through one's whole being. The disposal of the covers at Hinton furnish very abundant, high-class sport of the best quality. Hunting, again, is another recreation for the plucky rider, and hounds and harriers are within easy reach of Hinton. To find the finest herds of deer and cattle, the finest flocks of sheep, the finest kinds of feathered stock, the finest crops, the finest fruits and flowers and garden produce, is an ambition worthy of a man of wealth, because his example stimulates his county to aim also at the highest and the best. A man of wealth who could afford such an estate as Hinton St George, would be able to have many of the intellectual enjoyments of town by entertaining from time to time the hard-worked thinkers in the ranks of science, philosophy, art and religion. Such gentlemen could appreciate the intervals of rest which a few days now and then in the luxurious apartments of the mansion would give them. Thus the possession of so distinguished a home would enable its possessor to dispense physical, intellectual and religious benefits to the people, rich and poor, over a wide tract of country all around him. Wealth is not to be measured by its income only, it has opportunities of imparting benefits which bring back interest in kind as well as in coin.

The Land Roll continues with remarks addressed as 'Special to American and South African Gentlemen:

Landed estates may be had for the taking in Central Africa. In parts of America they may be had for a few dollars an acre. In the old countries they must be paid for. The difference in value is the difference as between the daub of a tyro and the painting of a great master; or the mind of a savage with the mind of a cultured man of science. Land adorned presents to us the ancient palatial mansion, the park, with a turf made springy by centuries of care, trees from timber of majestic proportions to underwoods, coppices, belts, plantations and nurseries, verdant meadows and arable fields, suitable for producing every growth adapted to its latitude, orchards and gardens in profusion. Comparisons are to be realized by intelligent consideration, and the capitalist who wants land will draw from comparison his conclusion whether it is better for him to obtain a natural tract of country with unsophisticated surroundings, upon which, as a man of taste, he will have to lavish a fortune every year, and then never live to see it other than bearing the marks of 'spic and span', or whether it is better for him to buy an estate upon which the refining influences of generations of wealthy nobles have, for a thousand years past produced one of the most superior residential domains which is to be found upon the globe's surface, and which, withal, produces a liberal rent roll to replenish his banking account twice in the year.

It is hard to believe that such an Arcadian Utopia was available for a mere £600,000 and it is surprising that it was not sold quickly.

William Henry, the 6th Earl Poulett visited Hinton St George for the last time in April 1898, when he stayed with his family at Hinton House for two months. On Sunday, 22 January 1899 Lord Poulett died at his London home, 60 Queens Gate. Most of the people at Hinton did not know of his passing until they heard the church bell tolling at ten o'clock the next morning. Indeed few people even knew that he had been ill.

The earl's body was brought by train from London to Crewkerne. It was conveyed to Hinton where it arrived about 11 p.m. on Wednesday evening. The coffin, made of elm, with a leaden shell and an outer case of polished oak, rested in the chancel of the church overnight, watched over by estate workers. On the coffin rested the earl's coronet on a scarlet and gold cushion. The next morning the church was opened and large numbers of parishioners and others came in to pay their respects. The funeral service took place in the afternoon, and was conducted by the rector, the Reverend Robert Ratcliffe Dolling, assisted by the Reverend Joseph Billing, Rector of Seavington and chaplain to the late earl. The coffin was borne from the church by estate workers acting as bearers, and interment in the family vault followed. There were many wreaths and floral tributes, including one from William Henry's widow inscribed 'From your ever loving, devoted and heart-broken wife'.

So passed the 'Sporting Earl'. With him it is perhaps true to say, passed many of the old traditions of the great estate. Something of the old order continued until the First World War, but within seventy years the estate was finally sold and the family home left deserted and empty.

THE CROSS - HINTON ST GEORGE

CHAPTER 8

The Poulett Claimant

'I am Viscount Hinton, eldest son of Earl Poulett'
Barrel Organ Placard

Although not accepted as a member of the noble line of the Poulett family, William Turnour Thomas Poulett nevertheless has his place in the family story. His claim to the title and estates on the death of the 6th Earl gained him a great deal of publicity and notoriety. The newspapers of the day were full of information considered to be of interest to their readers and much of the following account is taken from contemporary newspaper reports.

William Turnour Thomas Poulett was born at Grove Cottage, Southsea, on 15 December 1849, seven months after his mother Elizabeth Newman had married William Henry Poulett, a nephew of the 5th Earl, who at that time did not appear likely to succeed to the title himself. The couple were married on 23 June 1849 and after two months William discovered that his wife had been pregnant when they married. He left her on 8 August and did not live with her again, although he provided her with an income for life. William Henry always denied that the child was his and refused to recognize him as such, and made no provision whatsoever for him.

The boy's early education was obtained at Church House College, Merton, where among other subjects he learned to speak French fluently. After leaving school, William Turnour attempted a career in the theatrical world. He commenced this life as a public singer, but his voice failed and he then took engagements as a clown and comedian at the Surrey Theatre under the name of 'Mr Cosman'. He was not particularly successful in this field but he persevered. In December 1869, just before his 20th birthday, he married into the theatre, taking as his wife a ballet dancer named Lydia Ann Sheppy.

When he became 21 in 1870, William visited Crewkerne and Hinton House. He was described as a tall, fair, rather good-looking young man, who dressed stylishly. He stayed at the George Hotel in Crewkerne and hired a trap and was driven out to Hinton St George. Here he tried to see William Henry, now the 6th Earl Poulett. His lordship, however, positively refused to accept him as his son and would not see him, and ordered his servants to show him, if not throw him from the grounds of Hinton House. This they did but without any force or roughness – in fact he was shown every consideration during his visit to the village. It is said that he took refreshment at one of the inns kept by a Mr Grinter (another report says Templeman). This fact was duly reported to Lord Poulett who promptly terminated the tenant's lease and turned him off the estate. William Turnour also visited Hinton again in 1872, for a newspaper report of December that year says that 'Earl Poulett's son and heir visited the village, and spent a night at Lord Westbury's at Hinton House [the mansion was apparently being let]. He left the following morning. The church bells were rung in his honour and flags put out around the village. Outside the Poulett Arms Inn an immense sheet of bunting was stretched across the road!

Lord Poulett is said to have offered William a settlement of £800 a year if he agreed to disclaim the title of Viscount Hinton but this he refused to do. The Dowager Duchess of Cleveland, a family relative, was sympathetic towards him and helped him financially from time to time. There were three children of his marriage, a boy named William Henry George, born in 1870, and two girls. The boy eventually inherited £5,000 from the Duchess of Cleveland and went to Ceylon as a tea planter. The girls were educated at a French convent. His mother died in 1871 and was buried in the local cemetery at Portsmouth. The inscription on the grave stone records the memory of the Right Hon. Elizabeth Lavinia, Countess Poulett, wife of William Henry, sixth Earl Poulett. A strange story is related of an occasion when William Turnour visited his mother while she lay dying. In reply to his anxious enquiries, his mother answered that all was well but added in a whisper, 'There is an eye sometimes stares through that crack in the door that troubles me'. William tried to assure her that no one would come and spy on her in that manner, and that it was all her imagination. 'But it is true,' his mother persisted, 'I have seen that eye too often.' On making enquiries of the landlady, William was told after some hesitation, 'Yes, it is true. Emma Johnson comes down from Rosebank, Waterloo, to find out how soon she is going to die, and she has peeped through the door.' When the unfortunate lady did die, Emma Johnson, just over a month later, married Lord Poulett and became the new Countess!

William did not rise in his stage career but gradually sank lower and lower and was eventually forced to earn his living by means of entertaining in the streets and elsewhere with a barrel-organ. He commenced this precarious living on the streets of his native Southsea. He gained notoriety from the fact that on his barrel-organ he displayed a placard stating: 'I am Viscount Hinton, eldest son of Earl Poulett; I have adopted this as a means of earning a living, my father having refused to assist me through no fault of my own.' During the summer months he used to ply his trade on the steamers between Dover and Calais, and a French paper printed a cartoon of him, shoeless and in rags, torturing tunes from the organ while on his head was an immense coronet. The facts printed on the placard do not appear to have added much to the income he derived from organ-grinding and the 'Viscount' and his family were often destitute.

They finally settled in Islington and William carried on with his trade, still managing to attract the attention from time to time of the comic papers who continued to print cartoons on the subject. One such illustration portrayed 'Viscount Hinton' grinding away at his piano-organ, outside a vulgar-looking mansion, while Mrs Newly-Rich and her daughter look out from a window. Mama was made to exclaim with great emotion to her daughter, 'Look dear, at the haristocratic way in wich 'is lawdship turns the 'andle!'

About 1890 the Poulett family brought to court an action of what is known as *Perpetuation of Testimony*, for the express purpose of proving that William Turnour Thomas had no claim to the title and was in fact illegitimate. The 6th Earl himself gave evidence, but to all intents and purposes the case failed as nothing conclusive was decided at that time.

When the 6th Earl died in January 1899 he left as his heir his 16 year-old-son by his third marriage. William Turnour Poulett, the other claimant, was living in a dingy tenement building at 17 Henry Buildings, Penton Street, Islington. Newspaper reporters were quickly on the scene and on the day after the earl's death one reporter found 'Viscount Hinton' on his pitch in Upper Street, Islington. He was lighting a cigarette while his wife collected coppers. The interview and subsequent conversation was reported as follows:

'Viscount Hinton, I believe,' said the reporter. 'Yes, I am he,' answered the organ-grinder. 'I have to inform you that Earl Poulett died yesterday at his town house, 60 Queens Gate.'

'Nonsense! Do you really mean that?' An emphatic assurance was given. 'Then I am Earl Poulett,' was the rejoinder. So in the blatant thoroughfare which has been labelled the 'Devil's Mile' was the announcement made to this latest peer that he had presumably succeeded to his title. The news, when fully grasped, seemed to stun the recipient. He could hardly realize that at last, after years of humiliation, he stood once more with a chance of regaining the position to which he had looked forward so long. His wife, who walked painfully with a stick, seemed to adapt herself more quickly to her dignity.

'I am deeply sorry to hear that the earl is dead,' she said, and then, turning to her husband, 'but Willy, I am heartily grateful that at last your troubles are over.' It was quite dramatic, this little scene, amid the hum and blaze of the Islington traffic.

'Come with me and we'll talk about it,' said the Earl, 'but first I must pack the machine up. Mr. Freeland!' – this to an old man, who for many years has helped to drag the organ home at night – 'You can get yourself a half-pint of bitter' – and with this first act of generosity to signalize his new dignity, Earl Poulett led the way to a quieter spot.

'What do I think of the news? Well I hardly know – it is certainly unexpected, and I may say frankly, welcome, for though I have not wished the death of my father, despite the manner in which he has treated me, I am glad that at last, I shall be placed beyond the sordid existence I have been obliged to lead. Curiously enough, I expected some news, because last night, I had a dream, which always when it comes to me, is the presage of some eventful occurrence. I shall, of course, take immediate steps through my solicitors to assert my claim to the title and entailed estates. Yes, I dare say there will be some opposition on the part of the family, my father leaves a wife – his third – and I think three other children – a boy and two girls, but I do not think there is any doubt about my right of succession. Of course, the income from the property is greatly reduced owing to the involved state of the late Earl's affairs, as the result of which his rents have been practically estreated during the past year or more to the benefit of his creditors. What the amount of my inheritance will be it is therefore impossible to say, but at any rate I should receive an income which will enable me to live in comparative luxury. Of course, I shall discard my organ at once. It would hardly look the thing for an Earl Poulett to play in the streets, would it? I am only sorry that I have no better clothes than those I am wearing, for a week before Christmas my rooms were entered, and the whole of my wearing apparel, including five frock coats were stolen. Still that is a minor consideration now, though it has been a very real trouble to me up to this moment. Yes, I shall certainly call on my solicitors the first thing in the morning. I am only surprised that they have not been made aware of the late Earl's death in order to communicate with me. But perhaps it is a little soon for the news to have reached them, as I have had no relations with my family for some time. Well, it's all over now, and I think I have earned a rest. I shall go home and look through my papers.'

And the Earl and Countess Poulett walked slowly away towards the little room in a tenement house near the Angel, which has been their home in times of adversity.

The following day a reporter called at 17 Henry Buildings. The 'earl' was not at home having gone to see his solicitors. His wife, however, was in, and the following conversation with her is reported:

I am not sorry that there is a prospect of our street life being ended. Since I injured my ankle I have not been so able to assist in pulling the organ, and Willie has been poorly for some time. He suffers from rheumatism in the legs and very often he is unable to stand. But I have stuck to him through all these years, and I would have stuck to him to the end in any case. Yes, we were many times in sore straits, well nigh half-starved often. But we would have starved rather than take the assistance that the late Earl sent indirectly through policemen and others. How long have I been married to Viscount Hinton? It's so long I scarcely care to tell. We were married 28 years ago. No, there was very little romance about our marriage, it was one of those cases of love at first sight. We have lived very happily. Willie is so good tempered. We have had three children – two girls and one boy. Our son was left £5,000 by the Dowager Duchess of Cleveland, and he is now in Ceylon engaged as a tea planter. The girls are in a French convent.'

At this point the claimant to the title arrived home. 'I have,' he said, 'been consulting my solicitor, Mr Hall of Warwick Court, today. I was naturally anxious to know what I ought to do. Mr Hall told me there was plenty of time, and I needn't trouble myself. I have, therefore, decided to wait till the late Earl is buried before I take any steps. What do I then purpose doing? I cannot say exactly, but it is more than likely that I will go down to Hinton St George, my property, and quietly take possession. Do I anticipate any opposition? I do not, but if there is I will do what I did one time before. I will break down the gates and enter. It was sometime in the seventies that I resorted to that. Along with a friend named Billy Blorr, I was in the vicinity of Hinton St George, I wanted to get into the park that is part of my possessions, and I was informed by one of my father's servants that it was a right of way. With very little ceremony I cut down the gates, and placed them under St George's cross and then walked in. Oh yes, if there is any legal fighting to be done I shan't shirk it; but I shan't commence it. My case is clear, those for the Hon. William John Lydston have to establish theirs. I shall let them begin, and then when I have heard what they have got to say I will answer them.'

Questioned about his parents the prospective Lord Poulett said that it was not the case that his father married his mother after a brief acquaintance. 'As a matter of fact they lived together,' he said, 'at least two years before they were married, and the banns were published at Landport in the ordinary course three weeks before the marriage was solemnized.' He was born in wedlock. This fact was not disputed. Very soon after he was born his father and mother separated, his mother enjoying a good income which died with her. She died at Southsea in the August of 1871. He continued: 'No, my father did not provide for me. He did make an offer, but it was on the condition that I dropped the title and went to a distant part. If I complied he was to settle £800 a year on me, but I refused. I then took to theatrical life, the Dowager Duchess of Cleveland assisting me greatly. When did I first take to organ-grinding? It was about 1889, and my first pitch was on the beach of my native Southsea. Yes, I have had a hard life since then, but I trust it is all over. Will I sit in the House of Lords? I hope to. Oh yes; I'm a Conservative. I have always been a Conservative. It's some time since I was in the House of Lords, but I have been there in the capacity of the eldest son of a peer. Yes, I have been authoritatively recognized as the late Earl Poulett's successor. On Thanksgiving Day in 1872, I was invited by the then Lord Chamberlain to be present at the Cathedral. I went with my father to the House of Lords, and afterwards proceeded with the other peers and the eldest sons of peers to St Paul's Cathedral. I have ample proof that my father recognized in me his lawful heir. When did I last see my father? About two months ago, when I was playing the organ in Brompton Road. He did not recognize me in any way.

After the Earl's death on Sunday, 22 January, it was reported that the village of Hinton St George had been agog with the news that the organ-grinding viscount was in the neighbourhood and was only biding his time before taking possession, by force if necessary, of Hinton House. In view of the state of affairs, the gamekeepers and servants living on distant parts of the estate were hurriedly called to the mansion, in order to prevent an entry being effected by the viscount. A strict look-out was kept at all possible points of entry to the mansion and grounds, persons seeking to enter the gates being closely questioned as to their business. Some men who were merely walking along the roads were carefully scrutinized by estate workmen, some of whom were told to keep a strict look-out during the night. The local agent to the trustees of the estate, presumably for the purpose of better directing any defensive operations which might be rendered necessary, remained in the village close at hand over Monday night. But no Viscount Hinton or any of his minions (if he had any) appeared. It is said that practical jokers were going to test the defences by one of their number dressing up as the claimant accompanied by a barrel-organ (specially smuggled into the neighbourhood) and presenting himself at the gates of Hinton House. A newspaper reporter commented caustically as follows:

> What an opportunity the valiant defenders of Hinton Mansion and grounds missed of showing their prowess to the astonished and admiring natives! It would be unkind to judge of the amount of latent bravery lurking in the breasts of the defenders, some of whom unkind rumours say were crippled old men and scarcely able to stand.

Apparently the mansion itself was barricaded at all strategic points.

The funeral of the late earl took place at Hinton St George on Thursday 26 January. The prospective earl was, however, unable to attend due to an accident sustained while pushing the organ along Rosebery Avenue on the previous Tuesday. He had expressed his avowed intention of being present at the service, and rumours grew that not only had he met with an accident but also that he was very seriously ill. A *Daily Telegraph* reporter consequently visited his home at Henry Buildings, Pentonville on Thursday evening and the following is his tongue-in-cheek account of the visit:

> It was not difficult to find the Buildings, but this particular set of apartments occupied by the aristocratic street musician required diligent search owing to the scarcity of light in this particular quarter of Pentonville. The presence of a stranger, however, soon attracted a crowd of small boys who swarmed around the buildings and enquired the object of the visit. 'I guess, guv'nor, you're looking for the viscount,' said one of them, to which a companion quickly retorted, 'He's no viscount; he's a bloomin' Lord now. If you want to see his lawdship,' the youngster added, 'you goes along this dark passage, up those stairs to number 17, and mind you don't break your bloomin' neck on the way. Lights is scarce in Henry Buildings.' Aided by these instructions no further difficulty was experienced in finding the viscount. He is a man of presentable appearance, respectably clothed, and neither in demeanour nor conversation does he resemble those other organ-grinders who may be found any day in the purlieus of Saffron Hill. On the present occasion he was reclining on a horsehair sofa in a small back parlour. The room was poorly furnished, but scrupulously clean, and was lighted by a small paraffin lamp, such as you can buy for the sum of 4½d. at most Italian warehouses. Apparently a 'reception' was in progress when our representative entered because in order to give place to the visitor, quite a large number of people – nearly all of the poorer class – filed into the passage, and went their way to other sections of Henry Buildings. 'His lordship is indisposed, but he will see you now,' said a middle-aged lady, who had escorted the visitors from the room. The viscount keeps a level head amidst the stir excited by the death of the 6th Earl Poulett, and comports himself with a dignity which one would

hardly expect to find in Henry Buildings, Pentonville. 'I am very glad to see you,' he said. 'I am not so badly hurt as they make out, and I hope to be out again soon. The fact is, I was going along Rosebery Avenue yesterday afternoon when I twisted my ankle. That's why I am stretched out here. But I can't complain, for I have plenty to interest me.' Here the viscount pointed to a small table upon which there was a huge pile of letters. On the floor there was a great litter of envelopes, from which the epistles had evidently been recently taken. There were piles of letters also on the mantelpiece, letters on the sofa, letters in fact everywhere. 'Where did they all come from?' 'They come from all parts of the country, from Ireland and Scotland, as well as England, and these you see about here all came today. What's more,' added the Viscount, waxing quite hot with enthusiasm, 'they all breathe the same message, congratulations and sympathy.' 'From whom did they come?' 'From all classes, rich and poor, learned and ignorant. I value them all, but those from the poor touch me most. For years I have lived amid poverty, and I know how warm are the hearts of the poor. For two hours this morning I was opening these letters – simply opening them and glancing through the contents. There's sympathy in all of them and encouragement. Look at this one for example.' Here the viscount rose from the sofa and limped painfully towards the mantelpiece. 'Read that,' he said, handing over a rather crumpled sheet of paper, which he took from a vase. 'Read that, and consider it as a type of many I have by me.' The letter read as follows:

> My dear Earl Poulett,
> I have seen a copy of your appeal in the *Western Gazette*. I should like to tell you that I was domestic at Hinton St George, and left at the death of the Earl. Then the late Countess Poulett recommended me to the late Dowager Duchess of Cleveland. I have read of you having to get your own living. I have often thought the Earl should have allowed you an annuity out of the lovely estate. I hope I may only live to know that you succeed to it – I remain your humble servant.
> A Poor Old Woman.

'That's a specimen of the letters,' resumed the viscount, 'and the poor old soul actually enclosed postage stamps to the value of one shilling. Believe me, I value those stamps more than £20.' On business matters the viscount was very reticent. 'I leave everything,' he explained, 'to my solicitor, who is acting for me. It has been said that people have come to me offering me money to promote my cause. I should like to say that is not true.'

'Why did you not go to the funeral of Earl Poulett?'

'I should have gone, but this accident yesterday upset my arrangements. I am glad to have an opportunity of putting myself right on this point, because it has led to some misunderstanding. I am quite certain that if I had gone many of the local people would have welcomed me, and especially those who have seen me playing on Southsea beach with the piano, also those who have seen me in Upper Street, Islington, during the Cattle Show and the Dairy Show.'

'What are your plans?'

'My solicitor is acting for me. If things go to the bad there is always the piano organ. It is in a stable close by here and in good condition. I might add that I have had quite a number of offers from entertainers who want me to appear on the stage. There is also a demand for my photos. See this,' he said, handing a circular: 'The sole rights of taking and producing photographs of Earl Poulett have been assigned to Mr Paul, and no illustrations are authorized to be published without his consent.'

'Good evening, Lord Hinton.'

'I beg your pardon,' replied the injured organ-grinder: 'I am now Earl Poulett.'

By the end of the week rumours were circulating that a compromise had been arranged between the rival parties to the Poulett peerage. It was being said that the agreement involved the surrender of the claim by the organ-grinder in consideration for an undisclosed sum of money, although some well informed persons were professedly in possession of the knowledge of the exact settlement. His accident kept William Turnour Thomas indoors on Thursday, the day of the earl's funeral, and also on Friday. However, in the evening, the heir presumptive to the Poulett estate and title once again graciously consented to receive a *Daily Telegraph* reporter within the precincts of Henry Buildings, Islington. The reporter's story reads as follows:

'Notwithstanding the lateness of the hour, between half-past ten and eleven o'clock on Friday evening – there was the usual crowd of small boys outside Henry Buildings ready to welcome any stranger who might present himself. Of late respectably dressed visitors, wearing silk hats and riding in hansoms, have been pretty frequent at the Buildings, most of them bound on a mission of enquiry or congratulations, and to these the services of the ragged urchins who abound in this quarter of Pentonville are distinctly serviceable, inasmuch as the suite of apartments – they consist of three small rooms – tenanted by the aristocratic grinder are difficult of access. First you must thread your way along a badly lighted passage, and then climb a ricketty set of stairs, circumstances which render the assistance of a guide late at night of decided value. 'You won't see 'is lawdship tonight,' yelled out the youngsters; 'he's laid up agin with rheumatics, he's reglar chronic wiv' 'em!'

Even in adversity Viscount Hinton appears to have been surrounded by many friends but as things now stand he is apparently overwhelmed with the number. From an early hour in the morning the procession commences, and on Friday night the little back-parlour where the viscount has been accustomed to regale himself after the exertions of the day's round are over, was filled to its utmost capacity. The tenants of Henry Buildings all refer to the grinder as 'the noble earl', and most of them appear thoroughly alive to the dignity which the presence of the heir-presumptive to a peerage and a vast estate has conferred upon them. 'I can't turn out my guests from the parlour,' said the viscount apologetically, 'but I can speak with you on the staircase. It is very cold, and the wind tonight is keen, but street musicians are pretty tough!' The 'noble earl' closed the parlour door, and walked with difficulty half-way down the stairs, where dim illumination was provided by a flickering gas jet. 'You see,' he said, 'I haven't recovered from that sprain yet, and my rheumatism troubles me. I was able to go out for a little time today, however, in a cab – a somewhat strange experience for me of late,' he added with a smile.

'Is there any truth in this report of a compromise,' was the first question.

'To my knowledge,' replied the viscount, 'the report is absolutely devoid of foundation. I am the man chiefly interested, and if any arrangement had been made I should be the first to know. It was only today that I received a communication from my lawyer telling me to rest my foot for a time, and then to see him. I have the fullest confidence in my solicitor and he would make no arrangements to which I was not a consenting party. I should like to say here that I am not anxious for publicity. It was all very well before the late earl's death, but now we are coming to deal with strictly business matters involving very delicate and complicated interests, and we don't want anything that is not strictly regular and circumspect. Allow me to introduce you to my partner in the organ business, who has just returned from my solicitors,' continued the viscount. 'He's a good sort, and, like myself, comes of a good family – but you must not mention his name.'

A tap at the parlour door and there came forth a man with grey hair, erect and soldierly in his bearing, just the type of individual one associates with a period of 'better times'.

'When the noble earl commands me, I obey,' said the partner. 'All I have to say is that I went today to Mr Hall's in Warwick Court – that's the lawyer – about the noble earl's business. I was going upstairs when I saw Mr Hall, and I recognized him at once, because we have met before. I went into a private room and I said that I had brought a letter down from the new Earl Poulett, which he had received from a solicitor who had clients ready to provide money to fight the case with the younger claimant. Mr Hall replied that he had an engagement on Earl Poulett's account with the Eagle Insurance Company and therefore he wished to be excused at that particular time.'

'I presume,' rejoined the viscount, 'that he was going to investigate my claim in connection with the securities held by the Eagle Insurance Company.'

'What is the attitude of the representatives of the rival claimant?'

'On that point,' rejoined the viscount, 'I am absolutely in the dark. All I know is that they have been communicated with on the subject. I have not seen the reply. As a matter of fact, nothing could be done until the late earl was decently buried, and as everyone knows, the burial took place on Thursday. There's plenty of time, and we are not rushing matters. So far as I know, I have never seen the younger claimant. He might have seen me, perhaps, when I have been playing my organ in Kensington. However, I bear him no malice, and wish him well.'

'Is there any truth in the statement that you are forming a syndicate for the promotion of your cause?'

'Absolutely none. It is as groundless as the talk about compromise, people have discussed the question of a syndicate apparently, but they are acting on their own authority. I want you to deny the statement that I, Earl Poulett, am forming a syndicate. Perhaps the rumour arises from the fact that a certain gentleman who was in London today has just gone down to Hinton St George, with the intention of seeing the farmers and tenants and interesting them on my behalf. This gentleman is now in Crewkerne, and bear in mind that he has gone on his own account. At the same time I wish him well. If money were badly wanted I don't think we should need to trouble the good folks of Crewkerne, because judging from the letters of congratulation which are inundating me just now, I think there would be plenty of money to be found in London.'

'Have you any definite plan of campaign?'

'None beyond the plans known to the lawyers. I shall be guided completely by Mr Hall's advice. We have not one atom of doubt as to the justice and validity of our claim, and we shall pursue strictly legal and orthodox methods.'

'And if you succeed?'

'If I succeed,' said the viscount, drawing himself up to his full height, 'I have but one ambition in life – to do good to the poor. As you know I have been in sore straits during the many years of my life, and I know how tightly the shoe of poverty pinches. I love the poor.' ('The noble earl,' here interpolated the partner in the organ business, 'is speaking the strict truth'.) 'It would be my hobby to relieve as much suffering as possible. You little know how much suffering there is in the country, and how patient the poor generally are. I am not an ambitious man, and have seen enough of the world in my time to estimate its tinsel and hollow glories at their true worth. I believe more in the substance than the shadow, and I can assure you that I would esteem it a greater privilege to entertain a few poor families at a good dinner than to take my seat in the House of Lords. One more word in conclusion,' continued the viscount. 'You can tell the people who have said that I intend to break down the barriers at Hinton that they are talking bunkum. We want British law, not brute force.'

The affair proved to be a nine-days wonder, and people soon forgot Viscount Hinton and his barrel-organ. He made no more visits to Hinton St George, but he did continue to press his claim through proper legal channels. However, it was not until July 1903 that the case was at long last brought before the Committee of Privileges of the House of Lords. The evidence on behalf of both claimants was fully investigated. It was stated that nearly fifty years before, the whole estate had been resettled in such a way as to exclude William Turnour Poulett. Evidence given by the late earl at the *Perpetuation of Testimony* in 1890 was re-examined. In particular the details of his movements with his regiment in the few months before his first marriage were studied, and it was evident that he was not even in the country when the child was conceived. On 31 July their Lordships reached a verdict and the Lord Chancellor summed up their decision as follows:

Before her marriage with the late earl the latter's first wife admitted misconduct with Captain Granville, and after the marriage she made an admission to her husband to that effect. The whole history of the late earl's action was consistent with the story of the child not being his, and there was no recognition of it by him. In the course of the whole case there was nothing to cast a doubt upon the denial of the late earl. The course of conduct pursued by him was that which one would expect from a man who had married a woman in such circumstances. From first to last he refused to accept the suggestion that he was the father of the child. He did not think there could be any doubts deciding this case when once the facts were ascertained. The facts were all consistent with the one hypothesis put forward in the sworn testimony of the alleged father. There was no doubt that the claimant was illegitimate. There was no doubt that the legitimacy and the title belonged to the counter-claimant, and he moved that it would be the duty of their Lordships to report to the House that the claimant, the son of Elizabeth Lavinia Poulett had not made out his claim, and that the counter-claimant had. Their Lordships agreed.

So the hopes of William Turnour Thomas Poulett were finally shattered for good. Not for him a seat in the House of Lords nor a mansion in green and pleasant Somerset. There was nothing else but to continue his wretched existence in London, where he died a few years later of heart disease in the workhouse at Holborn at the age of 59. Lydia his wife died ten weeks before him. His story is a pathetic one, for he was after all, merely a victim of circumstance.

CHAPTER 9

The Seventh Earl

'A Perfect English Gentleman'
A Tenant of the 7th Earl

William John Lydston, 7th Earl Poulett was born on 11 September 1883, at 30 Belsize Park Gardens, Hampstead. His birth was the occasion for great rejoicing at Hinton St George, where his father gave a great reception, and a dinner for his friends and tenants, as has already been described. His father died when William John was 16 years old. At that time he is described as 'a good-looking young fellow, of fair complexion, and with a very intelligent, aristocratic face. He, however, gives us the impression that he is rather delicate in health.' He received his education at Cheltenham, Eton and Trinity Hall, Cambridge.

When the 6th Earl died, the son born to his first wife claimed that he was the rightful Viscount Hinton, and therefore the next Earl Poulett. He pursued this claim over the years and it eventually reached the Committee of Privileges of the House of Lords. It was finally decided in July 1903 in favour of William John Lydston, and he was able to call the title rightfully his own. The story of the Poulett claimant has been told in the previous chapter.

In the early years after the death of the 6th Earl when the fortunes of the estate were at a low ebb, the whole of the management was taken over by Sir George Dallas, Bt., a relative of the late earl's mother, and Chief Clerk at the Foreign Office, who was both trustee and receiver. Sir George and his wife, Lady Felicia Dallas, did much to help the family and the estate through these difficult years. The threatened sale was finally averted, and the young earl learned much about estate management from the man who became almost a guardian during his formative years.

Things improved generally, though gradually, and at the annual rent audit in July 1903, during the customary dinner, held that year at the Poulett Arms Inn, special tribute was paid to Sir George and Lady Dallas by the Reverend Joseph Billing, the Poulett family chaplain. He praised the efforts and steadfastness of Sir George, while of Lady Dallas, he said she 'had brought the family into prominence and had introduced them to the chief families of the neighbourhood. She had assisted in adding to the beauty of the church by giving a splendid concert in the Saloon at Hinton House.'

A few days later, on 31 July came the news everyone was waiting for. Sir George received a telegram informing him that the House of Lords had made their decision in favour of William John, and that he was indeed the rightful 7th Earl Poulett. The villagers of Hinton St George showed their delight and pleasure at the news by decorating the whole place with flags and bunting. The church bells rang wildly all the afternoon and evening, and everyone expressed their happiness at the news of the decision in favour of their young landlord. William John himself received dozens of telegrams and messages of congratulation, for, as it was said, 'because of his genial and affable manner, he had made himself most popular in the village and neighbourhood. He was away from Hinton when the news was received there, but the next day it was made known that he and his sisters Eleanor and Violet were coming home in the evening. Hinton once more busied itself preparing a welcome. The houses were

William John Lydston, 7th Earl Poulett 1883–1918

decorated anew with more flags, flowers, banners and mottoes. In Merriott Road at the entrance to the village a triumphal arch of evergreens and flowers was built, with a banner on one side proclaiming 'Welcome to our Noble Earl' and on the other 'Long Life and Happiness'. Soon after 6 p.m. a great crowd of people, not only the tenantry and estate workers from the village, but many more from the surrounding countryside gathered round the arch to await the arrival of the earl. With the church bells pealing out, the children marched from the school in procession, waving flags, and joined the crowd in Merriott Road. Loud cheers welcomed his Lordship's carriage when finally it arrived. The horses were quickly unharnessed and a band of willing and enthusiastic admirers soon prepared to draw the carriage through the village to Hinton House. The Rector, the Reverend Robert Ratcliffe Dolling gave a fine speech of welcome, and congratulated William John on behalf of everyone present on the decision of the Committee of Privileges. He said Hinton people had always looked on him as the rightful Earl and now all the world recognized him as such. In reply his Lordship said that it had been the happiest moment of his life. He thanked everyone most heartily for the splendid welcome they had given him, he would never forget it, nor their heartfelt congratulations on his having retained the title to which he had always laid claim. Then the carriage was drawn through the streets of the village in a triumphant procession, headed by the school-children, accompanied by the cheering crowd of well-wishers, all the way to Hinton House. Sir George and Lady Dallas were at the mansion to welcome the earl and his sisters home, and so for the moment the crowds dispersed. Later on in the evening William provided refreshments at the Poulett Arms for the bell-ringers, for the large party who drew the carriage, and indeed for many others who had joined in the celebrations. All in all it was a day to be remembered, especially for the way in which it demonstrated the affection and regard which the village felt for the Poulett family.

In August that year a Grand Bazaar was held at the mansion. It was opened by no less a personage than General Sir Redvers Buller, one of the Boer War army commanders. Stalls with all manner of goods lined the Grand Entrance Hall and entertainments of various sorts were arranged in the grounds. A particular feature of the event was the opening of Hinton House to the public for a tour of its interior for the price of 1s. A special guide book was produced for the occasion by Sir George Dallas. The tour commenced in the Grand Entrance Hall and visitors were shown the Library, Dining Room, the Grand Saloon, Grand Staircase, the State Bedrooms with the bed prepared for Queen Anne, and the State Rooms on the ground floor. It was perhaps the only time the mansion was opened in this way.

A year later, in September 1904, William John celebrated his coming of age. It was another occasion for a demonstration of loyalty and affection by his tenantry and workers, although the celebrations were of a more private nature, and the main presentation to his Lordship was postponed at his request until the following January. The tenants' rent audit which had been revived, was held that month at the mansion. After the business was finished a fine dinner was provided at which the earl presided, about 100 people being present. The rector, the chaplain and other representatives of the estate also attended. There were many toasts and much speech-making. The chaplain, the Reverend Joseph Billing, said that he sincerely hoped his Lordship would soon take his seat in the House of Lords, and that he would be spared many years to attain the same eminence as his noble ancestors. The rector, the Reverend Robert Dolling, in his turn said with a humorous reference to his age that he attributed it to the salubrious Hinton air, and he strongly advised his Lordship, if he wished (and they all wished him) to have a long life and good health, to get as much of the Hinton air as he possibly could. One of his Lordship's toasts was to 'Foxhunting, harehunting and General Sports' which was very well received. The Master of the Seavington Hunt replied, and said it was a great pleasure to him to hear the toast so well received and a greater pleasure still to know as he did, that he was hunting a country in which every man of them was a sportsman to the backbone. Next came the main toast of the evening and a presentation to Lord Poulett. The toast and the presentation was made by Mr William Penny of Coombe Farm, the oldest tenant on the estate. He reviewed his long residence of thirty-five years there and recalled his Lordship's birth twenty one years ago. He said that the estate had always had a considerate and generous landlord in the late earl, and he hoped and believed the young earl would in that respect follow in his father's footsteps. He then asked his Lordship to accept a piece of plate as a token of their good wishes for his happiness and prosperity, and he concluded by saying they would one and all be proud to present another such mark of their appreciation as soon as his Lordship should choose to bring home a worthy bride to that grand old mansion. This brought loud and prolonged applause. The text of the presentation address was then read as follows:

To the Right Hon. William John Lydston, 7th Earl Poulett. We the undersigned tenants on your Lordship's Hinton St George Estates, desire to offer you our hearty congratulations on the occasion of your attaining your majority and succeeding to the estates. Some of us well recollect the joy with which the birth of an heir was celebrated twenty-one years ago, and we are happy to be able to affirm that the hopes and aspirations then expressed have not been disappointed. In testimony of these kindly feelings we ask your acceptance of the accompanying piece of plate which we offer you as a memento of the goodwill and affection which have hitherto existed between landlord and tenant on the estate upon which we have the privilege to reside. Hoping you may, by God's blessing, be allowed to enjoy the like goodwill during a long and happy life.

This address was framed in oak with a design including the Poulett arms. The presentation itself was a very handsome piece of silver representing his lordship in hunting costume, seated on horseback with foxhounds in attendance. The presentation was then made, and the toast drunk with great enthusiasm and with musical honours, and his Lordship rose to respond. He said:

I cannot thank you sufficiently for this magnificent present and address and for the hearty way all of you have proposed and received this toast. I accept them all as a proof of your hearty goodwill. I fully appreciate your kindness, and shall do my best to retain that goodwill and to foster those good relations which always existed between my late father and yourselves. Knowing you as I do, I hope and believe that these happy relations will be continued between us. I thank you all from the bottom of my heart for your kindly expressions and good wishes, and I assure Mr Penny that I will do my very best to gain that other present to which he so neatly alluded.

The Reverend Joseph Billing then paid a warm tribute to the late earl's memory and asked them all to remember the countess who had so lovingly watched over and nurtured with true motherly care the son whom they were now honouring. He also asked them to drink the health of William's sister, the Lady Violet, who was on honeymoon with her new husband, Mr Cecil John Talbot Rhys Wingfield. Another toast was made to Sir George and Lady Dallas, and in reply Mr John Richards, the family solicitor, said they had had an anxious time during his Lordship's minority, and sometimes the difficulties had seemed almost insurmountable. But thanks to the great experience of Sir George Dallas, the trustee and receiver of the estate, all those difficulties had been overcome. Sir George had carried out faithfully his stewardship, and Earl Poulett owed a great service to him. Lord Poulett was a rich man, and yet as things go nowadays he was not a rich man. But whatever responsibilities those riches brought, he believed fully that Earl Poulett would meet them as a man should meet them. He hoped the tenants would endeavour to make their requirements to suit his Lordship's means, and then he (the speaker) would have no fear but that they would be fairly and generously met. Mr. Richards then proposed 'The Tenants of the Estate' and said he was associated with estates in various parts of England, but nowhere did he find the tenants meeting their landlord in the matter of rent so promptly and cheerfully as on this estate. Other tenants in turn replied. They all expressed pleasure at having his Lordship at the head of the table, and hoped he would come frequently amongst them. They were glad to know that they all paid up so handsomely though it was a struggle sometimes to do so. If his Lordship would reside amongst them as much as he possibly could, and look to their needs and requirements, they would continue cheerfully to supply the needful means for ensuring happiness and prosperity.

After the speeches, the festivities continued to a late hour and ended with singing and recitations by various members of the assembled company.

The next day a dinner was given to the employees of the estate, and the cottage and allotment holders, numbering about 100 people. Dinner was laid in the Grand Saloon, and presided over by Mr Charles Irish, the Estate Bailiff. After the meal Lord Poulett was presented with a handsome silver cigar and cigarette box, with an inscription as a gift from the employees. With it was an illuminated address (by Charles Irish, junior) which read as follows:

We, the employees on your Lordship's estate, very heartily congratulate your Lordship on attaining your majority and succeeding to the estates, and we are pleased with the opportunity this auspicious occasion affords of presenting to your Lordship the accompanying cigar and cigarette box as a small token of our loyal respect which we beg you to accept with our united wishes for a long and happy life.

His Lordship in replying, said he would never forget their kindness.

On Friday the schoolchildren were entertained with a tea and a Christmas tree in the schoolroom. Lord Poulett attended and all the children received a present from the tree. There were rousing cheers for the earl before he left for a holiday in Jamaica. He told them that it gave him great pleasure to be present at this annual event and he hoped to be there again next year.

On Tuesday, 10 January, Lord Poulett as Lord of the Manor of Chard, had been present at a great reception in the town Hall of that town. There was a long address of congratulation by the town clerk to William John on his coming of age, which recalled the long association of the Poulett family with Chard, and they hoped they would see more of his Lordship in the future. A framed address was presented to him, carved in oak and bearing the Poulett arms, in the following words:

To the Right Honble William John Lydston, Lord Poulett. We, the Mayor, aldermen and Burgesses of the ancient borough of Chard, desire to offer to your lordship our hearty and most sincere congratulations on the occasion of your majority. We cannot forget that for a long course of years the family of Poulett has been closely associated in various ways with the borough and parish of Chard. We desire to see that close association both deepened and strengthened and we earnestly pray that for many years to come your Lordship may, by the blessing of Almighty God, occupy with much happiness and prosperity the high and influential position to which you have succeeded.
    Sealed with the common seal of the Council, this 10th day of September, 1904.
    S.H. Denning, Mayor.
    Walter J. Tucker, Town Clerk.

The Mayor, in making the presentation, said the people of Chard had taken great interest in the event, for a long time they had been without an owner as it were, but they would now have the benefit of the owner and, he hoped, occupier of Hinton House. His Lordship had not only attained his majority but had entered into possession of the ancient home and estate of the family, who had been connected with the county of Somerset for many generations. Large estates brought with them responsibilities and a great power for doing good; and property had its duties as well as its rights. They read that many of his ancestors had filled many distinguished positions in the State and taken a large share in the government of the country – some had been courtiers, statesmen and warriors. They all hoped his Lordship would emulate their virtues and follow their examples, and take his share in the work of the country, and also in the counsels of the nation. In reply William thanked them all for the address and congratulations. He heartily reciprocated the wish that the ties of friendship which had so long existed between his family and the borough might long continue, and as far as it lay in his power he would do what he could to strengthen and develop those associations.

In 1906 the Mens' Reading Room was built in the High Street at Hinton, by Lord Poulett, as a meeting place and games room for the men of the village. The scheme had begun some years before in 1900 when a room was used for the purpose at Oldway Lodge next to the school. The opening ceremony of the new room was performed by his Lordship and the key used by him, together with his portrait may still be seen in the building. Lord Poulett became its first president. A full-sized billiard table was provided and the room is still in full use today.

Two years later Lord Poulett fulfilled the wish of his old tenant during that coming-of-age speech, by finding himself a bride.

On Wednesday, 2 September 1908, he was married to 18-year-old Sylvia Lilian Storey, who was well known at the time as a popular young actress at London's Gaiety Theatre. The

Sylvia Storey, wife of 7th Earl Poulett

marriage caused a stir in Society and Theatrical circles, and Miss Storey was reported to be the 'ninth actress who had recently made a notable marriage'. William and Sylvia had known each other for about four months before their wedding and it was said his family raised no objection to the match. The ceremony took place at St James's Church, Piccadilly, and was a very private affair. The best man was the family solicitor and friend of the earl, Mr John Richards, and another friend, Mr Donnithorne, gave the bride away. Neither the bride's father nor the bridegroom's mother was present, although they had both given their approval. The new Lady Poulett was dressed in a light blue tailor-made costume with a black hat trimmed with red flowers and a dark veil, and was accompanied by Miss Vesey FitzGerald and Lady Violet Wingfield, the bridegroom's sister. After the ceremony the couple left for their honeymoon on the south coast.

Miss Sylvia Storey's family had long been connected with the world of art and the stage. Her father was Fred Storey, the nephew of A.G. Storey, R.A. He was known as a good scene painter and a clever actor and dancer. Her mother, too, was an actress. Sylvia, who spent much of her childhood in Brighton, first appeared on the stage at the age of six in her father's production of *Rip Van Winkle* at Kennington. She also appeared as a child on the stage of the Palace Pier Theatre in a Christmas play of her father's called *Gerda in Fairyland* when she took the part of Gerda. She had since appeared in various productions at the Prince of Wales Theatre, The Aldwych and the Gaiety. Just before her wedding she was understudying Olive May, and appearing in the chorus of the musical show *Havana* at the Gaiety.

Her father, when asked by the Press why peers came to the stage for wives, is reported to have answered, 'because they find there both brains and beauty'.

Lord Poulett brought his new countess home to Hinton St George on 2 October. The village had been preparing for this day ever since the news of the wedding, and a committee had been formed to organize the festivities. As a result the village was decorated as never before. Flags and streamers were everywhere, and triumphal arches were erected at strategic positions throughout the village. In fact prizes were awarded for the best arches. The first prize went to the one in Merriott Road at the entrance to the village. On one side were the words 'A Hearty Welcome Home from All' and on the other 'God Bless the Happy Pair'. The second prize was won for the arch outside the Reading Room. Here the mottoes read 'Hinton St George Reading Room offer warmest greetings' and 'Welcome to our President'. Outside the school a banner across the road proclaimed 'The Children welcome our Earl and Countess' with the Poulett arms on the reverse side. In Church Street appeared mottoes reading 'May they Prosper', and 'East, West, Home's Best', and 'God Bless You Both'. Another archway was erected at the Park Gates by Brooms Lodge, bearing the words: 'Welcome to our Noble Earl and Countess. Long Life and Happiness attend you Both.' Yet another arch was built at the gates of the mansion grounds, saying 'All Blessings and Joys attend you Both'. On the clocktower above the entrance to the mansion were the words 'Home Sweet Home'.

The couple were expected on the 3.57 p.m. train at Yeovil Junction where his Lordship's car was waiting. At 4.30 p.m. the car arrived at the archway in Merriott Road, where by this time a huge crowd had gathered. All the school children were present waving flags and banners, and the Crewkerne Star of the West Band were in attendance. As the car stopped the cheers were deafening, while the church bells continued to peal out their welcome. When quiet was restored, the Reverend Robert Dolling mounted a dais and read a speech of welcome. He said:

My Lord, on this happy occasion of your homecoming after your wedding, we parishioners and tenants desire to offer you our warmest congratulations upon that happy event. We desire also to extend a most hearty welcome to your charming bride and we trust that our acquaintance with her Ladyship which begins this afternoon may be the beginning of many years of mutual friendship and regard. That every blessing may attend you both during a long and happy life is the earnest wish of everyone among us.

Lord and Lady Poulett now alighted from their car and his Lordship replied to the address. He said:

Parishioners and tenants, may I say friends – it is quite impossible for me to find words at this moment which would enable me to thank you all sufficiently for giving us this magnificent reception on our return home. And I am much touched by the very kind way in which you have welcomed for the very first time my bride amongst you this afternoon. I am sure when you know her Ladyship much better, and it is my hearty wish that you should, there cannot fail to spring up between you that mutual friendship and true regard which has been the hearty wish of you all this afternoon. Lady Poulett wishes me to thank you all from the bottom of her heart for your kind welcome to her today. Believe me, there is no place like home. For though we shall go away and return again so often in our future lives amongst you, yet there will only be one return known to us as 'our homecoming' and this happy day will remain vivid in our memories to the end of our lives. Again on behalf of my bride and myself I thank you most heartily for your welcome.

Lady Poulett, wearing a grey mole *Directoire* skirt with a white blouse and felt hat to match, was then presented with a beautiful bouquet of pink malmaisons, lily of the valley, smilax and asparagus fern tied with pink ribbon. This bouquet, a gift from the women of the parish, was presented to the countess by the head keeper's little step-daughter Betty Tozer. There was loud cheering as her Ladyship accepted the flowers and kissed the little girl. The school children then sang a 'Song of Welcome' which had been specially composed for the occasion, with two verses as follows:

What a dear old place is Hinton
How proud we ought to be
To think our little village
Is blessed in such degree.
We have got a grand old mansion
And an Earl of noble life
And now we delight to welcome
Him and his charming wife.

'Tis a grand old home they'll enter,
A happy wedded pair,
We Hinton scholars wish them
True joys beyond compare.
May they happy be at Hinton
And settle with us here
May God bestow all blessings
Upon them year by year.

A procession then formed up, led by a rider in hunting dress on horseback, the band followed, surrounded by the children, the car carrying the happy couple was drawn down the street by various tenants and the remainder of the large gathering brought up the rear. The bells rang out again, and the band played 'A Fine Old English Gentleman' as the procession made its way to Hinton House. In the evening of that memorable day, there was dancing on the lawns around the mansion and at the Cross in West Street. The archways at Merriott Road, the school and the Reading Room were illuminated, while in the stable yard at the mansion, scores of fairy lights and Chinese lanterns lit up the scene. Surely there had never been such a demonstration of devotion in Hinton before and nothing quite like it was ever seen again.

In June of 1909 the bells in the church tower rang out to announce to the village that an heir had been born. The birth of George Amias Fitzwarrine was the occasion for much rejoicing in Hinton. Once again the houses were decorated and by request of the proud father, the school children were given a holiday.

In May 1910 King Edward VII died and in June 1911 the country celebrated the coronation of the new King George V and Queen Mary. Lord and Lady Poulett attended the ceremony at Westminster Abbey and two portraits of them in their robes were painted by the artist Wood and placed in the State Ante Room at Hinton House.

About this time William made various alterations inside his ancient home. The cartoons of Dido and Aeneas in the Grand Saloon and various pictures there were moved to make way for the seven great sixteenth century Brussels tapestries showing the story of King Cyrus. They were surrounded by oak panelling, and more panelling from neighbouring Henley Manor was put in the state rooms in the south wing. The 7th Earl also laid out the sunken garden with its ham-stone balustrading and ornaments in 1913.

From the time they arrived home after their wedding, William and Sylvia spent most of their free time at Hinton House, interesting themselves in the affairs and well-being of the estate, and taking part in public functions in the surrounding area. When his army duties permitted, Lord Poulett took an active interest in various local organizations. He was for a while Master of the Seavington Harriers, and on the day of Court Leet went to Chard with his hounds to keep up the old manorial custom of hunting in the district on that day. Lord and Lady Poulett were entertained in the Corn Exchange and received a hunting crop from the Mayor to mark the occasion.

William John became a J.P. for Somerset and was a member of the Crewkerne and Chard Lodges of Freemasons. In Crewkerne he was President of the Hospital Management Board and a member of the Governors of Crewkerne Grammar School. In Chard, he was, as well as Lord of the Manor, a member of the Board of Guardians, and of the Rural District Council.

In 1912, on 29 January, another happy event occurred. This time it was the birth of a daughter, christened Bridgett Elizabeth Felicia Henrietta Augusta.

At the outbreak of the First World War in 1914, Lord Poulett was serving as a captain with his regiment, the Warwick Royal Horse Artillery which was then doing its annual training, and full mobilization followed at once.

In common with other villages and towns throughout the country, active men joined up very quickly, so that by the time conscription came there was hardly a young or middle-aged man left to call up. A detachment of VAD's had been formed earlier in Hinton, and a hospital was opened at Hinton House in October 1914, which received wounded troops from the battlefields for the rest of the war. The state rooms in the south wing were used as wards and offices and the treasures and furnishings removed for the duration, and as it happened were never to be replaced there.

On 2 January 1915 Rosa, the Dowager Lady Poulett, the widow of the 6th Earl, died at her home in Eccleston Square. Her body was brought from London and laid to rest in the family vault at Hinton Church. Her son was unable to be present as he was away on war service. William John in fact as an artillery officer served in France for most of the war, visiting Hinton when on leave and taking a great interest in the hospital at his home.

The strain of active service eventually had its effect on his health and he was invalided home from France early in 1918. After his recovery he joined an anti-aircraft battery on the East Coast of England.

Sylvia, separated from her husband and left to her own devices, soon tired of wartime village life. Relations with William became increasingly strained to the point eventually when they were actually contemplating divorce. In July 1918 William was taken ill again. His condition, possibly aggravated by his personal worries, quickly deteriorated and after a few days influenza and pneumonia set in. On the 11th he died at the early age of 35.

The tragic news was received with profound shock and grief at Hinton St George and indeed in the whole neighbourhood. A few days later, the village which but a few short years ago had welcomed him and his bride with such joy on their homecoming, turned out again to say farewell at the melancholy but splendid military funeral of their late landlord.

The body was brought by rail from Saltburn in Lancashire, where full military honours were accorded by the troops there, to Ilminster station. Here the coffin was met by Mr R.M.P. Parsons, the Estate Agent, and brought to Hinton St George and placed in the Grand Saloon at Hinton House. Here there was a watch of estate workers lasting through the night until the funeral service the next day. At three o'clock on 16 July the coffin was placed on a bier and carried to the church by estate employees, followed by the principal family mourners, Countess Poulett and the Ladies Violet Wingfield and Eleanor Poulett, the late earl's wife and two sisters. They were joined by a large assembly of relatives, friends, tenantry, villagers and others from far and wide.

The choir and the rector, the Reverend Frank Shelmerdine, met the procession at the church gates and then led it up the church path between assembled ranks of boy scouts, wounded soldiers from the hospital, with the Commandant, nurses and sisters, and a firing party of men of the Somerset Light Infantry.

The church was so crowded that many people had to stand in the porch and in doorways to hear the service. The hymns 'Through the Night of Doubt and Sorrow' and 'A Few More Years Shall Roll' were sung, while the 90th Psalm and the *Nunc Dimittis* were chanted. After a moving tribute from the rector the service ended and the organist Vera Best played 'Blest are the Departed' and Spohr's 'Last Judgement' as the coffin was taken from the church. There was an even greater company outside to witness the interment which was made in a flower-adorned grave on the north side of the church. The late earl had expressed a wish not be buried in the family vault. The hymn 'Rock of Ages' was sung, and after the final prayers and benediction by the rector, three volleys were fired over the grave by the firing party, and the Last Post was sounded by a bugler. For a long while after the family mourners had left the grave side, scores of people waited their turn to file past for a last look at the coffin in its grave.

There were many beautiful floral tributes. That of Countess Poulett carried the message: 'My Darling, I shall remember you while the light lasts and in the darkness I shall not forget you – Your most loving and sorrowing wife, Sylvia.'

From his young son, the new earl: 'My Darling Daddy, from George – And with the Morn these Angel faces smile, which we have loved long since and Lost Awhile.' He had been unable to attend his father's funeral owing to illness.

From his daughter: 'My Darling Daddy – Bridgett. On that Happy Easter morning all the graves their dead restore. Father, sister, child and mother meet once more.'

From his sisters: 'My Darling Bill, the best of brothers and the truest friend that ever lived – Vi, – and they rose to their feet when they crossed the bar;' and: 'My ever Darling Bill from Lena. Love lies beyond the sea of Death, yesterday, today and for ever. On every heart and every home has Death left his mark.'

From Sir George and Lady Dallas, who were too infirm to attend:

'In loving memory of our beloved Willy, from George and Felicia Dallas,' with a note regretting they were unable to attend and pay their last farewell to dear Willy at the graveside.

There were many more wreaths and flowers, both from individuals and organizations, from the village and the estate, the hospital and from the neighbourhood and county.

Some days later a sad delivery was made to Hinton House from the earl's military station in the north, consisting of all his belongings. There were clothes and uniforms, personal effects, military items, books, cooking utensils and cutlery. Listed among the collection were, poignantly, seven photographs and two coloured portraits of his wife, Sylvia.

So passed the last Poulett to die as owner of the family mansion and its great estate. So much loyalty and devotion had been showered on him, so many hopes expressed for his future, only to be dashed by his untimely end. Once again the head of the family and owner of the estate was a small boy. With the war drawing to its close with all its attendant problems, the future must then have appeared bleak to all those who depended on the estate for their livelihood, and to those loyal workers whose task it was to carry on with their responsibilities.

ST GEORGE'S CHURCH – HINTON ST GEORGE

CHAPTER 10

The Eighth Earl and the Twentieth Century

Gardez La Foi
Poulett Family Motto

George Amias Fitzwarrine, the 8th Earl Poulett was born on 23 June 1909. He succeeded to the title when only 9 years old at the death of his father in 1918, only four months before the signing of the Armistice which ended the First World War.

The troops returned home and the village and the estate set about returning to normal. The estate manager and agent was Mr R.M.P. Parsons, who had come to Hinton with his father in 1894. However, his father died in 1895 and since then Mr Parsons had virtually managed the estate on his own. He was ably assisted by Mr Charles James Irish, the estate bailiff since 1915. Mr Irish had taken over from his father also, who had been connected with the estate for over fifty-eight years. These men then, were the loyal employees on whose shoulders rested the running of this vast property, together with the staff, both on the land and in the mansion.

In 1920 two memorials of the First World War were built in Hinton. The first was the Calvary erected in the churchyard and bearing the names of those men who had died, fifteen names in all, including the 7th Earl Poulett. The second memorial was the Victory Hut, built behind the Reading Room, and which was to serve faithfully as a village hall and general meeting room for the next thirty-seven years. In the Hut was hung a Roll of Honour with forty-nine names of the men and women of Hinton St George and Dinnington who gave public service during the war.

Lord Poulett and his sister Lady Bridgett were a familiar sight as small children around the village in these days after the war, often with their nanny, Mrs Bilsden, whose husband Arthur had been the late earl's coachman and chauffeur, serving the family for over thirty years. The children were very fond of Mrs Bilsden and she became something of a substitute mother to them. Lady Bridgett recalls: 'Mrs Bilsden was an angel and gave us great happiness during our rather miserable childhood. She was always being called in when we were small and the nurses left due to dreadful rows with our quick-tempered mother.'

The children also found a special friend in the young Frederick James, a boy a few years older than themselves. His family worked on the estate and they lived at Brooms Lodge. (Mr James, who today lives in Salisbury, was born at Hinton and later he also worked on the estate as a young man after the First World War. His family has a long record of service with the Poulett family, the first recorded ancestor being Charles Sealey, Mr James's great-great-grandfather who was Head Gardener to the 4th Earl at the end of the eighteenth century. The last was Miss Alice James, Frederick's aunt, who was cook/housekeeper to the 8th Earl during and after the Second World War.) The three children used to play together in the house and around the grounds, and their friendship continued throughout the lifetime of the Earl and his sister.

After the death of her husband, Sylvia was free to do as she wished, short of remarrying when she would have lost her inheritance. She much preferred life in London among her theatrical friends and Society acquaintances, so that George and Bridgett received little in the way of a normal happy family upbringing. Lady Poulett would descend on Hinton House bringing a party of friends to spend a noisy weekend in the country. It was during one of these occasions that an incident occurred which helped fuel the young earl's resentment of his mother. His father, the late earl, had expressed a wish that his favourite horse which had been to war with him, should, on his death be brought back to Hinton, where no one should ride it and it would spend the rest of its life in retirement. Frederick James remembers taking the horse for exercise in the park. However, one of Sylvia's military friends staying at the mansion took the horse out one day and rode it in the park, making it jump the hedges resulting in the horse breaking a blood vessel and dying soon after.

In November 1921 the engagement was announced between Sylvia, Countess Poulett, and Major Percy Howard Hansen, V.C., D.S.O., M.C., of the Lincolnshire Regiment. 'Piccadilly Percy', as he was known to his friends on account of his sartorial perfection, was a hero of the First World War. He was awarded the Victoria Cross for conspicuous gallantry on the Gallipoli Peninsula in August 1915. After heavy fighting, his battalion was forced to retire, leaving behind several wounded owing to the intense heat from the scrub which had been set on fire. On his own initiative, with three or four volunteers Hansen dashed forward several times some 300 or 400 yards over the burning scrub, all the time under terrific enemy fire. He succeeded in rescuing from inevitable death no less than six wounded men. A month later Major Hansen won the Military Cross for another deed of outstanding gallantry. Stripping himself and carrying only a revolver and a blanket for disguise, he made a reconnaissance of the coast in the vicinity of Sulva Bay, swimming and scrambling over rocks which severely cut and bruised him. By this daring he obtained very valuable information and located a gun which had been the cause of much damage. He eluded a patrol of twelve Turks, but was later seen by a single Turk whom he shot dead with his revolver. He returned eventually to the British lines in an exhausted state.

Photographs of the countess and her handsome fiancé accompanied the news of the engagement in the Press.

In October 1922 Lady Poulett gave birth to a daughter, naming her Phoebe Amie Sybil. The young Earl Poulett is reported to have slashed the Coronation portrait of his mother with a knife.

In April 1924 it was announced that the engagement with Major Hansen had been cancelled. 'By her remarriage,' a report in the Press stated, 'the countess would have lost a large portion of her income under the terms of her husband's will.' Major Hansen continued his career in the army. He later married and had one daughter, and eventually died in 1951.

Earl Poulett received his early education at Eton. Upon leaving there he entered the Great Western Railway workshops at Swindon, where he served as a pupil apprentice as a mechanical engineer, and later at the Signal Factory at Reading. His proficiency in engineering and his knowledge of railways resulted in his becoming a Member of the Institute of Railway Signal Engineers. It was his ambition in those days to drive a railway engine! Before he was twenty Lord Poulett had a fully equipped workshop at Hinton House. Later he recalled those days on the railway at Swindon. 'I wanted and expected to be treated as an ordinary man – and I was. The lads called me "Old Pollet".' He worked in the shunting yards and cooked eggs and bacon on a shovel – 'How nice they tasted!'.

It is of interest to note that in 1925 a member of the literary world came to live in Hinton and remained there until his death in 1933. He and his wife occupied the cottage in Church

*George Amias Fitzwarrine, 8th
Earl Poulett 1909–1973*

Street now known as 'Gainsford'. He was Henry W. Fowler who is famous principally for his two books *The King's English* and *A Dictionary of Modern English Usage*. The latter has become a standard work of reference and is still in print today. He had a chequered career after leaving Oxford. He was briefly a schoolmaster but his religious doubts led to his resignation. At 41 he started a new career as an essayist but without great success. He collaborated with his brother Frank and produced various literary works including *The King's English*. This proved a great success and assured his future in the literary field. He married in 1908 at the age of 50, a lady four years younger than himself. When war broke out in 1914 Henry was 56 and took part in the recruiting campaign. He was, however, troubled by the thought that he was urging others to run risks from which he himself would be spared. So with his brother he enlisted in the army, giving his age as 44. He was eventually invalided out having spent eighteen months attempting to fight for his country. The brothers settled in Guernsey but Frank died in 1918. Henry and his wife now moved to Somerset and at Hinton St George he worked on the book that was to make him famous. He was often seen going for his morning run along the lanes at Hinton and used to swim regularly in the pool at Springfield. His wife Jessie died in 1930 after an exceptionally happy marriage. A memorial plaque to her memory was placed on the west wall of the nave in Hinton Church, which states that the bells were rehung and that 'By them she being dead yet speaketh'.

8th Earl Poulett and his sister Lady Bridgett as children

Lord Poulett's coming of age in 1930 was marked by great celebrations at Hinton St George. While photographs of the family appeared in the London magazines, nearly every house in the village was decorated in the old tradition, and there were streamers across the roads bearing the words 'Good Luck' and 'Good Wishes'.

One of the first gifts he received on his birthday was presented by Charles Irish in his capacity as House Steward, on behalf of the estate employees. It took the form of a solid silver inkstand inscribed:

Presented to the Right Hon. the Earl Poulett by employees on the Hinton Estate, on his attaining his majority, June 23rd 1930.

Later in the day the grounds of Hinton House were thrown open and over 500 people were entertained at the invitation of the earl and his mother. There was a large marquee in which tea was provided for all, with a huge iced birthday cake made by Frederick James. (He had become a Foreman Confectioner, and continued to make a birthday cake for Lord Poulett every year until the earl finally left Hinton in 1968.) The birthday cake was of two tiers, decorated with shields bearing the Poulett arms around the sides, and with miniature bandsmen in china, each playing a different instrument. The twenty-one candles stood in fuschia holders, and the cake was cut and handed round by Lord Poulett and his sister. There were numerous sideshows and amusements including a Punch and Judy show and a conjurer. Music was provided by the Crewkerne Town Silver Prize Band under their conductor Mr C.W.L. Pinney. After tea a presentation was made on behalf of the parishioners of Hinton St George by Miss Dorothy Lowe, who had been Commandant at the Hospital in Hinton House during the war. The ceremony took place in the sunken garden in front of the State Apartments, the presentation having been arranged by Miss Lowe and Mr Prowse Deacon. Miss Lowe, introduced by Mr Deacon, made a speech in which she said it gave her great pleasure to have the honour of making the presentation to Earl Poulett on the occasion of his coming of age. She assured him that it was accompanied by their sincerest congratulations and warm wishes for his future happiness. His Lordship had a very difficult time before him. Life was difficult for all of them just then and especially was it difficult for those with positions of responsibility and trust. In meeting the difficulties that faced him, Lord Poulett could be assured that he had behind him the loyal co-operation of the village of Hinton St George, also the neighbouring parish of Dinnington. She was voicing the feelings of everyone in saying this to him. Lord Poulett (the 7th Earl) would have been delighted if he could have seen the pleasure in which all had subscribed to that presentation. There must be a touch of sadness in those proceedings in that the late Earl Poulett, the young earl's father was not there by his side that day to help and encourage him for his future career. There would always be a feeling of affection for the late earl. She would always remember his thoughtfulness and kindliness for the sick and wounded soldiers when Hinton House was thrown open as a Red Cross Hospital during the war. 'You did, my Lord,' she continued, 'suffer a great loss when you lost your father. We need, therefore, to give you every help and encouragement. We wish you every possible happiness in the career you are entering upon. May I ask you to accept this gift in the name of the parishioners of Hinton St George.' Then followed a presentation made on behalf of the parishioners of Dinnington which was made by Mrs Tozer, who said that it was just a small token, but the people of Dinnington gave it to him with the heartiest good wishes for his future happiness. Hinton's present took the form of a dining-table set consisting of cut-glass candlesticks, central flower bowl and finger bowls, while Dinnington's gift was a gold mounted fountain pen and pencil in a case. His Lordship in reply said:

It is extremely kind of Miss Lowe and Mrs Tozer to have said such nice things about me. I cannot tell you how pleased I am to be here at Hinton St George on this my 21st birthday and to be able to welcome you all to my party, which I hope you are enjoying as much as I am. I think it simply splendid of all you parishioners of Hinton St George and Dinnington – all friends of mine – and my employees, to have given me such lovely presents. No words that I can say can possibly express my heartfelt thanks. I can assure you that your gifts will be most useful. I hope that this day will be the beginning of a lasting friendship between you and me, as was the case with my late father, whom perhaps many of you remember even better than I do. I look forward with pleasure to coming and living here in a short time. This has always been my wish and I trust that it may be my good fortune to spend many happy years among you. The knowledge that I have so many real friends here at Hinton – my home – will give me every encouragement in my future life. May I thank you all once more for your beautiful presents, and may I also wish you many happy years to come.

There was great applause following this speech and three rousing cheers were given for the earl. The band struck up with 'For He's a Jolly Good Fellow' which everyone joined in, followed by more cheers for Countess Poulett and Lady Bridgett who were presented with bouquets of roses and sweetpeas by Miss K. Irish and Miss Betty Tozer.

The Grand Saloon in Hinton House was the scene next evening for a dinner given by Lord Poulett for the tenantry and farmers. On the table in front of his Lordship stood the handsome piece of silver statuary presented to his father at his coming of age in 1904. After the meal another presentation was made on behalf of those present by Mr Ben Lock. It took the form of a solid silver tray inscribed: 'Presented to the Right Hon. The Earl Poulett by the tenantry of Hinton St George Estates on the occasion of his attaining his majority, 23rd June, 1930.' Accompanying the tray was a Morocco leather-bound album containing a list of the subscribers and the following illuminated address:

> To the Right Honourable George Amias Fitzwarrine, Eighth Earl Poulett. We the undersigned tenants of your Lordship's Hinton St George estates, wish to express our heartiest congratulations on your attaining your majority; and we ask your acceptance of the accompanying piece of plate, which we have great pleasure in offering your Lordship as a token of respect and goodwill, hoping that you may be blessed with a long and happy life and that much of it may be spent amongst us.

There followed a list of subscribers' names. Mr Lock, making the presentation, said it gave him much pleasure and he felt it an honour to be asked to make it on behalf of the tenantry and farmers to their worthy landlord. He then read the address contained in the album and said he would like to reiterate what was there stated, that they hoped that most of his Lordship's future life would be spent amongst them, they for their part would do the best they could to make him happy. He could say more about his Lordship's father than he could about him, as he knew him so well for a number of years. The late Lord Poulett was a perfect English gentleman and a perfect sportsman and a good landlord. They had the misfortune to lose him in his early life. The hoped the present earl would be spared to live for many years among them. He had the greatest pleasure in handing over the gifts and to assure his Lordship that their very best wishes accompanied them.

After long applause Lord Poulett replied. In returning thanks he said he was deeply grateful to Mr Lock for all that he had said about his father and himself. Also he thanked them most heartily for their handsome and useful gift which he would look upon as one of his most treasured possessions. The value he placed upon it was far above its intrinsic worth by reason of the fact that it showed what kind feelings they all had towards him and that they had taken so much notice of his coming of age. His Lordship continued:

> I consider this silver tray will stand as a symbol of the way in which you have welcomed me on my attaining my majority. Also I should like to take this opportunity now of thanking most of you who twenty-one years ago gave me such a beautiful present on my christening. As many of you heard me say yesterday I hope to come and live here in the near future. It is my earnest wish that I may be able to help you with your work on the land to our common good. I feel that had my father been here he would have seconded my desire, for I know had he lived he would have continued to do the best he could for you all, and which I hope to do in the future. Times are hard for you and me and have been for some time. But let us hope they will become better in the future, and I feel certain they will if you and I can get together and go happily forward with courage and vigour, for that is what is required nowadays. Once more let me thank you for this lovely present and for all your kindness to me these last few days.

His speech brought hearty applause and the company rose and drank the health of Lord Poulett and his sister Lady Bridgett. Later in the evening there was music from a small orchestra, and members of the company entertained with songs. Finally Mr J.F. Rutter thanked Lord Poulett for the excellent dinner and the convivial evening he had given them. He said they would all go away with the feeling that his Lordship had made an excellent beginning and had shown the right spirit. They all wished him success and a long and happy life.

A few days later, to end the celebrations, three charabancs carried some seventy estate employees and their families on an outing to Weymouth, where his Lordship provided them all with lunch and tea.

The *Western Gazette* summed up the celebrations in the following words:

> Throughout the whole of the festivities it was apparent that the close ties of friendship and good feeling that have always been shown between former earls and the people of Hinton St George still exists. The warm hearted manner in which everyone entered into the coming-of-age jollifications proved beyond doubt that the present earl is as popular as any of his forbears.

Two years later, in 1932, Lord Poulett formed a company to be called the Hinton St George Estate Company with a nominal capital of £125,000, to take over his estates and he himself to be permanent governing director.

During the 1930s Lord Poulett, his sister Lady Bridgett and their mother Countess Poulett were leading figures in London society. Lord Poulett had a reputation as a man of unconventional fashion in dress. He was particularly famed for his attempts to popularize the cloak for formal wear, and was often seen, when visiting a theatre or restaurant, dressed in a crimson-lined flowing evening cloak, but apparently he had few followers. Beverly Nicholls the writer recalls: 'Above all there was Earl Poulett who had an assortment of gorgeous velvet cloaks lined with scarlet or white.' Lord Poulett later commented: 'I still have the one with the scarlet lining when I come up to London. It has quite a history. I was in Germany during the '20s and admired the German policemen's cloaks. My mother was on the stage, and I had the habit of leaving the theatre during the show. But if you have a cloak you can fold it up and put it under the seat, which is what I did. Then I could leave without causing a disturbance.'

His mother and sister were two ladies much famed for their beauty, and their features were well known in the glossy magazines, photographed by leading society photographers such as Lenare, Madame Yevonde and Cecil Beaton. They even appeared in advertisements for beauty soaps and cosmetics. Lady Bridgett 'came out' in 1928 and was at once acclaimed the beauty of the year. For the next ten years she was to be seen at every smart Mayfair event, often displaying clothes or jewels for charity. In 1934 the *Daily Express* reported on the Easter Parade: 'Debutantes and ex-debutantes dressed more immaculately than their usual immaculate best – Lady Bridgett Poulett the most distinguished of them all.'

In 1935 in Paris at a first night, it was reported that 'Lady Bridgett held a spray of orchids and all eyes for quite some minutes'. When a guest at society weddings, Lady Bridgett's photographs often had more prominence than the bride's. Both the earl and his sister at this time were described as 'Very popular cadets of Society's younger brigade'. Throughout the decade hardly a week went by without a photograph of the Pouletts, either together or singly, appearing in such magazines as *The Tatler, The Bystander* and *The Sketch*! They were seen attending all manner of functions – theatrical first nights, balls (sometimes in fancy dress), the races, charity events and weddings etc.

*Lady Bridgett Poulett sister of
the 8th Earl Poulett*

On 21 June 1935 Earl Poulett was married to Miss Muriel Swinstead, the daughter of John Howard Swinstead. His bride, like his father's before him, was an actress, well known professionally as Oriel Ross, and was described as 'tall, blonde and very lovely!' The romance had been kept a close secret and only a few intimate friends and members of the earl's family, including Countess Poulett and Lady Bridgett, were present at the ceremony at St Paul's Church, Knightsbridge. Mrs C.B. Cochran gave the bride away, while the best man was Mr Walter Haden.

The romance began at a party after a theatrical first night five months before, when the couple were introduced by a mutual friend. After the wedding the bride told reporters: 'Of course I am tremendously happy. We are going to Spain for our honeymoon. I hope we shall be away for a long time. Both of us intend to carry on with our careers. He is tremendously interested in electrical engineering. I am tremendously interested in the stage and film work. He is as keen about my career as I am about his. I first met George in January at a stage party after the first night of '*Between us Two*'. We became friends immediately and finally decided on marriage though we agreed that it would be as well to keep the whole matter a dead secret.'

Miss Ross had been playing Empress Catherine of Russia in '*Casanova*' at the London Coliseum with great success, and the show ran for several years. Oriel Ross was also the model for Jacob Epstein's sculpture 'Rima'.

*Oriel Ross, first wife of 8th
Earl Poulett*

The news of the wedding came as a surprise to everyone at Hinton St George. However, when it became known, the church bells rang out, flags were flown and the estate employees assembled at Hinton House where they toasted the health of the bride and groom in champagne and went off for a half-day's holiday.

When the earl and the new countess came home to Hinton after their honeymoon they held a grand reception for their tenants and parishioners at Hinton House. The function which proved a most happy one recalled the atmosphere and hospitality of pre-war years. As the guests arrived they were each received personally by the earl and countess. Little Kathleen Hutchings of Dinnington presented her Ladyship with a bouquet of yellow and mauve chrysanthemums which she continued to hold throughout most of the evening. There was tea for the children in their own specially decorated room, while refreshments were available for the adults. There was a film show held in the Grand Entrance Hall which included a Walt Disney cartoon and the feature film '*One Night of Love*' starring Grace Moore. After the performance everyone returned to the Grand Saloon where Lord and Lady Poulett led the dancing which continued for the remainder of the evening. The party ended with cheers for the hosts and the singing of 'Auld Lang Syne'. Lord Poulett, replying to the thanks of his guests, said how happy his wife and himself were to have so many friends around them. The countess and himself could not spend all their time at Hinton House but would certainly come there when they could. The presents from the estate were on view, and included a silver tea-set from the tenant farmers; a white and gold bone china breakfast service from the parishioners, and a silver-plated electric kettle from the estate employees. Before the reception every child in the village who was too young to be present had received a gift.

Later that year there was a serious fire at Hinton House which broke out upstairs in the caretakers' and servants' quarters, gutting several rooms and destroying the contents. A woman walking through the park in the evening raised the alarm when she saw a light at the top of the house. Crewkerne Fire Brigade and the Estate Brigade successfully got the fire under control after two hours. When the news spread around the district that Hinton House was on fire, hundreds of people flocked to the scene. Lord and Lady Poulett were not in residence and the caretakers were out also. But for the timely discovery of the fire the whole mansion could have been severely damaged.

At the end of the year the new Countess Poulett continued her theatrical career by appearing as Principal Boy in the Pantomine '*Jack and the Beanstalk*' at the Palace Theatre, Manchester. *The Sketch* carried a full length photograph captioned 'Countess Poulett as Principal Boy' and showing her Ladyship in her costume of short tunic, tights and feathered hat. This was not at all to her husband's liking and less than a year after their marriage, reports began to circulate of marital difficulties between Lord and Lady Poulett. In April 1936 the following notice appeared in the Press:

> To all it may concern – I, the Right Honourable George Amias Fitzwarrine the 8th Earl Poulett of Hinton St George in the County of Somerset, hereby give notice that I hereby expressly withdraw all and every authority which my wife Oriel, Countess Poulett may have at any time, either expressly or by implication or otherwise acquired to contract for me or in my name or as my agent or in any way to pledge my credit, and that I will not be responsible for her debts whensoever and howsoever incurred.

A few months later the couple appeared to be solving their difficulties and another announcement appeared in the papers:

> Notice is hereby given that the Earl and Countess Poulett having re-established a home together, Earl Poulett is prepared to accept his legal obligations to the same extent as previous to March 31, 1936.

Miss Ross had been due to play in '*The Shadow*' at the London Playhouse theatre but a few days before the opening, she retired from the cast.

The year 1937 saw the Coronation of King George VI and Queen Elizabeth. Lord Poulett duly attended the ceremony in Westminster Abbey, and recalled carrying a packet of sandwiches in his coronet!

In Hinton St George a day of celebrations had been arranged. Every house in the village was decorated, while the bells pealed at intervals all through the day. At 1 p.m. practically everyone in the two parishes of Hinton and Dinnington met at the Riding School at Hinton House where an excellent lunch was provided by the farmers and victuallers of the two villages. The Riding School had been transformed into a comfortable banqueting hall for the occasion, and the tables were decorated with flowers. There was a coronation beaker for everyone present, given by the rector, the Reverend Austin Balleine and his sister. In the afternoon there was a grand carnival procession round the village and back to Hinton House for judging in the stable yard.

In July 1939, with his marriage at a low ebb, Earl Poulett advertised Hinton House as being available 'To Let'. A full page advertisement in *Country Life* stated that the 'Historical Mansion' was 'To Let furnished, partially furnished, or possibly unfurnished for a year or longer!'

The Second World War commenced in September 1939 and Hinton village was quickly filled with evacuee children from Downham and Bromley. Hinton House was leased by Malvern Girls' College for the senior girls, their own premises having been requisitioned.

Grace Phillips, the Malvern College Secretary and Assistant Bursar, has recalled her early impressions of Hinton House and Lord Poulett when she was in the advance party to see that all was ready for the arrival of the school furniture and equipment. She was horrified to find the mansion still fully furnished and Lord Poulett still very much in occupation. When asked when his furniture was to be removed Lord Poulett replied nonchalantly: 'My good woman, that's your headache. I propose to do nothing. Mind you, woe betide if anything is lost or damaged!' Her troubles were not over when a fleet of caravans arrived later in the week, which had been hired for the college domestic staff. The hire firm had been given instructions that the drivers were not to enter the grounds of Hinton House, but Miss Phillips recalls:

Instead, they all rolled in over Lord Poulett's superbly kept lawns! We watched with horror from the windows of the Chinese rooms high up. Although we ran like the wind, Lord Poulett got there first. The abuse which flowed from him had to be heard to be believed! The drivers thought it prudent to remain in their cabs!

When Lord Poulett finally moved out, the College staff had to move and pack the entire contents of the mansion into the Grand Saloon until the Earl had them removed later. Miss Phillips appreciated the earl's feelings with hindsight and later observed: 'He had obviously been treated appallingly as a child, and his married life had gone awry. Now he was forced to let Hinton House. It had belonged to the Pouletts for centuries and was full of treasured heirlooms. Of course, poor man, for him it must have been traumatic!'

With the packing up of Lord Poulett's possessions, they were able to move in all the more mundane school equipment, desks and iron bedsteads, blackboards and easels etc., into the empty rooms.

Pupils at the College then have recalled their impressions of Hinton House, the village and the earl. Several remember first encountering his Lordship around the mansion, engaged in various tasks connected with the electric wiring, and not knowing who he was, imagined him to be the local electrician. Others recall the huge rooms taken over as classrooms and dormitories with the tapestries and portraits on the walls. They remember the parrot, Susan, who lived in her house in the grounds near the conservatories. Others remembered the honour they felt at sleeping in the earl's and countess's rooms, transformed into dormitories, and seeing the park and the cedar trees from the windows. The winter 1939/40 was a cold one, they awoke to find the water in their jugs frozen and their flannels rigid.

Miss Phillips also recalls that lighting was a big problem:

One great inconvenience was the lack of lighting in the State Apartments, which had been unused for years. The oil lamps were a sore trial in every way, except to warm those who tended them! Lord Poulett came back to live in the village. He liked and admired our Headmistress, Miss Brooks. She understood him and was interested. He offered to do our electrical repairs. Apparently he was an expert electrical engineer. Somehow she persuaded him to install electricity in the State Rooms. It was a major undertaking but it gave him pleasure.

'I make no promises, Miss Brooks. It will be a really tricky business, but I'll try if you like.'

Of course she was delighted. He worked like a beaver. At last he told her he thought it was ready. She suggested he should wait until everyone was at supper in the dining-room, which was the end State Room.

'You wait somewhere near, and give a signal for the switch to be turned on.' This he did. It worked. As Miss Brooks had expected there was a gasp of amazement and then instant applause. Miss Brooks went to fetch Lord Poulett from the door, drew him in and thanked him publicly. Spontaneously the whole school rose, clapped and stamped their feet in acknowledgement. It was quite a poignant moment. Tears glistened in his eyes, and he was obviously touched. I wondered whether he had ever before been the recipient of such gratitude.

His Lordship was gratified that the College named their houses while at Hinton after his ancestors; Amias, John, Hercules, Vere and William. Four of these names returned with the College to Malvern. To commemorate their stay in Hinton, on 9 May 1940, a tree was planted in the Cedar Piece at Hinton House by Lord Poulett and the head girl, Anne Cassidy. The ceremony was also attended by Lady Bridgett, Miss Brooks and the Rector and Mrs Carter, while the College girls were an attentive audience. Lord Poulett and Anne Cassidy planted the tree, burying a new penny and a college seal among its roots. Lord Poulett expressed his pleasure at meeting the College properly for the first time, and in answer to toasts drunk in lemonade, to him, Lady Bridgett and the village, he proposed Miss Brooks and the Young Ladies. A blessing followed in which the rector expressed the hope that the tree would flourish in the years to come. He asked for blessings on Malvern Girls College and all those who teach and learn therein. 'Prosper too, we pray thee,' he continued, 'the future of the noble family who have entered into this glorious heritage.' The ceremony ended with the singing of the National Anthem.

As it happened their stay was a comparatively short one, and the girls were able to return to Malvern before the end of 1940. Shortly afterwards the mansion was occupied by another girls' establishment, St Felix School from Southwold in Suffolk, who remained until the war ended. Among the pupils was Felicity, the daughter of Clement Atlee (the post-war Prime Minister), while on the staff as music mistress was the sister of Dame Myra Hess, the eminent pianist.

In 1941 Earl Poulett was granted a decree in the Divorce Court for the restitution of conjugal rights, to be obeyed within 14 days, for service against his wife. Countess Poulett filed no answer. Lord Poulett's case was that at Christmas 1935, his wife without his entire approval took an engagement in pantomine in Manchester. He said he was most anxious for a home and family but his wife's affection for the stage seemed to grow as time went on. In October 1936 they were staying in London, and she declined to return home to the country. She had never returned since that time, although he had done everything possible to persuade her to do so.

So much for the mutual interest in each other's careers that Lady Poulett had stressed at the time of their wedding. Oriel Ross continued to pursue her theatrical and film career with great success over the years.

Lord Poulett was now working as a Technical Assistant in the Chief Mechanical Engineers' Department at Woolwich Arsenal and at the Small Arms Section of the Ministry of Supply. Here he assisted in the making of breech blocks for sten-guns. That he was very popular with his colleagues was borne out by the fact that his fellow workers formed their own association entitled 'The Most Noble the Earl Poulett Order of the Breech Block!'

On 17 December of that year Lord Poulett remarried. His new wife was Miss Olga Lorraine Lawrence, the daughter of Waklin Lawrence of Svendborg, Denmark. Lorraine, Lady Poulett soon became a familiar sight in Hinton, attending various village functions, alone, or with his Lordship when he was at home from his wartime duties. They were present that year at the school children's annual Christmas party when Lady Poulett distributed gifts from the estate Christmas tree set up in the classroom.

Lorraine Lawrence, second wife of 8th Earl Poulett

During these wartime years Lord Poulett's mother, sister and half-sister were often at Hinton, and the whole family were frequently seen on Sunday mornings at church in the family pew, when Lord Poulett would read the lesson from the eagle lectern.

As patron of the living Lord Poulett appointed a new rector in 1942 after the retirement of the Reverend Carter. This was the Reverend William Draper who was to remain at Hinton for twenty-nine years before his own retirement, almost a record length of service for the village, exceeded only by the Reverend Henry Stanbury who retired in 1846 after forty-eight years.

Later that same year the most significant event for centuries occurred in Hinton St George. This was the sale by Lord Poulett of some 3,300 acres of the Hinton St George Estates including the villages of Hinton, Dinnington and Chillington, with land stretching from beyond Windwhistle across to Lopen. The new owners were Oxford University Estates who were represented locally by a resident agent with a cottage and office at 39 High Street in Hinton. After centuries of ownership by the Poulett family, Hinton was no longer his Lordship's responsibility. The tenants and farmers no longer looked to him for their homes or their livelihood. Never again would the church bells ring or the flags fly in the streets for the Poulett family. It could be likened to the abdication of the king! Although most of the former Hinton estate was gone, Lord Poulett retained Hinton House and Hinton Park, together with the estate workers' cottages in West Street, also Vine Cottage and Phoenix, the dower house. He also retained the title of Lord of the Manor and with it, as patron of the living, the right to appoint the rectors of Hinton St George.

In the greater world, the war dragged on. Part of Hinton Park was taken over by the War Office as a military camp, and successive armies of men were encamped there; English, Irish, Czechoslovakian and finally American troops, all in turn became part of Hinton's wartime scene. In the fields below the village was a searchlight battery, while the Victory Hut housed a troops' canteen. At Hinton House an Air Raid Wardens' Post was set up in the cellars. The population more than doubled in Hinton with the evacuees and the College and its staff, and although many of the men-folk were away serving in the armed forces, the village kept its spirits up with concerts, and dances for the troops in the park, and 'did its bit' with salvage drives, jumble sales, produce stalls and the like.

The war ended finally in 1945 and the years of reconstruction began. Hinton House was re-occupied again when Lord and Lady Poulett moved back into the old family home having spent the last few years at Phoenix. Much of the vast mansion remained empty, however, including the state rooms and the old basement rooms and kitchens, after their wartime service. A modern kitchen was formed close to Lord and Lady Poulett's private suite in the west wing. Of the remainder of the house only the Grand Saloon, the Library and the small Dining Room were re-furnished in pre-war style.

In the park all traces of the army occupation were removed, the evacuees and the College departed from the village, the troops came home and life slowly returned to something like normal.

Now that the village no longer belonged to the earl, it is true to say that the inhabitants had little day to day contact with the family. Lord Poulett still employed several estate workers who looked after the mansion and grounds, the estate yard and the woods and land in the park. A secretary/manager was now depended upon for the everyday running of the reduced estate, a full-time bailiff being no longer necessary.

As well as Hinton House, the earl owned a house in the Bahamas, a flat in Brighton and kept a suite for his use at the Dorchester Hotel in London. Lord and Lady Poulett frequently holidayed in the Bahamas at their home there named Lille Hus.

On 20 July 1947 the death occurred of Lord Poulett's mother, Sylvia the Dowager Countess Poulett, at the age of 57, at her home in London. The funeral took place at Hinton St George where her remains were interred in a fern-lined grave next to that of her husband, the 7th Earl. Lord and Lady Poulett were present with Lady Bridgett and Miss Phoebe, the earl's half-sister.

Shortly afterwards the press reported that:

> The decorative Lady Bridgett Poulett will not be seen dining out in the West End this winter. She sails for New York and Florida. Lady Bridgett is 35, unmarried. She has just inherited from her mother a diamond necklace which I have heard valued at £10,000. Last week Lady Bridgett wore it to a party. At Lady Poulett's death the £250,000 set aside for her lifetime passed to the present earl. The bulk of her private fortune of £26,000 went to the younger daughter Phoebe, who lives in Chelsea. It included eleven fur coats.

In July 1948 Lady Bridgett Poulett was in fact married. It was not revealed until some fifteen months after the event that she had married Senor Luis Robledo, a Colombian diplomat, who was first secretary at the Colombian embassy in London. The wedding was kept secret because Colombia bans its diplomats from marrying nationals of the country in which they are stationed. The press reported that Bridgett had been in Bogota, capital of Colombia, three months before the wedding. After the ceremony the couple lived for several months in the American Officers' Club at luxurious Kronberg Castle, overlooking Frankfurt. They eventually established a home in Bogota.

Sadly in 1948 the death occurred tragically young of the earl's half-sister, Phoebe, aged 26 years from meningitis. She was buried close to her mother's grave in the churchyard at Hinton.

1953 was Coronation year and perhaps the largest programme of events ever to be held in Hinton St George marked the crowning of Queen Elizabeth II. There was a whole week of entertainments, much of it centred on Hinton House, the grounds and the Riding School having been given over by Lord Poulett for the occasion. There were dances, whist drives, a flower show and concerts all held in the festively decorated Riding School, while on the lawns around the house were varied entertainments and displays. On Coronation Day itself, while the villagers watched the ceremony on specially provided television sets in the Victory Hut, Lord Poulett, who had received the Coronation Medal, attended with Lady Poulett the great service in Westminster Abbey, dressed in their robes and coronets. They were at Hinton most of the week, however, joining in the fun and attending the various functions at which Lady Poulett presented the prizes. The week ended with a grand carnival procession around the village finishing up at Hinton House where once more the countess presented prizes. The evening climaxed with a Fancy Dress Ball, again attended by Lord and Lady Poulett, her Ladyship looking every inch a countess in evening dress and a glittering tiara. Coronation week was one of the last times that Lord Poulett appeared in his role as Lord of the Manor among his villagers. The national magazine *Picture Post* sent a team to the village, and an illustrated article on Hinton's Coronation festivities appeared in the souvenir edition of the paper on 13 June 1953.

The Riding School was often the scene of village functions, chiefly the annual flower show. Dances were also held there from time to time, and in the grounds of the mansion events were held on behalf of the local Conservative Party and for the R.S.P.C.A. Unlike his ancestors Lord Poulett was bitterly opposed to blood-sports and hunting of all kinds, and none was allowed over his lands or in Hinton Park. The old kennels, vacated by the Seavington Hunt during the war, were allowed to fall into ruin. Both the Earl and Countess were extremely fond of animals and there were always pet cats, dogs and caged birds in residence at Hinton House.

A few years later in 1958 there was again upheaval in Hinton and the surrounding countryside when the Oxford University Estate sold out to a firm of financiers who immediately resold to another firm, Talbot Estates of Nottingham. They in turn set about reselling the land and properties in individual lots. Thus many occupiers of cottages, houses and farms were able to buy their homes, and for the first time in centuries, Hinton St George, Dinnington and Chillington had no common landlord.

In October 1958 occurred one of those incidents which has become part of the folklore surrounding the 8th Earl Poulett. It has become embroidered over the years to the point when imagination often overcomes truth. The story featured in all the popular newspapers of the day with racy headlines such as 'The Countess and the Trilby' and 'What a Countess told a Porter'.

The story as reported is as follows:

Lord and Lady Poulett travelled up by train from Somerset to Waterloo Station. Upon their arrival there the erratic behaviour of the countess attracted the attention of the station staff. When asked to move so a porter could attend to some luggage she refused and asked him, 'Don't you know who I am? I am a Countess.' The station-master was sent for and arrived wearing a trilby hat. Lady Poulett apparently took exception to his hat and asked why he was not wearing a top-hat. She then attempted, or actually did (reports vary) knock his hat off. The police were then sent for and her Ladyship was arrested. Next day at Tower Bridge Court the countess pleaded guilty to being drunk and disorderly. In defence her counsel said she had been ill and a moderate amount of alcohol had produced regrettable results. She wished to apologize to everyone involved in those results. She was fined £2 and ordered to pay £17 costs. Referring to the incident later, the countess told reporters that: 'It is a standing joke between my husband and myself that station-masters should always wear top-hats!'

After this episode it seems that the press kept their eye on the doings of Lord Poulett. During the 1960s a series of incidents attracted much publicity, and the village and Lord Poulett often hit the headlines. Most of the reports were made in a jocular, almost teasing manner. It must be said that the earl did not seem to mind these reports too much, and took delight in making somewhat outrageous remarks to the press, all of which the journalists enthusiastically reported.

On the night of Tuesday, 16 February 1960 occurred one of the saddest disasters the village of Hinton had ever witnessed. This was the terrible fire which destroyed the ancient and beautiful George and Crown Inn. Shortly before closing time the landlord smelled burning and went upstairs where he found a lounge ablaze. He quickly gave the alarm and staff and customers still in the dining room and bars hurriedly left the building. The fire rapidly took hold and within minutes the whole length of the thatched roof was a mass of flames. Some fifty firemen from six brigades were quickly on the scene, but there was little they could do to save the inn. They were severely handicapped by a shortage of water and six tenders ran a shuttle service between Hinton and Merriott to fetch water. Pipes were also run to the ornamental pool in the yard at Hinton House, which was soon emptied of water. The firemen also had to play their hoses on the opposite side of Church Street which was being showered by sparks fanned by a strong breeze. Snow lying on the roofs probably saved them from catching fire. As it was all the occupants were advised to leave their homes and remove their belongings to a place of safety. Practically nothing was saved from the inn which continued to burn until the morning. Almost the whole population of the village turned out and witnessed the frightening spectacle, with flames leaping high in the air and across the road, with bottles exploding like gunfire, and with a car belonging to a barman adding to the inferno. By the morning only the ham-stone walls remained with the coloured inn-sign still in place. The ruins remained for several weeks before they were finally removed, and the brewery sadly made no attempt to have the inn rebuilt. The site itself was left vacant and untidy for ten years before new houses were finally built there.

In 1960 another item came to the notice of the press. This was an appeal by the Earl against the rating assessment of Hinton House. A headline read: 'Tubs Catch the Drips in Earl's Home' and the report ran as follows:

When dinner is served at the stately ancestral home of the noble family of Poulett, guests are asked not to mind the sound of water dripping into buckets and the occasional clatter of a slate. For as the eighth Earl, 50-year-old Old Etonian George Amias Fitzwarrine Poulett observed stoically last night – 'These are very trying times though doubtless we shall live through them. Unfortunately the old family home for the past 500 years is beginning to show it has seen better times.

The Valuation Court at Yeovil heard Hinton House described as follows:

From the outside, with its towers and tall windows, surrounded by 500 acres of rolling parkland, it could still be the scene of hunt balls and fashionable parties. But inside it is – 'So cold that to walk from one room to another is like going into a refrigerator – you could catch a cold just walking down a corridor; so leaking that when it rains the floors are littered with tubs, buckets and baths to catch the water pouring through the roof; so shaky that wooden posts prop up the ceiling beams.'

The Valuation Officer opposed the application to reduce the assessment from £325 Gross Value to £150. 'Things had been allowed to go into decay,' he said and added: 'We do not agree that this house will fall around his Lordship's ears.' The court adjourned to inspect the house, an hour's drive away. Lord Poulett commented wearily, 'I spend an average of £2,300 a year on repairs. But the day I start charging 2s. 6d. a time for people to come in, then I go. It would not be my house then. So we've shut off seventy of the seventy-seven rooms, which leaves us with not much more than a largish flat. We've moved out all the paintings and treasures because they would have been ruined.'

At Christmas also in 1960, another sensation rocked Hinton St George and the attention of the nation was again focused on the village and Lord Poulett.

An incident occurred at the village church during the Christmas morning service. The service had started and the rector was giving an early sermon. Lord Poulett arrived while the rector was speaking, noisily opening and closing the door of his private pew and making more noise as he fell over the kneeling hassocks. Finally in his seat and after yet more noise, he called out to the rector, 'You clerks in Holy Orders, stop begging for money and preach the sermon as you should do'. The rector said to him, 'You have had your say, now hold your peace'. The earl continued to shout at the rector and generally disrupt the service. The lay-preacher and the churchwarden then entered the private pew and after a struggle escorted the earl from the church. The rector continued the service after the earl's departure but requested the congregation to show the spirit of goodwill by not discussing the incident further. However, a phone call was made later to a national newspaper by an unknown person which resulted in nationwide reporting of the events.

Once again the papers had a field day. As well as reporting the story, interviews were held with the earl and countess, and with the rector Sensational headlines proclaimed 'Earl in Scene at Church'; 'Interrupted Sermon at Hinton St George'; 'I'm the Wicked Earl, he says'; and 'I am so Very Wicked, says Earl'.

The *Daily Sketch* said:

The Eighth Earl Poulett sipped a gin yesterday and roared: 'I am the wicked Earl – very wicked am I.' He was sitting in the 'Den' of his 157-room feudal mansion at Hinton St George, Somerset and talking about an incident in the 400-year-old church on Christmas morning. So was his 43 year-old-wife. The earl said: 'My rector, the chap I appointed, said a lot of things I didn't like so I told him so. Throw me out of my own church? I am the patron . . . appointed the rector to the living eighteen years ago. Send him a cheque every year, and I'll probably send him another next year.' The countess ('I call her Willikins,' said the earl) said: 'I think my hubby thought someone was having a dig at him and waded into the attack, and if you fight with my husband you die. But don't worry, you won't die just now.'

The earl denied he was drunk when he was escorted from the church. The countess said he had 1½ glasses of champagne before he left for the service. 'All the servants are off so I stayed at home to cook the turkey,' she added. Her husband smiled and said 'Willikins, why shouldn't I have a drink or two?'

I asked him if anything in the sermon offended him.

'Down to red hell,' roared he. 'Let's have the damnation scene from Faust!'

Lady Poulett had just returned from seeing the rector. She accused him of taking part in a vendetta against her husband and said that he was annoyed because they would not allow him (the rector) to remove the Poulett's family chapel from the church. Lady Poulett said: 'I apologized to him for being rude to him in his own house, but I certainly didn't apologize on behalf of my husband, I can't. He just hasn't told me what happened in church, and I can't squeeze it out of him. My hubby doesn't like hurting anyone's feelings, you know.'

The rector said last night that there was nothing in his sermon to which the earl could have objected. He added: 'I have had no apology from the earl. I have told the villagers not to talk about this. After all it is a matter for Hinton St George and not the nation.'

The local *Western Gazette* said:

But for an unusual set of circumstances the rector would not have been giving his address at the time of the earl's arrival. Recently within the Diocese there had been a change in the rule whereby lay-readers wore a ribbon with a medallion attached – the type of medallion denoting whether the wearer was entitled to preach only within his parish or in other parishes as well. It had been decided that there should be uniformity in that the lay-readers would, in future, wear a loose scarf instead of the ribbon and medallion. St George's Parochial Church Council had agreed to purchase the scarf for lay-reader John Kiddle and to present it to him as a gift from the church members at the Christmas morning service when he was to relieve the rector, who had already officiated at three celebrations of Holy Communion. In order that the presentation could be made in time for Mr Kiddle to conduct the service, the rector was giving his address at the beginning instead of at the end. The address was based on humility and the equality of men in the Incarnation, and in the words of the rector, there was nothing in it which could have caused the earl's intervention.

Countess Poulett alleged that some people associated with the church were opposed to her husband, and would no longer accept a Christmas tree which he had given for many years. The Earl said the family had always given a tree since 1892. He had not given one in recent years because, he alleged, of the rector's attitude. Since then, it is understood, there had been a tree in church but this had come from Forde Abbey. Declaring that the earl was a very religious man, the countess said she herself had always supported the church and had made numerous gifts to it. She claimed that because of the actions of some people in the village, even the school children no longer had their Christmas party. In the past she had placed gifts on the tree for them. Later the countess took me to the earl's private chapel, which has its own entrance from outside the church. She explained that it was not an easy door to open. Finally the countess called on the rector at his home. She asked why there was so much opposition to the earl when what in fact he needed was help. The rector said that he had done all he could to help, but the countess refused to accept this. She further claimed that trouble had been caused because Mr Draper wanted the earl's private chapel removed, but again the rector denied this.

Back at Hinton House Earl Poulett commented: 'I am still the Wicked Earl, and I am hated.' He still would not say what it was, if anything, in the rector's address which caused his outburst. He did not go to church, however, to cause a disturbance, he said. He went to church for the same reason that everyone else did on Christmas morning. It was his opinion that there was too much begging by the church and too much pleading of poverty which he said, did not exist.

The *Daily Mirror* in a similar vein said:

An earl who was escorted from church, after interrupting the Christmas morning service, drank a gin yesterday and said: 'I'm the Wicked Earl around these parts. I'm not at all the popular boy, in fact they hate me.' Yesterday in his ancestral house at Hinton St George, the earl, in riding breeches and yellow open-necked shirt, told me: 'There is one thing that Clerks in Holy Orders are after these days, and that's money. I object.' Then the earl talked of his unpopularity in the district. 'It may be because I do not allow the local hunt on my land,' he said 'My father was a great hunting man. But I shall have none of it. I am against blood sports.'

The following week the *Western Gazette* carried a headline: 'Earl Poulett is Seriously Ill – Travel Arrangements are Postponed.' A report stated that the earl had intended to attend the New Year's Day service in Hinton Church but had been unable to be present owing to illness. He had been advised by his doctor not to leave the house. It was announced from Hinton House on Monday that Lord Poulett was seriously ill and nursing staff had had to be called. It stated that Lady Poulett was also confined to bed.

There was only a small congregation at the New Year church service and there were almost as many reporters and photographers present as there were parishioners. A doctor said the earl was suffering from a virus infection of the type which had been prominent in the area recently. Many people had been attacked by what is commonly called 'two day 'flu'. Lady Poulett, however, went to church as previously arranged and sat in the private chapel. The service followed the normal pattern.

'On Saturday morning,' writes a staff reporter with the *Gazette*, 'Lord and Lady Poulett invited me to Hinton House to show me some of the many letters received from different parts of the country. Most of them expressed sympathy with the views which the earl had stated in church. He was in a very serious mood as he told me the full story of a dispute over a footpath which runs across Hinton Park from Clamour Steps to Pit Gate, and said he had no wish whatsoever to deprive the villagers of any convenience or amenity. None existed in this case.

'Would you, as a gesture, withdraw your application to the Minister of Local Government?,' I asked him.
'If they can find a footpath, they can have it,' he said. He added that it would be difficult to find many people in the village who were interested in it at all.
Then he talked about hate. 'Those who hate me, may hate me if they wish, but there is no need for them to do so,' he said. 'A lot of people are standing by me. I don't hurt anyone. All these people on my estates and properties have never had any feelings against me, and I have never had any against them. If they are in trouble, I can most probably help them, and do.'

No more was heard on this particular issue. Only those who were actually present at church that Christmas morning know exactly what was said, and the name of the person who rang the *Daily Mirror* has never been revealed.

The following year saw the outcome of the dispute between the earl and the villagers over the right-of-way across the park, already mentioned.

It was claimed that the footpath from Pit Gate to Clamour Steps was shown as a right-of-way on a map dated 1798, and recently discovered in Taunton Castle. Villagers claimed they had once used the path for Sunday strolls and courting. For sixty years, however, the Ordnance Survey Maps had not shown the mile-long path. Since the war, it was said at the public enquiry, Earl Poulett had barred Hinton Park with locked gates and barbed wire. All trace of the path had been lost – but villagers told of their memories. Eighty-year-old Miss Dorothy Lowe told the inspector she knew the line of the path well. 'It used to be a favourite Sunday walk,' she said. Mr Donald Trask, born in the village in 1904, said closing the path was 'cutting off the villagers' rights'.

The earl told the inspector he was unaware of the 1798 map until a new county map was produced in 1958 which showed the right-of-way. There was no need for the path or for the villagers to use his park, he said. 'There are places in this country for people to walk. If they want exercise there is Dartmoor or Exmoor, or they can walk in the roads.' He denied that he had ordered his men to detain anyone using the footpath until the police arrived. He said the path had been enclosed in barbed wire before he knew it was supposed to be a right-of-way. He added that he saw no need for the path to be kept open 'except for people who wish to be a nuisance'.

However, the Ministry of Housing and Local Government eventually ruled that the path be kept open. A Ministry letter said: 'The inspector concluded there was no doubt in his mind that the failure of local people to use the footpath prior to 1958 was largely due to doubt regarding the status and fear of accusations of trespass.'

The decision was welcomed by the Rambler's Association who regarded it as a test case and said: 'This is a very important victory. Had we lost the case, it would have meant the closing of many footpaths all over the country.' The case was widely reported in the local and national press.

In 1961 also, on 18 May, Hinton St George was saddened by the news of the death of Lorraine, Countess Poulett, who had been ill for some time, and had recently come home from a Bristol clinic. The funeral was held at Hinton Church and a large congregation attended, headed by Earl Poulett. Psalm 23, The Lord is My Shepherd, and the hymn, Come Gracious Spirit, Heavenly Dove, were sung. Her Ladyship was laid to rest in the family vault. Later Lord Poulett commissioned a beautiful stained-glass window to be erected to her memory in the south aisle of the church.

This must have been one of the saddest times in Lord Poulett's life. It is clear that the last few years had been beset with problems, fears and doubts aggravated by bouts of ill health.

From being the 'Golden Boy' in the early 1930s, he was now 'The Wicked Earl' who believed himself hated by the very people who had expressed so much devotion and good wishes for his future in those early years. Why had this come about? He had been born into a privileged position with both wealth and a title. Against this, he had lost his father, and his mother was frivolous and uncaring. He was thus deprived of a happy childhood and the training for his future position as landlord of a vast estate with hundreds of people looking to him for their livelihood. As it was, he had spent little time at home, choosing instead to work away from Hinton and letting his staff run the estate. It is perhaps little wonder that his parishioners became disillusioned and eventually uncaring, particularly so when the bulk of the estate was sold in 1942.

There can be no doubt that the 8th Earl Poulett was kindhearted, deep-feeling and sensitive at heart, disguising his emotions with bluff, hearty behaviour. He was also a tremendously proud man, proud of his noble lineage and title of which he frequently reminded people. He guarded his home and land ardently, and hardly anyone outside his immediate circle of family and friends was allowed inside Hinton House. This may have been due in no small

THE POULETTS OF HINTON ST GEORGE

way to the fact that he did not want people to see how run-down much of the mansion had become. Even scholars and historians did not get in. The Curator of the Soane Museum in London, anxious to examine the link between the mansion and the plans in the museum, actually made an appointment to meet the earl at Hinton House. However, on arrival she was told his Lordship was unable to see her, and she had to return to London with her mission unfulfilled. Likewise Sir Nikolaus Pevsner, gathering material for the volume on South and West Somerset for his 'Buildings of England' series, was unsuccessful in persuading the earl to let him view the mansion. In the foreword to his book Sir Nikolaus thanks the owners of houses in Somerset where everyone was most obliging 'with the exception of the owner of a really important house who proved intractable'. In the section dealing with Hinton St George he says: 'An adequate appreciation of Hinton House is impossible as Earl Poulett would not allow me to see the inside.'

Later he admitted that all he had seen of the house 'was by snooping, and if I had been seen by his Lordship, he might have turned very rude indeed, as he had when I telephoned'.

For a man so conscious of his ancestry the earl appeared remarkably uninformed about the history of his family and his home. One might have expected him to have welcomed people who could have shed some light on the story of his ancestral domain. No doubt again, the loss of his father deprived him of the one person who could have instilled in him an early interest and a deeper appreciation of his inheritance. As it was many myths and half-truths existed about the family and the mansion which persisted until recently, after the Pouletts had left Hinton St George.

His first marriage, which the village had set so much store by, had ended in failure, and from then on he appears to have distanced himself from Hinton, and finally severed the connection by the sale of most of the estate in 1942.

He was known affectionately as 'Lordy' by the villagers and employees alike. They regarded him in his early years with a mixture of awe and respect, which as time went on, changed to amusement, mingled with sympathy and eventually, indifference; but there was never any hatred as his Lordship imagined. He developed a well-known weakness for drink which frequently brought out the worst of his quite substantial temper. His workmen knew the signs, and gauged the times when it was best to make themselves scarce. Many of the estate staff worked for the family most of their lives. Others, not so lucky, were dismissed out of hand for trivial offences. When the earl and countess returned to Hinton House after the war, they kept a minimum of indoor staff, for many years leaning on their old cook/housekeeper, Alice James. After she retired there was a succession of housekeepers, maids and valets who stayed in their service for varying periods, but who often found employment with the couple both taxing and difficult owing to their erratic and often tempestuous behaviour. Even their chauffeur/gardener of many years' service, Eddie Aldridge (one of the descendants of the family who had come from Hampshire with the 6th Earl) was dismissed on the spot after a disagreement with Lady Poulett about the presence of the couple's large Alsatian dog in their limousine.

It is obvious that during the 1960s there were clashes of personality between the earl, his rector and other people in Hinton St George who wished to exclude his Lordship from village affairs entirely. This upset the earl deeply and must have led him to feel rejected, culminating in the scenes in church at Christmas and the dispute over the footpath in the park.

After the death of Lady Poulett, to whom he was devoted, he took stock of his situation over the next few years. The increasing liability of the huge mansion, crumbling and half empty, plus the fact that to his own deep sadness and disappointment he had no heir to whom he could pass on his inheritance, must have influenced his decision to sell up and leave Hinton St George for good.

Before then, however, another episode in the life of the 'Wicked Earl' occurred in 1963 and remains indelibly on the minds of the older villagers of Hinton.

Lord Poulett decided to regulate the amount of water flowing to the taps of Hinton St George. William Hickey's headline in the *Daily Express* read: 'Lord Poulett rations the "Lady's Bath" Water,' and summed up the situation in the following words:

The age of benevolent feudalism is not yet dead, I am pleased to report. Take the example of Earl Poulett, 53 years old, the eighth and last in his line. Lord Poulett lives in the Somerset village of Hinton St George (pop. 420) where he is Lord of the Manor, and he controls the whole of the water supply to the village from a reservoir on his land.

To the surprise of some of the villagers and the local Chard Rural Council, the earl has decided to ration the village's water. He has the supply turned off from 2 p.m. until 5 p.m. And again from 9 p.m. until 7 a.m. – except on Saturday nights. This is done, as the earl explains, for the good of the people. Some of the pipes in the village are damaged, and it is dangerous, says the earl, to allow the reserves of water all to drain away. 'My family has supplied the Hinton water since 1874 when there was a typhoid epidemic in the area,' he told me yesterday. 'The water comes from a well in the hills called the Lady's Bath and it is pumped into my reservoir to a depth of 8 ft. At present it is less than 5 ft. People have to be shown it is for their own good to have the water supply cut off. Damn it, they are not really being inconvenienced. They all go to bed early – nothing else to do. In any case, too much bathing and washing isn't all that good for you, you know. Dries up all the body's natural oils.'

Some residents in Hinton feel the water situation is 'grim'. Mr Eric Whisker, the Chard Council surveyor, has been called in to see what can be done to alleviate the crisis. 'The water supply will be taken over by the local water board in October,' says Mr Whisker. 'But fully converting the village into the regional scheme won't be completed for another twelve months. Still, in fairness to the earl, he is trying to keep his reservoir more than half full because of the fire risk to the thatched cottages in the village.'

Lord Poulett's rationing is having its effect. The level in his reservoir is rising by about three inches a day.

'Some of these people are so helpless they make me angry,' says Lord Poulett. 'Don't forget, I have to supply them all. There is no law to say I must. But I do. But don't forget. I'm in charge!'

Many of the older villagers have their own stories of the hardships endured during the shortages. Frantic phone calls to his Lordship pleading for enough water for a bath or the weekly wash sometimes had the desired effect, and the water would flow for a while. Lord Poulett, some years later, good humouredly recalled the writer's father, then the village postmaster, telephoning him and telling his Lordship that water came from Heaven and should be free for all. 'In that case,' replied Lord Poulett, 'you must put out buckets and bowls to catch it!'

It was in July 1968 that the news broke that Earl Poulett was to sell his remaining estate at Hinton St George, including Hinton House and 1,298 acres of land, and that he was leaving England to settle in the Channel Island of Jersey. When asked the reasons for his decision to sell his ancestral home, Lord Poulett is reported to have said that the problems of staffing and heating the mansion were too great, also that he preferred travelling to living in the country. Of his intention to move to Jersey his Lordship said that three of his ancestors were Governors there, so he looked upon it as going home.

The sale took place on 2 August, and in three minutes flat, the 45-bedroomed mansion and the 1,298 acre estate, seat of the Poulett family for five centuries, was sold to a syndicate for £225,000. The buyers, represented by T.R.G. Lawrence & Son, local estate agents, included four sitting tenants who bought their farms; a property company who bought the timber; and a businessman who bought the mansion and the surrounding forty-eight acres of parkland.

On 12 September Lord Poulett was married quietly to Miss Margaret Christine Ball, the daughter of Wilfred John Peter Ball of Reading.

Following the sale of the mansion most of the contents were sold also, realizing a further £175,000. The most valuable items were removed to London for sale by Sotheby & Co. and the remainder was disposed of at a two-day sale held at Hinton House on 23 and 24 October. On the day before, the house was opened for the purpose of viewing the items for sale. It was felt truly to be the end of an era. Crowds of people came to have a last look. Most of the villagers of Hinton St George were there, also came former staff and estate workers, old friends, and relatives of the Poulett family. The great rooms seemed stacked high with furniture, paintings, crockery and glass. It was indeed a saddening sight. Great gaps in the panelling in the Grand Saloon showed where the tapestries had hung. The family paintings had gone from the walls and the whole place had the atmosphere of a huge store before a bargain sale. In all its 500 years of history Hinton House had never seen a sight like this. Its hitherto sacrosanct walls were stormed by a horde of invaders, bent it almost seemed, on vandalism and pillage! Outside in the stable courtyard, the trim grass around the pool was littered with furniture, garden tools and ornaments. Among them it was later discovered was a valuable bust of George I by Rysbrack (now in the National Portrait Gallery) hidden in a group of undesirable plaster heads. The earl's limousine was on display, as was the coach belonging to the 6th Earl. In the Grand Entrance Hall tea and alcoholic beverages were on sale. By the gates into the ornamental grounds, the land had been turned into a car-park complete with portable lavatories!

On the first day of the sale, proceedings were held up when it was announced that a telephone call had been received saying a bomb had been placed in the mansion and was due to go off shortly. Consequently the police could do nothing but request everyone to leave the building until a search had been made. Everyone duly left the Grand Saloon where the auction was taking place and sat or walked around the grounds until the scare was over. After this the sale continued without interruption. Centuries of accumulated history were dispersed at that sale. Items collected over the years by generations of Pouletts were sold and carried away by strangers. The variety of items was enormous. There was the little wheelbarrow presented to the 5th Countess in 1856 after cutting the first turf at Crewkerne for the railway; the coronation chairs of 1937 and 1953; an 85-piece Limoges dinner service bearing the Poulett monogram and a coronet. There was a host of Georgian furniture collected by the early earls, and a quantity of Chinoiserie no doubt originally from the 4th Earl's Chinese suite. There was a massive chandelier from the Grand Saloon, 6 ft high and 6 ft across; and 123 ft of carpet from the Grand Entrance Hall. There was Regency furniture and Victorian furniture; and the clock showing the phases of the moon, won by the 6th Earl's horse Benazet in 1869. Among the 160 lots of china were items of Royal Crown Derby, Staffordshire, Minton, Worcester, Adderley, Wedgwood, Coalport, Newhall, Dresden, Delft and Rockingham. There were numerous Chinese vases, dishes and bowls, Imari bottles, Nankin dishes, Japanese vases, Majolica jugs and a pair of Dogs of Fo.

Among the dozens of paintings were portraits of kings and queens: Edward VI, Charles I and his wife Henrietta Maria. There were many of the principal members of the Poulett family and their relatives; the Herberts of Wilton; the Bastards of Kitley; the Veres; the

Fulfords; the Parkers of Saltram; the Berties; and the Marquesses of Winchester. There were busts and urns and pedestals, beds and cabinets galore. A huge Elizabethan dining table and the long-case clock presented to the 7th Earl on his marriage in 1908. Persian and Axminster carpets and practically the whole of the contents of the library. There was a large quantity of early telephone equipment dating from the time of the 6th Earl; and a grand piano.

Outside one could bid for a 6 ft lead statue of Bacchus, or a huge lead group depicting Samson slaying the Philistine. Knocked down too, was a marble statue of a Greek athlete and an eighteenth-century brass sundial on a ham-stone plinth. Also sold were the beautiful carved ham-stone ornaments from the walls of the sunken garden. If the 6th Earl's coach was too large then there was a nineteenth-century Governess Cart last used by the 7th Countess Poulett. In all upwards of a thousand lots were sold during the two-day sale and at the end of each day satisfied buyers were seen shouldering a bulky piece of furniture or carrying a large portrait away across the lawns to the waiting cars.

A few weeks later the series of sales in London commenced, held by Sotheby's. Items from Hinton House were offered for auction at some seventeen sales held between November 1968 and June 1969. Altogether over 360 individual lots were sold, comprising the most valuable and historic treasures from the mansion. There were over 150 paintings and drawings including the fabulous set of giant cartoons by Romanelli which at one time had hung in the Grand Saloon. There were works by such artists as Gibson, Kneller and Lely, and others by Van Dyck, Stone, Hayls, Beale and later ones by Harry Hall. Sold too was the famous portrait of Sir Amias Paulet in its magnificent carved frame. One whole day's sale was devoted to 108 lots of furniture which included the remaining pieces made by Matthias Locke for the 2nd Earl; and other items from the seventeenth, eighteenth and nineteenth centuries. The set of eight Brussels tapestries depicting the story of Cyrus which hung in the Grand Saloon were included on this day, along with a magnificent model of a ship made in the eighteenth century. There were side tables attributed to Benjamin Goodison, and a George II console with the top supported by a carved elephant. From the library came a beautiful George III Carlton House writing table.

Another sale consisted of a large quantity of silver and plate. This included the 100-piece silver dinner service from the George III period, each piece bearing an engraved Poulett coat of arms. Here, too, was the wedding present to the bride of the 4th Earl from H.R.H. the Duke of Clarence – a George III silver and cut-glass inkstand; and the model of a mounted huntsman with three hounds presented to the 7th Earl in 1904.

Soon after the sales of Hinton House Lord and Lady Poulett left the historic family home for the last time and the great mansion was empty and deserted for the first time in 500 years. The house that had seen so many happy homecomings would welcome the Pouletts no more. How pleased to see it must Sir Amias have been after the unhappy events at Fotheringay. What a haven it must have been to the 1st Baron and his son after the battles of the Civil War. The proud 1st Earl prepared it for his queen; the 4th Earl, loving it no less, altered its appearance, while the sad 5th Earl rarely left it at all. It was a great homecoming for the young 7th Earl on the day he knew he was undisputedly the rightful heir, and an even greater one when he brought his beautiful bride there, through the decorated streets of Hinton, under triumphal arches bearing the words 'East, west, Home's best.'

So the Pouletts left Hinton House and Hinton St George for good after five centuries, quietly and without ceremony. A final gift from Lord Poulett to St George's Church was the beautiful model of the church which had stood in the Entrance Hall at Hinton House.

The 8th Earl and his new wife made their home in Jersey at Gorey, not far from the old castle where his ancestors had ruled in the seventeenth century.

Lord Poulett's connection with Hinton St George did not end when he left the village. He remained Lord of the Manor and as patron of the living, it fell to his Lordship to appoint a new rector on the retirement of the Reverend William Draper in October 1971. Several months later and after a meeting with Lord Poulett, it was announced that the Reverend Peter Swinbank had been selected. The institution and induction of the new rector took place at Hinton Church on 25 August. Lord Poulett, however, did not attend the ceremony.

At the end of the year Lord Poulett paid his first and only visit to Hinton St George since leaving for Jersey. This was in connection with the restoration of the Poulett family pew and memorial chapel in the church, which over the years had fallen into some disrepair. He inspected the progress of the work and expressed the hope that when it was completed, the chapel and pew might be open for the public to see. While in the village his Lordship took the opportunity to look up several of his former staff and estate workers.

This was to be the last time the earl would see his former home for on 1 March 1973 he was taken ill suddenly in Jersey and died. A week later his body was brought back to Hinton St George and rested overnight in St George's Church. The next day, Ash Wednesday, a simple funeral service was held, in great contrast to the impressive ceremonies which attended the departures of his ancestors. A large congregation filled the church, led by Countess Poulett and her family, with the earl's cousins Major Edward and Lady Norah Wingfield. The earl's sister, Lady Bridgett de Robledo, was unable to be present. The psalm 'The Lord is my Shepherd' was spoken and the hymns 'Thou art the Way by Thee Alone' and 'Abide with Me' were sung. In his address the new rector paid tribute to Lord Poulett's humanity, kindliness and unassuming nature. Then the coffin was borne from the church by former estate workers, and the 8th Earl Poulett was laid to rest with his forbears in the family vault. So the history of the Poulett family ends, for there is no heir to succeed to the earldom. Although the late earl married three times, he died without issue.

His Will published later showed he had left an estate in England valued at £686,666. With his property abroad and in the Channel Islands his total worth was estimated to be in the region of £1,000,000.

CHAPTER 11

Hinton House

A Right Goodly Maner Place
Leland

The present house at the south-west corner of the village, with views over its extensive park, occupies the site of an earlier and smaller manor house which was the home of the Denebauds and earlier owners of the Hinton Estates. Fourteenth-century documents refer to a 'Manor House in a farm, with stables, a barn, a pigsty and a dovecot'. In 1390 there was a 'messuage' in a court, called the 'gustenchamber' on the east side of the hall, with rooms above and below between the chamber and a gateway by the hall, and with areas adjoining a great porch. There were gardens to the north and south, and various bartons.

Sir Amias Paulet, in about 1490, began a new house, prompted by his elevation to the knighthood and the needs of a growing family. It was also a time of much poverty and the work of building provided greatly needed employment. This late medieval house occupied the area of the south-west corner of the present building, and some walls remain incorporated in the present house. It had a battlemented west front, three storeys high, with early Tudor features including two stair turrets and two ornate three-storey bay windows, an entrance porch and a cross passage at the north end, connected to a service wing and a detached kitchen (which survived basically until 1970). On the south an oriel bay led to the parlour wing. This Tudor west front remained virtually unchanged until about 1790 and is shown on floor plans in the Soane Museum in Lincolns Inn Fields in London, and at the centre of the engraving in Collinson (1791) of the west front.

Much of the stone used in the building is traditionally said to have come from Croft Castle on nearby Castle Hill. A mansion was said to have succeeded the castle, owned, according to Gerrard, by the Warres of Hestercombe and later the Courtenays, Earls of Devon. Excavations of the hill some years ago found no evidence of any substantial building having existed there. If this is correct, then the stone is more likely to have come from the quarries in Hinton Park.

In about 1544 John Leland the antiquary visited Hinton and described the mansion in the following words: 'Here hath Sir Hugh Paulet a right goodly Maner Place of Fre Stone, with two goodly toures embatelid in the Ynner Court. There hath been of auncient Tyme a Maner Place at this Henton. But al that there now is notable is of the building of Sir Amise Paulet, father to Sir Hugh now lyving.'

At the beginning of the seventeenth century, John, the head of the Paulet family was gaining importance in the county. He married in 1613 and in 1627 was raised to the peerage to become the first Baron Poulett. Now virtually the top man in Somerset and one of the only two peers in the county, he made substantial improvements to the family home in keeping with his status as Deputy Lord Lieutenant.

Thomas Gerrard visited the area in 1633 and in his 'Particular Description of Somerset' noted with regard to Hinton House that it is 'auncient yet very stately and of curiouse buildinge'.

Lord Poulett now added the beautiful south wing with its state rooms and Palladian south

Hinton House – West front c. 1785 (from Collinson's History of Somerset)

facade in the style of Inigo Jones and his school. Experts, however, doubt if the great architect had any hand in its design. Built of golden coloured ashlar stone from the quarries at Ham Hill a few miles to the east, the wing is of two storeys with nine bays. Each of the windows has a triangular pediment with supporting corbels. There is a decorated roof parapet of pierced quatrefoils centred alternately with roses and shields. The windows are not spaced regularly and so it is possible that further bays were intended. There are two other houses not far from Hinton St George which have this same architectural characteristic, a long unbroken front of two storeys, with architraved windows and a balustered roof parapet, and have also at some time been attributed to Inigo Jones. They are Ashton Court, near Bristol, and Brympton d'Evercy, near Yeovil. The wing at Ashton Court was added in 1633 by Thomas Smyth, M.P. for Bridgwater. His wife, Florence, was the daughter of Lord Poulett, and it is therefore not unlikely that Smyth employed his father-in-law's builder, being as they were on extremely friendly terms, and building work at the two houses was going on simultaneously. The owner of Brympton was Sir John Sydenham who was also married to a Poulett, Elizabeth, the grand-daughter of the 1st Lord Poulett. The wing at Brympton is thought to be of a later date, about 1670, confirmed in some measure by the improved quality of the stone carving to that of the other two houses. The architect of these mansions has never been named with any certainty and James Lees-Milne in his book *The Age of Inigo Jones* dismisses Jones as the architect without hesitation. He suggests instead that somewhere in this part of England was a family of builders engaged in building houses or new wings of houses for royalist gentry. Such a family was the Arnolds of Ilminster, only a few miles from Hinton, although there is nothing on record to confirm that they were in fact responsible for these particular houses. In fact Hinton was rather ahead of its time, whereas Brympton, built after the Civil War, was a carefully worked out scheme, designed with greater knowledge, and is typical of its date.

The new south wing at Hinton was one room deep with no hallway and its rooms arranged 'in line', *enfilade*. The west room which replaced the Tudor parlour became the State Dining Room with a fine plaster ceiling bearing the date 1636, which may be the date of completion of the south front. The rest of the ground floor was one long room, perhaps a gallery, divided later in the eighteenth century into an Ante Room and a Drawing Room at the east end. The first floor of this wing contained four state bedrooms. A leaden plaque on the exterior front wall bears the arms of the 1st Lord Poulett and his wife Elizabeth Kenn.

The building of the south wing of state apartments replaced the parlour and bedrooms of the old house, and in order to provide further reception and bedrooms for the family and servants, two projecting west wings of three storeys were added, north and south of the main entrance, creating a western courtyard. The walls of these wings were of large ashlar blocks carved to look like cobble stones. The Reverend Dr Thomas Fuller, a friend of the Pouletts, writing in 1640, described the mansion as a 'charitable curiosity with stones like the dowle of a cartwheel and done in dire times to set the poor to work'. In 1644 it is recorded that there were forty-seven hearths to be taxed at Hinton House, indicating a most substantial establishment.

During the last years of the Commonwealth, the 2nd Lord Poulett was able to carry on with the improvements, and the accounts for the 1650s record various building works. These included a new central entrance porch with an arched and pedimented doorway referred to as 'New Hall, Porch and Chambers'. He also erected a 'banqueting house in his bowling green', and made improvements and repairs to other rooms and courts. Lord Poulett's accounts of this period contain fascinating details of the materials used and supplied by local dealers in Crewkerne and Montacute, coal from Bridgwater, lead from Wells and stone from quarries on Ham Hill. Two brickmakers worked there for eighteen months assisted by two more brickmakers from 'Roome'. The estate carpenter carried out most of the woodwork, while paints and equipment for 'cullering' came from a Crewkerne merchant named Greneway. A pump maker from Chard provided a fountain. Glass and ironwork came from Montacute, nails from Bristol, and pitch, tar, oakum and tallow came from South Petherton.

From contemporary illustrations it would appear that the house remained practically unaltered from then until the eighteenth century. About 1714 the 1st Earl Poulett refashioned the State Apartments in the south wing to create a 'prestige' suite of rooms for a projected visit by Queen Anne, and the rooms on the first floor were named in her honour although in fact she never visited Hinton. The wing was also extended to the rear providing a chapel on the ground floor and extra bedrooms for ladies-in-waiting on the first and second floors. This extension was given windows at the rear to look like those on the south front, but having different carved brackets and no mullions or transoms.

Between 1714 and 1735 two detached wings, south-west and north-west, were added at right angles to the west wings. A drawing by Edmund Prideaux of 1735 shows a view of the house from the park. The elaborate Tudor west front with its three storeys of bay windows has a central doorway with two oriel windows above. The roof has a battlemented parapet, two flanking towers, and there is a central domed turret. To the north and south are long projecting three storey wings, and at right angles to these on each side are the detached buildings with three upper dormer windows and plain parapets.

Between 1748 and 1756 the architect Matthew Brettingham carried out work for the 2nd Earl Poulett. This has never been identified and a note in the architect's account book merely says: 'For drawings and attending Lord Poulett's business at Hinton and in Town – £50.' It has been suggested that he may have been responsible for the subsequent joining of the detached buildings to the west wings.

In 1736 a visit was made to Hinton by a traveller, John Loveday of Caversham. His account of this journey contains the following description: 'We rode from hence [Crewkerne]

HINTON HOUSE BUILDING SEQUENCE DIAGRAMS (Not to scale)[1]

Key to Diagrams:
H—Hall, P—Parlour(s), O—Oriel, S—Service, K—Kitchen, St—Staircase, p—Porch,
-------- Uncertain, ⟶ Entrance

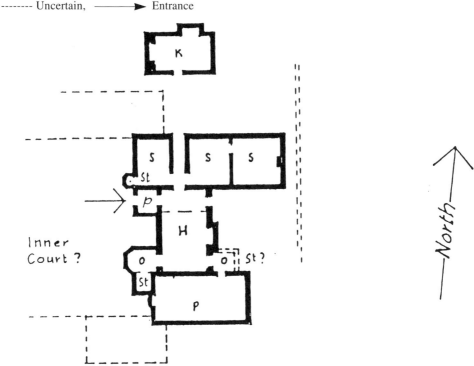

The Tudor House, c. 1490–1550. *Original medieval house rebuilt by Sir Amias Paulet and described by Leland in 1540 as a 'right goodly Maner Place'.*

2 miles to Hinton St George, Earl Poulett's stone house in a park. The front is old and not very regular. The wings which project great lengths at right angles, are newer; all but the higher part of these is built of round stones [Stones shaped douleways or in the form of a cart-nail, says T. Fuller in his *Somersetshire Worthies*], the windows only are sashed.'

The drawing in Collinson's *History of Somerset* already referred to, of the same view as the earlier Prideaux scene and made about 1790, shows some slight differences. The detached buildings have now been linked (perhaps by Brettingham?) to the main house and battlements have been added along the whole front. The main entrance is depicted more clearly and it can be seen that the bays and doorway were richly carved and ornamented.

It was the 4th Earl Poulett who was responsible for the drastic rebuilding and alterations which completely transformed the appearance of Hinton House and left it much as it appears today. He had substantial work carried out at various times during the period from 1788 when he succeeded to the earldom, until 1814, employing several different architects and builders. It is not possible to confirm accurately the exact chronology of the various phases of building, but from the architectural and other evidence available, some idea of what went on over this period can be deduced.

1. Diagrams reproduced by courtesy of John and Jane Penoyre

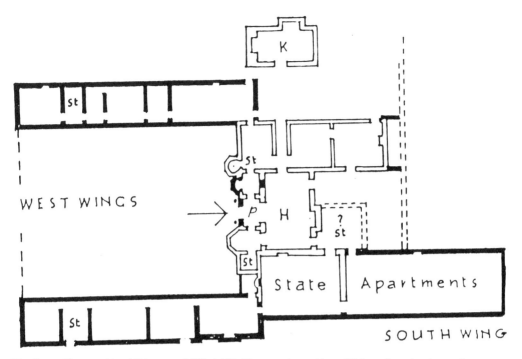

The Stuart House with additions, c. 1630–1650. House enlarged by addition of south wing and two projecting west wings. Entrance and Tudor interior also altered. Work carried out by 1st and 2nd Barons Poulett.

It would appear that at first the earl wanted to modernize the appearance of his house and give it a fashionable Georgian look, eliminating the vertical emphasis of the Tudor house, and providing it with classical proportions with the emphasis on the horizontal. The central hall area with its western Tudor entrance front, towers and oriels were all demolished along with one of the west wings and the south-west wing. The level of the land around the remainder of the house was then raised, leaving the upper two storeys above ground while the lower floor became cellars and basements. The central area was then replaced with an octagonal entrance hall and gallery 'to receive ye pictures' and a new Saloon to the rear. A huge beer cellar was made under the Saloon and the octagonal hall. Only the front of the south wing with the State Rooms was left at the original level, where much later a sunken garden was formed. The north-west wing was raised to match the remaining projecting west wing, and was similarly cobbled and castellated. Rainwater heads here are dated 1791. It is probable that the various dates so displayed indicate the date of the completion of work.

On the other side of the house an east wing was built, also with cobbles, to balance and match the west wing. (Rainwater heads here are dated 1791 and 1792.) This wing provided a Riding School and a billiard room with a servants' hall beneath the billiard room and cider cellars beneath the Riding School. A three-sided court yard was formed by the addition of coach-houses and stables on two sides to the north of the Riding School wing. (Rainwater heads in the stable yard are dated 1792 and 1793.)

Between the north-west wing and the new stables, a kitchen and laundry yard was now formed. This had several internal buildings ranged around a 'Drying Ground', a 'Still Court', and a 'Cooks Court'. There was also a 'Servants Hall Court' between the Billiard Room and the rear of the State Rooms to the south.

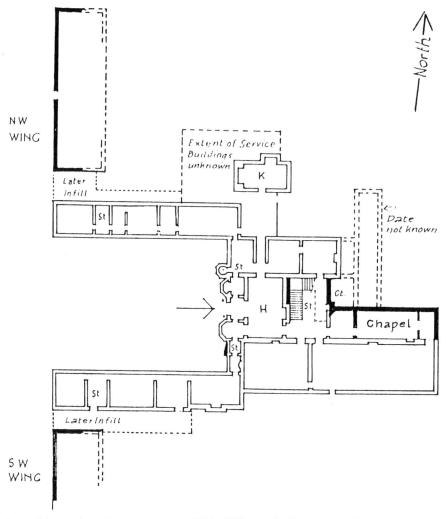

Georgian and Queen Anne improvements, c. 1700–1750. *Two further wings added, north west and south west. South wing extended by addition of chapel, and new staircase built to serve the 1st Earl's Queen Anne suite. Some work by Brettingham.*

New problems were created with the differences in levels of the floors in the various wings. The new octagonal hall and Saloon, at the raised ground level on the west, were some 9 ft above the State Dining and Drawing Rooms which were at the original ground level on the south. The state bedrooms were 8 ft above the Saloon level, so new staircases had to be built to provide access. There was also a difference of some 2 ft between the old first floor, now the ground floor in the west wing, and the level of the hall and Saloon. Thus, in spite of the improvements the house was now left with seven or eight different levels.

Rooms in the west wing that had previously been at ground level became cellars when the ground level was raised, or became service basements, or were abandoned with windows blocked up, or looked out on trench-like areaways. Much of these difficulties of traffic flow

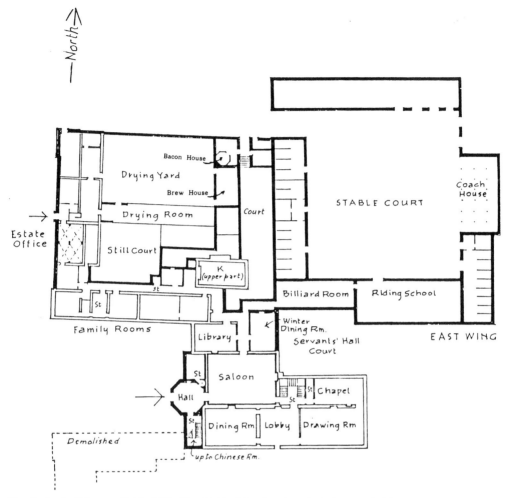

Classical rebuilding, c. 1743–1789. *The 4th Earl Poulett demolished most of old Tudor house and south west wings. Felton, a surveyor raised the ground around the remainder of house (except front of south wing). New octagonal entrance and Saloon built with cellars below, all in Georgian style to give new classical horizontal look to house. North west wing enlarged and matching east wing built with stable courtyard to rear.*

must have made it extremely hard to function as a household, even with a large staff, and may have contributed, along with declining interest, in the virtual abandonment of the entire south wing after the First World War.

Much of this early work for the 4th Earl appears to have been carried out by a builder or surveyor named Felton. Nothing is known of him. Reference is made to him in a copy of Collinson's *History of Somerset*, now in the Bodleian Library, Oxford, and once owned by Richard Gough, the famous antiquarian. A note in Gough's own hand reads: 'The house has been much altered by Felton a surveyor who took down most of ye walls and inside rear part, raised ye ground against ye house and on it built in centre a kind of dome to receive ye pictures, and a gallery.' (Gough died in 1809).

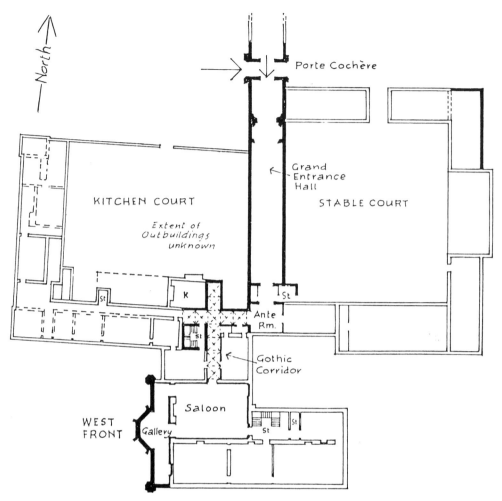

Gothic amendments of 1789–1814. Sir John Soane made various proposals for improvement but was replaced by James Wyatt. Wyatt gave Grand Saloon its Gothic styling and added two towers to octagon façade on west front. Main entrance changed from west to north via new gothic corridor linking up with new Grand Entrance Hall. Jeffrey Wyattville completed work with massive Porte Cochère. Stable yard closed in.

So now, when viewed from the park to the south, the mansion appeared with its new classical Georgian, horizontal proportions, the state rooms forming the centre of the composition.

However, in spite of all these improvements, the 4th Earl was apparently not entirely satisfied with Felton's work and his dome and gallery, and in 1794 he engaged Sir John Soane, the eminent architect, to redesign the Saloon and the south wing. A number of Soane's plans and drawings of Hinton House are preserved in the Soane Museum, London. He made measured drawings with floor plans, elevations and cross-sections showing the whole modernized 'Georgian' house as he found it, with the rebuilt central area, the octagonal entrance hall, and courtyard with stables, coach houses and riding school. Also among the drawings are plans of the old house showing the Tudor west front and the two projecting wings on either side. Soane's own plans for the house show that he wanted to raise the land in front of the seventeenth-century south wing and to build an entirely new front with pillared porticos and long windows. At least three of these designs for the south front remain. Inside there was to be a large 'Sallon' on the west side and three State Rooms with elaborately decorated interiors to the south. Soane and his clerk visited Hinton House several times during 1796 making drawings, plans and elevations. In May 1797 an item in his account book reads:

> May 26th – Making two designs for further alterations consisting of 2 plans, 2 elevations, 2 perspective views. An estimate of the expense of part of the Design approved and amounting to £1,540 which was directed to be carried out into immediate execution. Making out part of the working drawings for that purpose and frequent attendances on his lordship in person – £163 9.6.

However, at the last moment Lord Poulett apparently changed his mind again, evidently preferring the old Gothic style after all. Soane's services were dispensed with, and he was replaced by the architect James Wyatt. Sir John writes ruefully in his *Memoirs of the Professional Life of an Architect* as follows:

> I must do Mr Wyatt justice to acknowledge that he had expressed as much approbation of my designs as His Majesty had previously done adding, however, that inasmuch as good taste required that the exterior of the new structure [House of Lords] should be of a character to harmonize and unite with the adjacent buildings. This *ruse de guerre* of the Surveyor General is no novelty. It was successfully applied in depriving me of the appointment of architect to the Lazaretto erected a few years ago at Sheerness, and to the extensive alterations made at Hinton St George in Somersetshire.

Soane had to wait over a year for the payment of his last account despite three reminders, and eventually received a draft for the amount due on 12 July 1798.

So James Wyatt was given a free hand to complete the latest alterations in the Gothic style. He left the south wing untouched but reconstructed the Grand Saloon and installed the Gothic panelling, ceiling and candelabra. He altered the octagonal entrance hall and formed a gallery within the walls of the rebuilt central area. On the corners of the west front he added the two thin flanking towers.

Another radical change was now conceived. This was to move the main entrance from the west to the north. An entrance hall was planned through the stables on the west side of the stable yard. Wyatt linked the Grand Saloon to the new entrance hall by a fine Gothic corridor with cloister-type arched ceilings in plaster, very similar to those he built at Wilton House at about the same time as he was working at Hinton. The corridor was lit by stained glass in arched Gothic windows. Wyatt also added a handsome neo-classic well-staircase close by to serve the family rooms in the west wing. Wyatt's drawings of this staircase, dated 1804, are held at Yale University. He also furnished the library with fine fitted bookcases.

In 1800 the mansion of Clifton Maybank near Yeovil, the home of the Horsey family, was largely demolished. The gatehouse, ascribed to Inigo Jones, was taken down and the materials purchased by Lord Poulett for 120 guineas to be re-erected at Hinton St George. A workman was killed while the gatehouse was being dismantled. This gatehouse may have been intended to form the entrance to the proposed Entrance Hall at Hinton House, but no evidence remains.

The provision of the Grand Entrance Hall necessitated the building of more stabling and a further block was added in the 1790s across the north side of the stable-yard to form a complete quadrangle with an entrance in the north-west corner. The Entrance Hall was still incomplete when Wyatt died in 1813 and another architect, J. Kemshead, produced alternative plans. However, Jeffrey Wyattville, Wyatt's nephew, was engaged by Lord Poulett and he appears to have completed the work on the Hall. His last major piece of work at Hinton House was in 1814 when the massive Gothic *porte-cochère*, clock tower and gatehouse were constructed. He appears also to have linked the *porte-cochère* by a single-storey vestibule to the two-storied Entrance Hall. What happened to the Clifton Maybank Gatehouse and whether it was actually installed and then removed within a dozen years, remains a mystery. The stable-yard was provided with a new entrance arch in the middle of the north range when the original opening had to make way for the *porte-cochère*. A circular pool was formed in the centre of the stable quadrangle providing water for the horses and in case of fire. The old south wing and its State Rooms remained untouched after all!

Hinton House in 1968 may be said to consist then of two adjacent quadrangles, with on the west the kitchen courtyard and on the east, the stable courtyard, sharing in the centre the Grand Entrance Hall. To the south is the wing containing the State Rooms, while to the north projects the entrance *porte-cochère* and porter's lodge.

The following descriptive tour of the mansion recalls the home of the Poulett family as it was mainly in 1968 but with some references to earlier years. This was just prior to the sale of the estate, and while the mansion still contained most of its historic contents. Hinton House was occupied by the Poulett family for some 500 years. It was always a private house and was rarely opened to the public. It has not been possible therefore to describe all the rooms and their contents in detail.

The visitor to Hinton House approached the mansion by way of the main Park Gates at Brooms Lodge to the north of Hinton St George. A short drive through the park leads into the gardens on the west side of the house. Ahead is the main entrance in the *porte-cochère* under the clock-tower, built in 1814 by Jeffrey Wyatville. This massive archway forms an imposing entrance to the house. The wooden ceiling is decorated with carved pendants bearing shields with quarterings of the arms of the Poulett family. The Poulett arms may be seen also immediately above the archway on the south-side. Under the archway to the north is a doorway to a spiral stone staircase, leading to the clock-tower and roof. The tower with a battlemented parapet is surmounted by a flagpole from which, if Lord Poulett were at home, the house flag would be flying, white and bearing the three gold and silver swords. Another door in the north side of the porch leads to the porter's little lodge which contains a sitting room and a bedroom. To the south are the massive oak doors which bring the visitor into the Grand Entrance Hall. The Hall was formed within the walls of existing stables, which were built in 1792. James Wyatt probably conceived the idea of moving the entrance from the west to the north side of the house and the Hall was completed in about 1813 to form a more impressive approach to the new reception rooms. The Hall is some 132 ft in length, and most of it is now open to the vaulted roof. The first floor above, known as the Bachelors' Wing, and the interior walls were taken down because of dry rot in about 1935 and not replaced. The Hall originally consisted of a series of Gothic archways of Ham stone with ribbed ceilings in between. When the *porte-cochère* was added in 1814, Wyatville built the single-storey vestibule immediately inside the main doors. A false wall with windows was built up to roof height on the stable-courtyard side. A rain-water head dated 1814 can be seen outside.

A length of blue carpet stretches the whole way along the Hall to the doors at the far end, over a stone slab floor. At one time the mansion was centrally heated, and a note of 1895 says: 'On a cold winter's day the temperature can be made as wished; for in the halls and corridors and in many rooms (besides fireplaces) are coils of hot air pipes and appliances radiating a pleasant heat.'

The Hall is lined on either side with various objects of interest. On the right just inside the door is a little wheelbarrow and a steel-bladed spade made of oak, carved with oak-leaves and bearing the Poulett arms. Made by Giles Hayward of Crewkerne, they rest on a stand and were used by Countess Poulett, the wife of the 5th Earl when she cut the first turf at Crewkerne at the start of the construction of the Salisbury – Exeter Railway in 1856, and afterwards presented to her. To the left is a beautiful model of Hinton St George Church on a carved stand. This is the work of an employee of the Hinton Estates named Thomas Holland who made the model in 1844 during a period when he was unable to work because of a broken leg. Along the hall are many tables, some with marble tops on which stand ornaments and pottery; also here are several Georgian pedestals with urns and busts. Near the huge fireplace is another item of interest under a glass case on a carved mahogany stand. It is a fine model of a ship in boxwood and pearwood. It was made in the early eighteenth century and is of a two-decked man-o'-war with sixty-two guns. It has much beautiful gilt ornament including the royal arms and a figurehead in the form of a crowned lion. A similar model may be seen in the National Maritime Museum at Greenwich. Standing by the fireplace is a George III mahogany-framed surveyor's wheel, with a brass dial which measures links, poles, furlongs and miles. It bears the inscription: 'Made by Thos. Wright, Instrument Maker to his Majesty.' On the mantelpiece is a large Regency clock made by J.C. Jennings of London. Its dial shows the moon's phases, and silver lettering tells that the clock was won by Benazet in 1869. Benazet was a horse owned by the 6th Earl which won twenty-seven races including the Grand Steeplechase at Baden Baden in 1869.

We leave the Hall through purple-baize covered doors and cross a small lobby to an ante-room hung with pictures. To the left is the Billiard Room with a large fireplace bearing a shield of arms. In earlier days the room contained a full-sized billiard table with electric taps to mark the play upon discs fixed to the wall. Beyond the billiard-room door, beneath a large mirror, stands a beautiful George II giltwood and black-painted side table, which was designed by the London furniture maker Matthias Lock for the 2nd Earl Poulett. (It is fully described and discussed later with furniture in the Grand Saloon.) The doorway opposite the billiard room opens into the Gothic Corridor with its cloister-like arched and groined ceiling. The corridor leads straight on to the family apartments. To the left, it branches off to the Grand Saloon and to the right is a short spur (now demolished) hung with pictures. This is very similar to the corridors at Wilton House which were added by Wyatt at about the same time as he was working at Hinton. At the four corners of the crossing, where the corridor branches left and right, stand four white marble busts on tall stands. Those on the left are particularly fine. They depict the likenesses of Isaac Newton and Alexander Pope and are from the workshops of Louis François Roubiliac. There are inscriptions on the base of each, that of Newton reads: '*Naturam Newton, primus pateficit opertam, Quodcunque est, rectum est, jam tua Musa docet.*' (Newton first laid bare the secrets of Nature, whatever is, is right, thus my Muse teaches.) That of Pope reads: '*Promissum ille sibi voluit praenoscere Caelum, Nec novus ignotas hospes adire domus.*' (He wished to have a foretaste of the promised Heaven and not to approach those mansions as an unfamiliar guest.) They date from the mid–eighteenth century. Close by against the walls is a set of four George II mahogany armchairs. They have low oval backs pierced with radiating splats. The seats have oval cane panels and the moulded legs are joined by stretchers. To the right and left of the gallery area stand a fine pair of early George II painted term candlestands which were possibly designed by William Kent and made by Benjamin Goodison. They are 4 ft 4½ in high and have square tops with canted corners supported on Ionic capitals resting on modelled boys' heads with wings at the shoulders. The columns are panelled and taper downwards, and are carved with leaves and faced with lappet trellis overlaid with acanthus leaves and oak leaves at front and sides. The tall square bases are decorated with acanthus leaves, twisted ribbon and fluted mouldings. They are painted to represent bronze. (Similar pedestals from Chatsworth House are illustrated in the *Dictionary of English Furniture* Vol III, p. 159, fig. 2.) The stands now hold a pair of carved Oriental figures, probably Javanese, each holding a staff and with one arm raised. They are on tapering pedestals with walnut panels. Nearby is a magnificent longcase clock with a mahogany case carved in Chippendale style. There are eight bells with both Whittington and Westminster chimes. The 18 ct. gold plaque bears the inscription: 'Given by the Tenantry of the Hinton St George Estates to the Rt. Hon. William VII Earl Poulett on the occasion of his marriage in 1908.'

Taking now the corridor to the left which leads to the Grand Saloon, a door on the left again opens to the Main Dining Room. The room is elegantly furnished and hung with family portraits. In the centre is a beautiful George III mahogany dining table, while round the walls are a set of six George II walnut dining chairs, with scrolled backs and cabriole legs with carved paw feet. The seats are covered in calf. (A similar chair is illustrated in the *Dictionary of British Furniture*, Vol. I. p. 277, fig. 158.) The fine mahogany pedestal sideboard is also George III, decorated with classical urns and swags of corn and bullrushes. It has rare oval lacquered brass handles and painted plates with geometric designs in red and white. Over the sideboard hangs a portrait of the Hon. Peregrine Poulett, one of the twin sons of the 1st Earl, depicted with his pet fallow deer, and painted by Thomas Gibson.

Leaving the dining room the corridor now leads to massive oak doors which open to the Grand Saloon. This is the most magnificent room in the mansion and measures some 53 ft by 36 ft and is 26 ft high. The top of the glass lantern light is some 40 feet above ground. The room dates from the late eighteenth century when the major alterations to the house were carried out and is almost certainly the work of James Wyatt. It may be compared to his work at Wycombe Abbey, Bucks, and Ashridge Park, Herts. It is in 'Gothic' style with a polished oak floor and the walls have a high plaster dado (made to look like wood) with a castellated cornice, decorated with 287 quarterings of arms connected with the Poulett family. The roof is of dark plaster also with carved raised motifs and beams terminating in carved figures holding coats of arms. The huge lantern light is full of stained glass. The main features of the room are the seven magnificent late sixteenth-century Brussels tapestries on the walls. The room was formerly hung with large cartoons and pictures, but it was altered by the 7th Earl early this century and new oak panelling was installed in the spaces between the tapestries. The tapestries are extremely fine examples of their kind and depict the story of Cyrus by William Segers, and the episodes here were drawn from the writings of Herodotus. The tapestries have wide borders with oval medallions containing scenes from classical mythology. The borders are filled with allegorical figures, birds and animals and fabulous creatures surrounded by flowers. They are woven in beautiful colours on an ivory ground and bear the Brussels factory mark and the weaver's mark.

Commencing on the north wall by the door and continuing clockwise around the room the tapestries are entitled as follows:

'The Defeat of the Messagetae.' We see the camp of the Messagetae overrun by a surprise night attack launched by the Persians after the banquet they had given, when the defenders were overcome by wine. In the foreground the sentinels are overcome by the Persian scouts.

'Queen Thomiris receiving the messenger from Cyrus.' The queen stands on a hillock with

Hinton House – West front in 1968

Hinton House – South front

Hinton House – Porte Cochère and Clock Tower

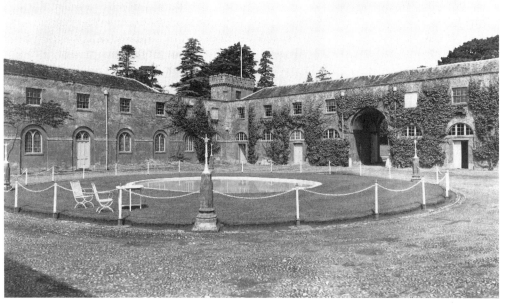

Hinton House – Stable yard – now Brettingham Court

her chamberlain while the messenger kneels before her. In the left foreground King Astyages lies asleep in his tent dreaming that his grandson Cyrus would become Master of Asia. In the background Cyrus in his chariot crosses a bridge over a river with his army.

'The Liberation of the Jews.' Cyrus is seated on his throne with his chamberlain holding a proclamation restoring liberty to the Jews and returning them their treasures from the Temple which had been removed by Nebuchadnezzar. Their leaders are kneeling in gratitude before him.

'The Meeting of Artemesia and Xerxes.' Queen Artemesia of Caria kneels before Xerxes while in the background can be seen the Persian army landing on the Grecian shore from a bridge of boats constructed over the Hellespont.

'The Siege of Babylon.' King Cyrus stands in the foreground with his advisers while in the background his army is diverting the course of the River Euphrates by which means he was able to enter Babylon along the bed of the river and so capture the city.

'The Meeting of Astyages, King of Media, and his grandson, Cyrus.' The king is seated on his throne with a scribe beside him, with Atembares and his son confronting Harpages and Cyrus. In the background the soothsayers are explaining the king's dream that his grandson would become Master of Asia. To the left the son of Artembares is being scourged by village boys at the order of the young Cyrus, who had been chosen by them as their leader, because of his disobedience to his commands.

The last tapestry on the west wall depicts 'The Death of Cyrus'. Here is seen Queen Thomiris with her courtiers after crossing the Araxes when Cyrus was defeated. A captain of her army brings before her the head of Cyrus which she orders him to plunge into a blood-filled vessel so that at last even in death he might satiate himself with human blood. In the background her soldiers are laying siege to a citadel while the defenders bombard them with boulders.

There are in fact eight tapestries to this set and the other one hangs elsewhere in the house. It is entitled 'Astyages and Harpagus', and shows the king ordering his attendant to kill his grandson Cyrus in consequence of his dream. In the background Harpagus is seen committing the infant to a herdsman.

The Grand Saloon is lit by a magnificent chandelier suspended from the centre of the lantern. It was designed for the room and is made of gilt metal. The base is an inverted dome of opaque glass from which issue 30 scroll and foliate arms terminating in leafage candle holders. It is 6 ft across and 6 ft high. A smaller and similar chandelier, with eight candle holders, hangs in the crossing of the Gothic Corridor.

In the centre of the floor is a pale blue Persian-designed carpet with a central patterned medallion.

The collection of furniture in Hinton House contains items dating from the mid-seventeenth century to the late Regency period. First there is carved and lacquered furniture of the late seventeenth and early eighteenth-centuries which were acquired by the 1st Earl Poulett. During the period he occupied high positions at Court and in the Government the mansion must have been almost entirely furnished in Chinese lacquered furniture, English japanned furniture in the Chinese manner, carved walnut seat furniture such as already seen in the dining room, and various tables and stands carved in the baroque manner. After 1714 when he failed to gain the favour of George I, the Earl retired to the country, which would explain the absence of important items of furniture dating from the latter years of his life, with the exception of two pairs of candlestands. He was succeeded by his son, the 2nd Earl, in 1743 who commissioned Matthias Lock, the well known carver and designer to supply the second group of furniture, which includes some of the finest identified examples of Lock's work. Many of the most important pieces of the Hinton House collection are here in the Grand Saloon.

Around the walls of the room is a set of nine George II mahogany armchairs with upholstered backs, seats, arms and arm supports, raised on cabriole legs with claw and ball feet. The legs are carved at the knees with scallopshells and leaves.

Commencing at the north-west corner of the room to the right of the door and continuing clockwise again, the following items of furniture are displayed. Between two of the armchairs is a George II chest with a pierced engraved brass escutcheon. It is covered with panels of eighteenth-century Chinese lacquer with powdered gilt borders and decorated with landscapes. Left of the door is a late seventeenth-century black japanned cabinet decorated with Chinese designs of landscapes, figures and birds. Inside there is a cupboard with several drawers, decorated with a variety of figures including a reindeer pulling a sledge, a camel and a woman milking a cow. In the north-east corner stands a particularly fine early eighteenth-century cabinet on a chest made of Chinese coromandel lacquer. The chest has a pair of doors with engraved and pierced brass strap hinges and a lock plate, and the whole is decorated with birds, peonies and chrysanthemums in bright colours on a black ground. The stand has two short and two long drawers decorated with birds, animals and flowers. The chest is thought to be Dutch. Just in front of the cabinet is an item of great interest. This is a fine and rare George III carved and painted pedestal, probably made by Edward Wyatt, a carver and gilder who did work at Litchfield House, Windsor Castle, and Carlton House. The pedestal has a circular stepped top with a frieze of anthemion and leaves carved and applied on a yellow ground. There are three massive lion legs in dark olive green each capped by a bearded head of Hercules wearing the skin of the Nemean lion. The whole stands on a yellow grained marble circular base with a green gadrooned border and block feet carved and painted in Greek key.

Before the large open fireplace, which has a massive decorated and carved mantelpiece, stands a George I firescreen. The screen panel is double-sided and is late sixteenth-century work painted in oil. One side shows two figures holding staffs with the background of a mountain village. The other side shows the Disciples receiving the Holy Spirit on the Day of Pentecost, in a classical building with a landscape seen through an arched window. The frame is in the style of James Moore and is decorated in gilt and black.

Near the corner of the south wall is a Regency cupboard of about 1810 with panels of eighteenth-century Chinese black lacquer, decorated with trees, pavilions and figures outlined in brass and with an arcaded gilt-brass galleried top. Next are two chests on side tables. The second table is a fine example of the William and Mary period. The rectangular top has a panel of mirror glass with a gadrooned frieze, raised on Ionic capitals above rectangular balusters carved with leaves and strapwork, and decorated with tassels and chains of husks. The four legs are joined by a waved X-shaped stretcher carved with trellis and gadrooning, all in giltwood and painted black.

To the east and west of the carpet is part of a set of William and Mary seat furniture. Here are two wing armchairs and facing them a pair of stools. Ten side chairs completing the set are elsewhere in the house. The chairs have tall arched backs and both chairs and stools have S-scroll legs faced with fluted lappets and joined at the front by an arched stretcher pierced with leaves and with strapwork ending in small scrolls. Some of the side chairs have their original red silk covering and silver thread *galon* fringing.

At the west end are two mid-eighteenth century mahogany X-frame armchairs with oval backs, worked in the nineteenth century with the Poulett arms. Two similar chairs without the arms are elsewhere in the house. In the recess under the tapestry on this, the west wall, is a very rare Queen Anne black japanned side table. The rectangular top has projecting rounded corners and is decorated with a river landscape in gilt and red on a black ground with a border of flowers and tendrils. The stand has a shaped frieze and the front legs curve in to the centre and join in a scallopshell.

Standing at each end below the west tapestry are the greatest and most valuable treasures in Hinton House. These are the two George II painted and giltwood candlestands. They were designed and made by Matthias Lock for John, 2nd Earl Poulett in about 1744, for the Tapestry Room. They are 5 ft 9 ins high, the circular tops with gadrooned borders hung with tassels supported on fluted upper sections overlaid with rococo foliage; the centre of each with three heads, two of women, the third of a bearded man with plumed head-dress capping C-scrolls from which is suspended drapery and carved at the sides with flame mouldings; the inner surfaces with an unusual basket-weave decoration and continuing in three elongated S-shaped supports faced with leaves and scroll work and dividing in paper-scrolls to be centred by a ball and joined above the S-scroll tripod legs. The legs are faced with acanthus leaves headed by and ending in scrolls and centred by large acorns, with triangular concave-sided platforms and panelled feet. They are now painted dark olive-green and parcel-gilt.

The other piece of furniture by Lock remaining at Hinton House is the beautiful giltwood and black-painted sidetable already seen in the Gothic corridor. It has a rectangular top projecting above the legs at the corners and has a deeply fluted frieze pierced at the centre with a female mask and with a leafy coronet amongst scrollwork divided by scallopshells and hung with chains of flowers carved in relief, and raised on groups of three legs at each corner divided by scallop-shells and faced with similar swags of flowers and ending in paw feet.

Matthias Lock, the carver and designer of London is best known for the part he played in introducing to England the French rococo style. He published a series of designs for carved furniture between 1740 and 1769 and there is a collection of his original drawings in the Victoria and Albert Museum. Among these drawings are seven small sheets of rough sketches of various pieces of furniture accompanied by notes stating the number of days spent on their manufacture by Lock and his craftsmen. The fact that these sketches were preserved amongst the Lock drawings suggest that he supplied the articles direct to the customer. Until comparatively recently only three of Lock's clients were known with any certainty. They were Lord Hoderness, a Mr Bradshaw and the Earl of Northumberland. Now may be added the name of John, 2nd Earl Poulett. Amongst the sketches are three showing a looking-glass, a table and a stand. They are rapid pencil sketches presumably drawn as preliminary studies for the detailed drawings to be submitted to the client. The drawings are described as 'A Large Sconce', 'A Table' and 'Two Stands'. Each of these, it is further noted, were in 'the Tapestrey Roome'. The notes with the drawings do not give any clue as to the whereabouts of the house in which the 'Tapestrey Roome' was situated. However, recently the actual pieces were identified by Miss E. Murdoch of the Victoria and Albert Museum. The mirror and table are no longer at Hinton, the former having been acquired by the Victoria and Albert Museum, and the latter is at Underwood Hall in Yorkshire. The four other drawings executed at the same time refer to other pieces made for Earl Poulett and refer to a lantern described as 'Lanton in the Grand Stair Case', a side table, a bracket, described as 'A Bracket for a Glass Case with ingey (i.e. Chinese porcelain) figers in it in the Dressing Roome over the Toilite Table', and a wall bracket for porcelain described as 'A piece of Carving Worck in a Closet in the Dresing Roome'. The table has been described, and the wall bracket was in the mansion within living memory. The other two pieces have disappeared. The mirror, table and candlestands are partly gilded, while the carved heads and the background are bronzed. It is probable, however, that when first supplied, they were gilded all over. The combination of gilding and bronzing was a fashion of the early nineteenth century and the bronzing was probably added about that time in order to bring the decoration up to date or to match newly acquired pieces made in the Empire style.

It is interesting to read Lock's notes on the drawings of the number of days worked by himself and his assistants on the various pieces and also the price charged. No figure is given for the gilding so presumably a separate charge was made for this. The table took eighty-nine days work and cost £22 5s. 0d.; Lock did fifteen days work, while the assistants, Loman, Hill and Wood worked twenty, ten and fifteen days respectively. The pair of candlestands was the most expensive item, costing £50 the pair and taking 188 days to make. Lock did twenty days work and four workmen, Low, Hill, Wood and Loman put in fifteen, twenty-five, twenty-eight and forty-eight days respectively. (Note: At Sotheby's sale in November 1968, the table and the pair of candlestands realized £7,400 and £23,000 respectively.)

The 2nd Earl Poulett inherited the estate in 1743 and probably ordered the furniture from Lock soon afterwards. The tapestry room for which the pieces were made no longer exists but it may have been one of the State Rooms in the south wing.

At the west end of the Grand Saloon, two arched openings lead into the Gallery which measures about 68 ft long and has a huge half octagon bay with arched windows and glass doors leading to the gardens. From about 1490 until James Wyatt remodelled it in the early nineteenth century, this was the main entrance to the house, first through an asymmetrically placed Tudor porch, later through a central archway and, after about 1790, through an octagonal entrance in a classical front. The octagonal shape remains on the exterior wall but its inner half is hidden behind Wyatt's panelling.

Like the Grand Saloon the Gallery has a panelled dado with miniature coats of arms, and a carved ceiling. The windows and glass doors are Gothic in style with a painted Gothic design and the Poulett crest in the upper panes. The walls are hung with paintings and there are various items of interest. At the northern end is a William and Mary black japanned bureau-cabinet with mirrored upper doors and decorated with landscapes, birds and flowers. In the centre of the east wall is a pair of George II candlestands in the style of Benjamin Goodison. Goodison worked from about 1727 to 1767 and supplied furniture to the royal palaces. The stands have circular tops with egg and dart borders and bowls each supported on the head of a girl modelled in full relief dressed in classical costume. The lower sections each have a bowl faced with acanthus leaves, and tripod supports carved with fish scale capped by seraphim and ending in scrolls. Like the Lock furniture they are painted in dark olive-green and parcel gilt. They are similar to the pair of candlestands already seen in the Gothic corridor. It is possible that both pairs of candlestands were the work of Goodison and were acquired by the 1st Earl Poulett about 1730. Further along the same wall is a very beautiful and rare seventeenth-century Dutch cabinet inset with silver panels, in ebony. It has a central cupboard flanked by pilasters with gilt metal capitals and is surrounded by eleven drawers and faced with sixteen panels of silver. The scenes on the panels depict the Amazonian war and bacchanalia including groups of cherubs carrying the wine harvest, others with Silenus, and cherub musicians. The panelled sides have carrying handles and the whole is supported on an early eighteenth-century black-painted stand with an unusual arched and waved X-shaped stretcher.

Opposite is a very rare George II elephant console table. It has a rectangular top simulating Siena marble with a deep frieze with Vitruvian scroll and leaf borders painted to resemble bronze. The support is also bronzed and is centred by a carved elephant mask in high relief, the trunk supporting a carved swag of flowers and leaves hung by rope from the projecting scroll corners. It has elephant paw feet and is on a rectangular base grained to resemble porphyry. There are a number of Georgian pedestals in the Gallery carrying ornaments and busts, one, in marble, of the Virgin is in the style of Due Quesnoy and is probably eighteenth-century work.

Recrossing the Saloon to the door in the south-east corner, the main staircase is now reached. The Grand or Oak Staircase built by local craftsmen probably dates from the alterations carried out at the end of the eighteenth century. It serves three floors and is a good example of a cantilevered stairway. In one of the stained-glass windows the initials 'A.P.' and 'H.P.' may be seen. These are purely decorative and do not date the staircase since the latter are those of Sir Hugh Paulet (d. 1571) owner of the house at the time of Leland's visit, while the former are the initials of Amias Paulet, either Sir Hugh's father who built the house (d. 1537) or his son (d. 1588).

John Loveday's account of 1736 describes another staircase existing in the house at that time as follows:

> The sides of the stair-case are blue stucho streaked with Gold; it looks not unlike Lapis-Lazuli, or a Sky richly spangled; the light at the top of the staircase gives an Eclat to it: altogether it has a very good effect and is entirely new to me.

Around the walls of the present staircase hang three of a set of five mid-seventeenth-century Antwerp tapestries, attributed to Philip Wauters, and acquired by the 1st Baron Poulett. They depict scenes from the life of Moses. Along the top are laurel swags suspended from a cartouche. The lower border has a larger cartouche and ribbon-bound swags of fruit. The sides have garlanded caryatid figures upholding baskets of fruit and are supported by plinths with brightly plumaged parrots perched on them. The three here depict:

'The Israelites in the Wilderness'. Here is Moses calling for manna from Heaven while the children of Israel collect it in baskets according to the Lord's commandment.

'Moses and the Serpents'. Moses with Aaron, and the Egyptians smitten by a plague of serpents. In the centre is a serpent twined round a cross.

'The Striking of the Rock'. The Children of Israel thirsting in the wilderness and Moses smiting the rock in Horeb with his rod, and water issuing from it.

There are also a number of family portraits hanging on the walls of the staircase. On the landing is a fine early George II mahogany marble-topped table. The rectangular top has a *verde antico* and Ste Anne marble border and is inlaid with a tile pattern of marble and semi-precious stones including Peterhead granite, lapis lazuli in the centre and a mosaic tile in white and shades of red. The stand has an egg and dart border, the frieze moulding centred by a carved shell and supported on cabriole legs carved with acanthus leaves and ending in lion-paws feet.

Descending the staircase the lower hall is reached, the walls hung with many paintings. The door ahead leads to the old Chapel, once used regularly for the religious gatherings of the family and their servants. In 1736 Loveday mentions the 'Chappel, where the Altar-piece and Chimney front each other, they are each in a corner of the long Sides'.

A door in the south-east corner of the chapel leads us through an immensely thick wall, which was an outside wall prior to the building of the chapel in the early part of the eighteenth century. We enter the first of the three ground floor State Rooms, arranged in line *enfilade* with connecting doors along the south front. These rooms were emptied at the time of the First World War when the house was used as a military hospital and contain no furniture today. Many family portraits, however, remain on the walls. We are in the State Drawing Room where there is a large open fireplace with a marble mantel. A photograph of the room taken about 1900 shows the walls covered in heavily patterned flock or paper. The floor is carpeted and the room is well furnished. From the centre of the ceiling hangs an enormous gas chandelier, with some fifteen branching lights. When electricity replaced gas a few years later the gas lamps were removed and crystal chandelier hung in their place. John Loveday mentions a room next to the chapel in 1736, which may be this one, thus: 'The Grand Room below stairs is considerably long and proportionately wide, but not high. The gable ends of Glass communicating here with another Room, there with the Garden, as it makes this room appear longer, so in proportion it takes from its height.' Windows at the east end of the wing were blocked in about 1790, but their features remain on the exterior.

The present wooden windows replace original 'cross' windows with stone mullions and transoms. The butt ends of the transoms were left in situ and can be seen on either side of all the windows in the south front. (Comparison can be made with the south front of Brympton d'Evercy.) Holes in the stonework were for the securing bars of removable shutters. The partition at the west end of the Drawing Room was added during the eighteenth century to create two rooms out of the original larger drawing room or long gallery. Fireplaces were also rearranged. A door in the south-west corner leads through this partition to what is now the State Breakfast Room (or Ante-Room) and is the second of the state rooms. It has early oak panelling brought from Henley Manor in about 1900. Glass doors lead out to the sunken garden which was ground level before in about 1790. On each side of the room are full length portraits of the 7th Earl, William John Lydston, and his wife Sylvia. They are dressed in peer and peeress's robes for the coronation of George V in 1911. The portraits are signed by Wood. (These portraits have since been restored to the mansion and now hang in the Gallery.) Opposite the large open stone fireplace hangs a portrait of Mary, Queen of Scots over a curious small blocked exterior door, which seems incongruous with the Palladian facade. In the north-west corner is another blank door, a large interior doorway which led to the Grand Staircase at the north of the State Rooms. Over the south-west door is a portrait of Joan and Sarah, the two little daughters of Sir Amias Paulet. This door and another small service door lead through the thick c.1540 exterior west wall (probably the original parlour) to the third state room, the State Dining Room.

This room is also panelled with panelling brought from Henley Manor and has a large open fireplace with the Poulett crest and an Earl's coronet carved in the stone. Its chief feature is the magnificent moulded and decorated ceiling. The ceiling bears the date 1636, when the wing may have been completed. The ceiling has an egg and dart cornice and the theme of its decoration is 'Man and the Universe'. It is figured all over with many sorts of birds and animals. Among them may be seen a dragon, phoenix, rabbit, peacock, snake, fish, fox, turtle, lobster, mermaid, lion, bat, dodo, dog, hounds and hares, all entwined with flowers and fruit. The figure of a man surrounded by moons and stars carries the inscription 'Homo Microcosmus' and that of a woman bears the word 'Eternitas'.

A large painting dominates the west wall. It is entitled 'The Return of the Poulett Family from the Wars' and is 15 ft 6 ins by 12 ft. It shows the family reunion after the Civil Wars of 1642–49, in which the Pouletts fought on the Royalist side. The 1st Baron Poulett is seen on horseback with his three sons, John (later the 2nd Baron) Amias and Francis. His wife Elizabeth waits on the steps of a house with their five daughters, Florence, Margaret, Susanna, Helena and Elizabeth. The seventeenth-century artist of the English School is unknown.

An old photograph of this room taken about 1900 shows that the walls had a plain covering, the floor was carpeted and there was a large dining table. The huge painting is clearly visible, and there was a gas chandelier similar to the one in the drawing room.

Hinton House – Kitchen yard – now Wyatt Court (note medieval chimney stack)

Hinton House – Grand Entrance Hall – c. 1936

Hinton House – Main Dining Room

Hinton House – Private Drawing Room

Returning via the Grand Staircase and through the Saloon to the corridor, the door opposite the Dining Room opens on to the Library. This room was remodelled by James Wyatt at the beginning of the century, when he fitted it with the oak bookcases with brass meshed doors and lined with crimson moreen. The room has a moulded and decorated ceiling and cornice. The bookcases house the family collection of books while above and around them hang many more family portraits. Above the fireplace hang eighteenth-century swords and bayonets and several riding crops with silver and bone handles. In the bookcase recesses hang early nineteen-century brass bugles and a hunting horn. The most important piece of furniture in the room is the fine George III mahogany Carlton House writing table under the window. The top section is semi-circular and has a pierced brass gallery and a letter slot at each side. It has six drawers and two curved cupboards, two drawers at the sides and three more drawers in the frieze. The four tapering fluted legs are headed by gadrooned capitals. A similar table is illustrated in the *Dictionary of English Furniture*. Close by is a George III mahogany arm-chair covered in buttoned red leather. A door concealed by brass mesh leads to the west wing and the private apartments. When the alterations were carried out at the end of the eighteenth century and the land was raised around this part of the house, the floors were then 2 ft above the level of the new entrance hall and Saloon. These floors were accordingly lowered to a uniform level which gave new height and dignity to what became the private apartments. The rooms underneath now had ceilings below the window-heads, and became part of the service basement.

We are now in the small Dining Room or Ante-Room. Here is another fine collection of family portraits and small framed family shields of arms. There is a handsome George III dining-room side table with a drawer at each end of the frieze, which is carved at the centre with a classical urn and paterae, from which are suspended chains of garrya husks. At the corners are pineapple motifs. The tapering and fluted legs are headed by bands of elongated laurel leaves and stand on leaf-clad bun feet. On this table are three interesting items. In the centre is a silver model of a mounted huntsman with three foxhounds, mounted on a large ebonized plinth bearing eight silver plaques showing figures and hunting trophies. The front central plaque bears the inscription 'Presented to William John Lydston, 7th Earl Poulett on the occasion of his attaining his majority, 11 September 1904' and was a gift from the tenants of the Hinton Estate. On either side is a pair of silver-plated huntsmen on horseback on ebonized plinths. One is signed 'J. Willis Good, 1874'.

A communicating door leads to the Family Drawing Room. The principal room of the private apartments has a handsome open fireplace with a stone surround and a marble mantel supported by Ionic pillars. There is an egg and dart moulded cornice and painted plaster panelled walls. Early this century the room is described as having an illuminated ceiling in colour and gold. The room is elegantly furnished with plain green carpet and crimsoned figured curtains. There are many more family portraits on the walls and a portrait of Queen Anne over the fireplace. The principal items of furniture here are as follows: The five arm-chairs are of the George III period and have their original needlework covers. Made of satinwood with baluster supports to the arms and bow-fronted seats, they are decorated with anthemion and leaves in black paint. The seats and backs are worked in silk and wool *gros* and *petit point*. The seats have vases of summer flowers, and the backs have rustic scenes, including a man with his dog seated by a river, two girls milking cows in a field, and another with a girl attempting to save her dog from an attacking goose. Between the windows is a fine William and Mary brass-bound strong box on a beautiful painted and giltwood stand. The box is painted black and richly overlaid with scrolling brasswork. The interior is veneered in purpleheart and there are two drawers. The stand has a deep pierced frieze of interlaced scrolling leaves and flowers with a female mask within a shell at the centre. The legs are silhouette balusters capped by seraphim with Ionic volutes and swags of fruit, on leaf and ball feet. On the other side of the central window is a similar strong box and giltwood stand, differing only from its fellow by a male mask in the centre of the frieze. Against the west wall is a William and Mary parquetry secretaire chest containing cupboards, drawers and secret drawers. The front and sides have inlaid designs of radiating circles of richly figured wood.

Double doors lead into the Sitting Room or Boudoir. Here there is an Adam fireplace, a decorated surround to the ceiling and an egg and dart cornice. The north door leads to the main corridor of this wing. Passing through a small lobby the door ahead leads to another Sitting Room. To the left is the Master Bedroom with windows to the south and west. There is a dressing-room and bathroom attached. In 1895 this was 'Her Ladyship's Bedroom' and it is noted that 'by one side of the bed are speaking tubes to various parts of the house, and on the other, electric bells, and also a telephone communicating with the house of the medical man, 5 miles distant, so that while lying comfortably in bed, a conversation can be sustained with one's doctor, while he is in his house'.

From the sitting room double doors and a short flight of steps lead to the Wedgwood Room. So called because of its blue walls, it has a decorated frieze and moulded plaster plaques with classical figures, while the ceiling is groined and arched. Here hangs a portrait of Sir Amias Paulet attributed to the artist Zucchero, but it is the frame which claims the attention. It is very late 17th century made of pinewood and possibly the work of Grinling Gibbons. It is composed of beautifully carved musical instruments, flowers, fruit and corn with two birds perching beneath. Two more eagle-like birds are carved on each side. At the top are the Poulett arms and an armorial cartouche with massive garlands of oak leaves and acorns. This was once the Business Room. From the notes of 1895 again, we read that: 'This is a remarkable room, and its description will convey some idea of how a very ancient residence can be fitted with modern requirements 'up to date'. This room then, contains a telephone which communicates with the various parts of the estate; another telephone communicates with the railway station at Crewkerne, and also with the town of Chard, where the doctor lives. Besides these telephonic apparatuses, there is a very elaborate and costly telegraphic instrument for communicating with the post office – thence to London, and thence to any part of the world.' The telephone was indeed considered something of a miracle in those days. Early this century the 7th Earl used this room as his own private workroom where he carried on his hobby of carving ivory.

Beyond the Wedgwood Room is a lobby with doors to the gardens and a staircase leading up to two small rooms, once gun and ammunition rooms. The next room is oak panelled and was once the main Gun Room and contained cases of guns and shelves for ammunition. Following on is a store and flower room. Here was once the Old Bath Room. Quoting again from the notes of 1895 the following is the interesting description of this room. 'From the ancient and Roman character of this apartment, we almost expected to see King Agrippa, who introduced baths into Rome, where many were constructed by Augustus and his successors. Whoever constructed the bath, and it is very ancient, intended there should be no doubt about immersion for it is 7 ft 6 ins long, 4 ft 2 ins deep, and 4 ft 4 ins broad. This bath may have had some connection with the military knights of the House of Poulett, for the 'Order of the Bath' which was constituted in 1399 by Henry IV, was conferred by him upon forty-six esquires, who had watched and bathed the night before his coronation in the Tower. Be that as it may, many men find a bath essential to the preservation of a strong physique, and ancient houses of military families possessed one. Besides this large bath is a smaller one of a similar character in the room.'

No trace remains today of these baths and no one living can recall them. They must have been dispensed with by the 7th Earl.

At the far end of this north-west wing is a room once used as a dark room, where the 6th Earl kept a large collection of 'mysterious chemicals' and 'personally conducted, on scientific principles, some useful experiments in practical photography'.

The last room with a door to the outside yard was the former dairy, and now houses the water-conditioning plant. Two service flats occupy other rooms at the rear of this wing.

Returning to the lobby before the Wedgwood Room, a passage off leads to the Gun Loaders' waiting-room. In earlier times the 'Waiting Room' was so-called because it was here that prisoners waited to be tried in the Business Room when former Lords Poulett were active magistrates. The way through leads up a staircase and back to the Gothic corridor of the private apartments in the west wing. About half way along on the left is a staircase which leads to the present internal telephone switchboard and accumulator rooms. The walls of the corridor are hung with numerous paintings and prints and farther on, on the left is a door to the modern kitchen and pantry. Double doors now open to that part of the corridor entered originally from the Entrance Hall and ante-room. A door to the right before the passage leading to the Grand Saloon opens to the Red Staircase Lobby. The elegant neo-classic well staircase was designed and built by James Wyatt and his signed drawing, dated 1804, shows it just as it is today. The plan is held by the Yale University British Arts Centre.

Ascending these stairs to the first floor, another long corridor may be seen stretching the length of the west wing, along which are situated the three principal bedroom suites, comprising four bedrooms and two bathrooms. The first bedroom and its adjoining dressing-room are known as the Haunted Rooms, for here the unused bed is said to be sometimes found with the appearance of having been slept in. Hinton House is haunted by various ghosts – one is the Countess of Essex, who, robed in black as she appears in her portrait downstairs, shows herself before the death of a Poulett. Another ghost is said to be that of Susan, daughter of the 1st Earl who can be heard at times rustling her skirts on the Grand Staircase.

An inventory of 1819 made after the death of the 5th Earl, shows that nearly all the bedrooms were furnished with fourposter beds with various types of hanging, some had hair mattresses and some had goose-feather beds. A lobby at the end of this corridor has a door leading into the north-west wing. Here another long corridor stretches the length of the wing, and the rooms are known as the Nursery Suite. There is a Day and Night Nursery, five bedrooms, three staff rooms and a bathroom. Returning to the end of the corridor by the Red Staircase, a door on the left leads to the present Bachelors' Wing with three bedrooms. A blocked door in the lobby here led to the rooms over the Grand Entrance Hall which was the original Bachelors' Wing. Close by is a hydraulic baggage lift for hauling visitors' luggage up from the basement floor. The landing above the Red Staircase leads through to a large lobby. To the left is a guest suite of two bedrooms and a dressing room. In the corner to the right a short flight of steps leads to the Chinese suite. These three rooms were completely decorated and furnished in the Chinese style, and still retain their Chinese painted wallpapers, although now sadly sagging from the walls of the unused rooms. They were designed for the 4th Earl when the octagonal classical west front was constructed in about 1790 and were partially altered by the addition of a split upper floor when Wyatt constructed the Grand Saloon behind these rooms in about 1800. John, the 4th Earl was a friend of the Prince Regent, and he was no doubt influenced by Prinny's Pavilion at Brighton with its oriental extravagances. The main room faces due west and has a large half-octagonal bay overlooking the park. Under the central window is a fireplace which at first sight appears to be false. However, it can be used, as the smoke is drawn out of a vent at the side into a chimney concealed within the thickness of the walls. Opposite the window is a recess for the bed which in the 4th Earl's time was a 6 ft 4 ins mahogany-pillared fourposter, with rich Chinese chintz draperies and cornices. The edges were trimmed with little wooden bells of red, gold and green.

A door from this room leads to a short flight of steps down, through a small lobby to the Upper State Apartments. Here are the rooms which were prepared by the 1st Earl Poulett for the reception of Queen Anne probably about 1714. It is doubtful if the queen ever planned to visit Hinton at all. During her reign she travelled very little. She did visit Bath and perhaps it was hoped she would break her journey with a visit to Hinton. It is more likely that the suite of rooms was prepared as a matter of prestige rather than of reality. Nearby Forde Abbey has a similar Queen Anne's bedroom. The Hinton suite comprises four large rooms and three smaller rooms. The smallest of the five rooms facing south is called the Dome Room (in the 1900 guide-book) but no trace of a dome can presently be found. It has a painted panelled dado and a decorated cornice. At one time the three large rooms in the south-east may have been one large room forming a Long Gallery. All these rooms have also been vacant since the First World War with the exception of the occupancy by the girls' schools during the Second World War, but the walls are still hung with tapestries. The two tapestries in the Dome Room are the remainder of the set of mid-seventeenth century Antwerp tapestries on the walls of the Grand Staircase. They are:

'The Discovery of Moses in the Bullrushes.' Here is the infant Moses in an ark of bullrushes discovered by Pharaoh's daughter and her attendants in the rushes at the river's brink. In the background is his mother.

'The Crossing of the Red Sea.' Here Moses is depicted with Aaron while the fleeing Israelites beseech the help of the Lord against the pursuing Egyptians, whose chariots are engulfed by the waters of the Red Sea.

Communicating doors connect the four following large rooms:

The Royal Room; Queen Anne's Drawing Room; Queen Anne's Ante Room; and Queen Anne's Bedroom. These rooms were originally hung with the Brussels tapestries now in the Grand Saloon. Here now are the six huge cartoons which they replaced.

They are more or less in store in these rooms now and their appearance when on the walls of the Grand Saloon can only be imagined. Our visitor in 1895 writing of the tapestries and cartoons says: 'They are amongst the very finest we ever inspected in any public or private place. The pieces are of colossal dimensions, are in excellent preservation of artistic workmanship, and although ancient, retain a clear brightness of colour indicating the superior quality of the materials used. The cartoons are the work of Giovanni Francesco Romanelli, an Italian artist who lived in the seventeenth century. In 1630 he was put in charge of designing tapestries and these cartoons are part of a set of eight drawings for tapestries illustrating the story of Dido and Aeneas as told in Virgil's Aeneid. They are painted in gouache on paper laid on linen. The predominant colour is warm biscuit, which gives the scenes a golden appearance. The drawings, on a truly monumental scale, are touched in first with black chalk, and followed by a free brush drawing in raw umber wash. This set of cartoons is thought to date from about 1670. Some six sets of tapestries exist today which were woven from these designs, but very little is known of the history of the drawings. They may have come to England in about 1700 either for weaving or to be admired as paintings. It is not known when they came to Hinton House, but it is probable that the 4th Earl purchased them to furnish his new Grand Saloon at the beginning of the nineteenth century. The scenes depicted are as follows:

Hinton House – Grand Saloon

Hinton House – The Library

Hinton House – The Gallery

'Aeneas and Dido at a banquet.' Dido is seated with Aeneas beside her, Cupid in the guise of Ascanius is kneeling before her and offering Illion's sceptre and other gifts saved from Troy. Achates is standing on the left, and serving maids are in the background. (Size 9 ft 3 in x 19 ft 3 in – See *Aeneid* Book I, 629–729.)

'Dido sacrificing to Juno.' Dido, followed by her sister Anna and a maid, is pouring wine on an altar at which are a priest and two assistants; another man is sacrificing a calf in the foreground; a woman kneeling before a statue of Juno is in the background. (Size 9 ft 1 in x 11 ft 6 in – See *Aeneid* Book IV, 55–67.)

'The Building of Carthage.' Dido shows Aeneas the construction of the walls of Carthage; there are two men with a plan before her, while masons are at work in the background and a sculptor carves a capital in the foreground. (Size 9 ft 1 in x 16 ft – See *Aeneid* Book IV. 73–75.)

'The Royal Hunt and Storm.' Juno has plotted with Venus the marriage of Dido and Aeneas by sending them to shelter in a cave during a sudden storm which scatters their hunting party. Aeneas protects Dido with his cloak as they rush towards a cave, their eyes fastened to each other's. Ascanius is on horseback in the background with other huntsmen, while two cupids fly above. (Size 9 ft 1 in x 11 ft 6 in – See *Aeneid* Book IV, 152–165.)

'Aeneas taking his leave of Dido.' Aeneas is announcing to the weeping Dido his intention to leave Carthage; the Trojans are loading their ships in the background, two of Dido's maids are to the left. (Size 9 ft 1 in x 11 ft 5 in – See *Aeneid* Book IV, 269–390.)

'The Death of Dido.' Dido is on her funeral pyre, reclining on Aeneas's armour and stabbing herself with his sword; her sister Anna stands beside the pyre, while Iris hovers in the air above and two men in the background point out to sea. (Size 9 ft 1 in x 13 ft 10 in, – See *Aeneid*, Book IV, 642–705.)

There is a complete set of the eight tapestries in Vienna, bearing the name of Romanelli as designer and M. Wauters as weaver.

Queen Anne's Bedroom was originally hung with two tapestries representing scenes of Alexander entering Babylon, and Alexander entering the tent of Darius. These two tapestries bore the Poulett arms and a baron's coronet at the top, dating them from the time of Charles I or II. One measured 24 ft 6 in in length. The bed prepared for Her Majesty was particularly magnificent. It was a large four-poster with a lofty cornice and hung with red velvet draperies with gilt lace borders. On the bed was a silk damask coverlet. The bed itself was last heard of in 1921 when it was sold for 320 guineas at Lord Anglesey's sale at Beaudesert Hall, Staffordshire. Other items listed in the Queen's Bedroom in the 1819 inventory are: a hair mattress, ten chairs stuffed in velvet, two dressing stools, a circular stool, a French inlaid chest-of-drawers, and a printed drugget. The windows here and in the ante-room were hung with velvet festoon curtains. From Queen Anne's Bedroom a door leads to a passage and two small rooms, possibly for the Ladies-in-Waiting, or dressing rooms.

The second floor may be reached by a staircase close by. Up here are seven bedrooms for the mansion servants, arranged around the upper walls of the Grand Saloon. There is a door from which access may be obtained to the lead roof of the state rooms.

The tour of the mansion is completed by a visit to the Lower Ground Floor or Undercroft, which is the domain of the household and domestic staff ruled by the butler and the housekeeper, and is a veritable warren of kitchens, workrooms, stores and living quarters. All this area was virtually unused in 1968, as a modern kitchen upstairs served the needs of the 8th Earl's household. The area was last used extensively during the Second World War, but at the beginning of the century at the time of the 7th Earl, the following rooms and domestic arrangements are recorded.

The staff entrance was via the iron gate at the top of twenty stone steps close by the Porter's Lodge. A long passage – some 230 ft long – led to the main door. Here is a railway track for trucks carrying supplies, luggage and fuel to the house. A hydraulic lift by the door carried the luggage up to the floors above. On the eastern side of the passage under the Grand Entrance Hall are several cellar-like stores for coal and wood. Close by are the Game and Poultry houses while outside the main door are rooms for the porter and footman.

Inside the door, passages lead off in different directions. Here is a bell rope to ring the bell on the roof which was used for summoning the household and their guests for meals. It could be heard all over the village and the park where they might be out riding.

The main kitchen is a large lofty room, 30 ft x 26 ft 5 in and 17 ft 6 in high with a glass skylight. It is furnished with huge dressers holding large numbers of all kinds of copper pots, pans and moulds of all sizes and shapes, many bearing the Poulett crest. In the centre of the room are large tables with thick wooden tops, and along the outside wall runs a long lead-lined sink for washing up. There is a huge Eagle stove some 6 ft long for cooking, while close by is a settle where the staff can rest briefly from their labours. A dumbwaiter carries trays of food to the corridors leading to the dining rooms above. (The kitchen is situated in the remains of the original medieval house, with its huge chimneys, and which survived until the alterations made about 1970.) A scullery leads from the kitchen with larders and store rooms off, containing all the household kitchen ware and equipment. There is also a game larder, bakery and butcher's rooms. A door leads out and up to the Kitchen Court. Here there are several buildings used for the mansion's laundry. There is the drying shed, a wooden building some 40 ft long with open ventilators for airing the clothes; the laundry, equipped with revolving wooden tubs with large handles; a mangling room; and an ironing room.

This latter contains two triangular pyramidal stoves 3 ft high, which heat fifteen flat irons at one time. Outside is the drying ground, a large open area hung with clothes lines. There is a small glass-house and the electric plant house with a Petters oil engine for producing electricity for the mansion. This was installed by the 7th Earl just before the First World War. The engine had two large fly-wheels and often needed the application of a blow-lamp before it would start! (None of the buildings in the Kitchen Court remained in 1968.)

Back in the house is the boiler room for hot water, and four stove rooms for supplying the hot air to different parts of the house. The huge stoves consumed vast quantities of coal and had to be frequently cleaned out of 'rock', which formed from the boiling water. The house was lit by oil and candles until the gas plant was opened in the village late in the nineteenth century.

Along the passage could be found that most important place, the Housekeeper's Room. It was comfortably furnished with a fireplace with a brass fender, two large armchairs and a couch with loose covers; a dining table with chairs, a Turkish carpet and a cuckoo clock! Close by was her pantry with large cupboards containing much of the household and family china. This included a blue and white breakfast set of 74 pieces; a Crown Derby dessert set; a Worcester dessert set decorated in green with gilt borders; Japanese and Minton tea services; a Limoges dinner service of 160 pieces decorated with a gold scroll border and each piece bearing the Poulett crest; and a Minton dinner service of 50 pieces in white with coloured Poulett arms. Close by was the still room and the Butler's Room and Pantry. He had a bed covered with a red and white counterpane and a feather pillow and bolster. There was an antique easy chair in red morocco, and a large pigeon-hole bureau with five drawers. The walls were hung with prints of coastal views. His pantry contained three large cupboards full of household glass and china, including a Rockingham tea service in violet and gilt with a rose decoration, of some fifty pieces. Here too was the silver cellar with a vast collection of all sorts of silver table ware, ornamental pieces and cutlery. Included were a silver salver presented by the Seavington Hunt to Earl Poulett in 1908 and a silver rose bowl presented to him by the Reading Room. As well as the silver there was a huge quantity of plated articles. Next door was the Footman's Room with his bed and rocking-chair. Other rooms close by were the Cook's Room over the scullery, a Kitchen Maid's Room, a Scullery Maid's Room and the staff bathroom. Across the passage from the main door was the Servants' Hall. Situated under the Billiard Room it is some 43 ft long and 20 ft wide. Here the staff met for their meals. (This room was used as an extra kitchen for the hospital during the First World War.)

There are extensive cellars at this level also. The two wine cellars are in the south-east corner under the State Drawing Room and in 1918 contained twenty bins of bottles of various kinds. The beer cellars, a huge place with lofty brick vaults supported by stone pillars and with a blue stone floor containing drainage channels, was built in about 1792 under the octagonal entrance hall and Grand Saloon. There are extensive cider cellars under the Riding School and stables. (Tradition has it that a troop of Royalist cavalry was quartered in the mansion's cellars at the time of the Civil War.)

Mention must be made of the Strong Room in the corridor leading up to the State Rooms. Inside were shelves lined with green baize. Here was kept the collection of important family plate and silver. There were numerous silver and gold inlaid trays and salvers, entree dishes and large meat dishes and covers, nearly all bearing the Poulett arms, and dating from George II and III and Victorian periods, including George II candlesticks with decorative branches. There were a number of presentation pieces, including the silver-gilt porringer given to his Poulett godchild by King George III, and the silver inkstand by Paul Storr presented by the future King William IV to the 4th Earl Poulett and his bride. Here was kept the magnificent silver dinner service consisting of some seventy-two plates and twenty-two dishes, all elaborately decorated and bearing the Poulett arms on each piece. (Altogether some 160 pieces were listed in the 1918 inventory.) As in the Butler's Pantry there was also another vast collection of plated articles.

There are four staircases from the basement up to the main house, and sympathy may be felt for the staff who worked there, for the miles they must have walked to carry out their daily duties, not to mention the problems involved in serving hot meals from the kitchens to the dining rooms.

Some records of the housekeeping arrangements remain. Lord Poulett's 'Stables, House and Pleasure Grounds account of 1837 lists the following twenty-three servants together with their annual wages:

House Steward	£100
Butler	£50
Housekeeper	£36. 15s.
2 Nursemaids	£12 and £10
Cook	£47
2 Kitchen Maids	£14 and £9
2 Still Room Maids	£14 and £8
2 Laundry Maids	£17 and £8
3 House Maids	£12, £8 and £8
2 Footmen	£20 and £16
Under Butler	£24
Under Groom	£45
Coachman	£30
1st Gamekeeper	£63
2nd Gamekeeper	£42
3rd Gamekeeper	£42

In 1856 there were seventeen indoor and outdoor male servants who were assessed for taxes.

In 1874 an almost daily payment was made to one Sophie Wetherall of 1s. a day to 'weed the gravel walks', which appears to have been a full time occupation! When the 7th Earl lived in the house before the First World War, there were twelve indoor servants: a housekeeper, butler, footman, hall-boy and valet, a cook, two kitchen maids, two house maids and three laundry maids. Outside there was a coachman, a groom and a stable boy. The men wore full livery with buttons bearing the Poulett crest.

An even older set of accounts still preserved is the 'Kitchen Booke' which contains details of housekeeping from 1697 to 1727. Many of the pages are signed by Bridgett, the 1st Countess Poulett. Among the items listed and their cost are the following:

14 quarts of milk	1s. (5p)
Side of lamb, a hind quarter of veal and 8 sweetbreads	10s. (50p)
Flesh for ye doggs	2s. (10p)
6 pairs of soles, 6 playse and 5 lobsters	7s. (35p)
18 pigeons and 40 eggs	3s. 6d. (17½p)
Cock and 10 eggs	10d. (4p)
8 large chicken	2s. 8d. (13p)
2 doz. of lemons at	2½d. each 5s. (25p)
4 geese, 3 chicken and a pigg	7s. (35p)
Phesant	1s. (5p)
56 eggs	1s. 2d. (6p)
33 pounds of veal at 2d. a pound	5s. 6d. (27½p)
2 calves heads	1s. 6d. (7½p)
12½ lbs of salmon	13s. 6d. (67½p)

Leaving the house by a door from the ante-room off the Gothic corridor, the tour may be continued outside by a visit to the Stable Courtyard. This is a large quadrangle ranged round a central grassed area with a large oval pond encircled by a cobbled driveway. There is an entrance arch from the north drive, and buildings comprise the old stabling on the north side, stabling and former coach houses on the east (now converted to garages), the Riding School on the south, while the west side is formed by the Grand Entrance Hall which replaced stables originally there. Rainwater heads here are dated 1792, others on the north side are dated 1809, and on the Entrance Hall is one of 1814, the date of Wyatville's porch.

The Riding School measures about 72 ft by 30 ft and is 22 ft high, with an open timbered roof. It provided the family with an admirable enclosed area for viewing or participating in dressage or fancy riding of the 'Spanish Riding School' type and was a prestige amenity, not a school to learn to ride in the modern sense. On Sundays during the time of the 7th Earl, cock-fighting was organized here by his Lordship. In recent years it has been used for many village functions, dances, concerts, flower-shows and the like.

On the opposite side of the yard with the entrance arch, were four stables and a saddle-room, with a straw-loft and three stablemen's bedrooms above. On the east side was the coach house, now converted to garages. In here is the remaining family drag coach made for the 6th Earl in 1870 by Barkers of London. It is painted in dark blue, red and black, and bears the Poulett family crest. Along with it is a small nineteenth-century Governess cart, last used by the wife of the 7th Earl. In 1895 there were eleven coaches here and stabling for sixteen horses. Close by were ten loose boxes and stables, and two harness-rooms, while above were straw-lofts, and the coachman's quarters consisting of a bedroom, kitchen and sitting room. A stable-boy employed here in 1908 recalls that he earned 16 s. a week. His day commenced at 5.30 a.m. and he spent his time in a variety of tasks. When not grooming or feeding the 7th Earl's nine horses, he cleaned the gold-plated harness, scrubbed the black and red tiled floor of the harness room, or cleaned the fire-irons and fender in the saddle-room. He also cared for his Lordship's car, a shiny blue Fiat limousine with brass fittings and blancoed tyres and running boards, which was driven by a chauffeur in a blue and buff uniform with brass buttons. (Villagers recall one car equipped with a bell which was rung so that the approach of the Earl would be recognized! The last car at Hinton House was a 1950 Humber-Pullman limousine which was sold for £290 at the 1968 sale.)

Other rooms on the east side of the yard included a mess room and a farmers' room, while above were two more bedrooms, a granary, lathe room and several lumber rooms. A passage here now leads to the present Estate Office which has an arched and groined roof, and walls hung with maps of the Hinton Estates, and keys. Another passage leads through to the eastern side of the mansion where we find the Saw Mill Yard with ranges of stores and implement sheds.

The gardens and grounds of Hinton House have been developed and altered over the years. Leland mentions a park 'in the syde of a hill'. In 1669 another visitor, Duke Cosmo of Tuscany described the grounds thus:

There are also gardens for utility and pleasure. On the one hand they contain all those sorts of plants and fruits which the climate will allow, and on the other a parterre, very different from the common usage of the gardens in England. For, where these have sanded walks perfectly levelled by rolling them with a stone roller (threaded through the centre with an iron rod, whose ends are joined together in a triangle by which it is pulled to and fro), and between the walks several flat spaces covered with very green turf and without other adornment, this garden of my lord Pawlet is a meadow with different beds having borders of bricks on end, filled with flowers.

In 1684 the Cedar Piece, to the north of the house, was planted with young trees brought from the Holy Land by Margaret, the wife of the 8th Earl of Pembroke. The mother of Lord Poulett at that time was Susan Herbert, the daughter of the 5th Earl of Pembroke, so the trees were no doubt a present from their relatives at Wilton House, where other cedar trees were planted at the same time. A graveyard of family pets with memorial stones could be seen until recent years in the Cedar Piece.

John Loveday in 1736 describes the gardens as 'very pretty'. An illustration of this time shows the front of the house with the grounds divided from the park by stone pillars with ornamental gates and railings.

The 3rd Earl Poulett enlarged the grounds and provided kitchen gardens, when the main road to Dinnington was closed off, and a new road constructed to the north of the church about 1766. An uninterrupted pathway from the mansion to the church was probably made at this time also.

Collinson's illustration of about 1790 shows that the gates and railings had gone by then and the lawns of parkland flowed up to the walls of the house unhindered.

In 1895 the gardens were particularly magnificent, A contemporary description reads as follows:

The lawns stretch round by the state apartments to the rear where there is a pleasant walk a quarter of a mile long, through timbered shrubberies and flower borders. Many other flower beds, borders and specimen trees adorn the grounds, in which hydrants are laid all round the house. On a sloping bank is a collection of magnificent cedars of graceful symmetry and colossal proportions. By the cedars is a foliage-covered walk from the mansion to the church. Nearby is an arched entrance through a doorway to another part of the grounds which are studded with enormous exotics, charming flower borders and parterres. Also a conservatory with a fernery at each end [these contained ornamental ponds and fountains] summer-houses, etc. Adjoining this is the fruit and vegetable garden, containing several vineries, stocked with Black Hammo, Alicante, White Muscat of Alexandria, Lady Downe, Mrs Spence, Gros Colman (both black and white), Nadresfield Court, Gros Marock, Buckland, Sweetwater, Fisher Seedling, Black

Prince, Vens Muscat, etc. The crops of grapes are very large, and the head gardener has taken prizes in many parts of England. The vines are all healthy and in good condition. The hot houses provide roses and other flowers, cucumbers, etc. all the year round. The orchard house, the tomato house, rosery, etc. are all well stocked. The grounds contain figures and vases of artistic value.

The Rosery (or rose garden) was particularly attractive. It has long since disappeared but was situated near the Cedar Piece. It consisted of a circular area of lawn surrounded by a white trellis fence covered with climbing roses. Within the fence were beds of roses arranged symmetrically in circles to the centre, with trellised arches of roses between each bed. It must have been a most pleasant spot to enjoy the sight and scent of the flowers while the sun filtered through the great branches of the cedar trees.

Early this century the conservatories still flourished. They contained tall palm trees, large ferns, lilies, orchids, and all manner of flowers and shrubs. Coloured porcelain parrots hung on swings, and real peacocks strolled on the lawns. Magnolias flowered on the garden walls, while around the grounds were to be found azaleas, rhododendrons and hydrangeas, many growing in pottery urns, made in the Poulett kilns near Chard. There were ornamental pools, with water-lilies and goldfish; rock gardens, and herbacious borders.

After the last war quantities of beautiful fruit, flowers and vegetables were still grown at Hinton House, and a magnificent stand displaying the mansion's produce was always a feature of the annual Horticultural Show, held for many years in the Riding School.

The 'figures and vases' include a fine eighteenth-century lead group of statuary depicting Samson slaying the Philistine with the jawbone of an ass, standing amid the trees in the Cedar Piece. The work is after an original by John van Nost. On the lawn to the west of the house is a white marble figure of a Greek athlete, and an early eighteenth-century brass sundial on a ham-stone pillar. In a niche on the east side stands an eighteenth-century lead figure of Bacchus, clad in a wolf-skin loincloth, and holding a bunch of grapes. To the east of the house a path leads through a tunnel under the drive from the village, so one can walk from the gardens on the south to those on the north without having to encounter either villagers or tradesmen. The sides of the bridge are decorated with stone carvings and coats of arms, etc., which may have come originally from the old west front of the house. To the east a drive leads past flower beds and through the woods to the old Crewkerne road at Stockbridge Brook.

The sunken garden on the south side of the mansion in front of the State Apartments was laid out by the 7th Earl. The balustraded walls are adorned with handsome carved urns of ham-stone decorated with swags of fruit and foliage and in the opening of the walls are carved ham-stone baskets of fruit. A plaque set in the west wall reads: 'This garden was formed in the year 1913 by William John Lydston, 7th Earl Poulett.'

Hinton Park

At the time of the sale of the Hinton St George Estate in 1968 Hinton Park comprised some 1,290 acres including Hinton House and the surrounding gardens and grounds. The enclosure and layout of the park as such commenced early in the sixteenth century. Leland, in his itinerary written about 1544, says: 'This Hugh (Paulet) hath of late made a Parke not far from his House at Henton in the syde of an Hylle.' By 1561 a park called Hinton Park or Upcroft had been formed which was said to be four miles in compass by 1569. In a certificate of Musters forwarded to the Privy Council dated 30 September 1583 there was included a list of parks and enclosed grounds, furnished in connection with proposals for furthering the breeding of horses. The reference to Hinton Park is as follows: 'The Lady Elizabeth Powlett, widow [of Sir Hugh] hath one parke or inclosed ground for deere at Georgehenton of too myles compass and keepeth iii mares according to the statute.' In 1633 Thomas Gerrard, visiting Hinton House, reported that 'It stands in a daynte parke on a dry soile and hath all conveniences suiting such a place in abundance'.

Cosmo of Tuscany in 1669 said that 'around the house is the park, of three miles in circumference, shut in by a thick plantation of trees'. He saw deer in the park 'of two sorts, black and red, to which the mixture of plain, of hill, of coppice wood, and meadow land, together with two plentiful springs of water affords a most suitable abode'. In 1718 a 'New Park' is recorded which probably refers to further extensions. By this time there were two entrance lodges.

In 1736 John Loveday observed: 'By the help of an haw-haw you take in a good view for a low Situacion, particularly an hill at a proper distance beautifully cloathed with trees. The Wilderness and Maze are in the Park, the hedges of it are in great perfection, the building within serves as a banqueting room.' No trace remains today of these rustic diversions, other than a lodge with four pavilions about a mile west of the house. Now known as Keeper's Lodge because of its more recent use as a game larder, it may indeed be the original 'Banqueting Room'.

Over the years the park was gradually enlarged, reaching its present size by about 1800. As the park grew so did the areas of woodland. The last major extension was made in about 1766 when the 3rd Earl Poulett closed the old main road through Hinton at West Street and built a new road to the north of the church. Room was now provided for more extensive kitchen gardens and an uninterrupted path from the mansion to the church. About the same time a further enlargement was made by moving the Dinnington road slightly northwards beyond the brow of the hill to where it now skirts the present Broom's Drive Plantation to Pit Hill, out of sight of the mansion and park.

A new deer park is recorded in 1802 and there was much planting and ornamentation carried on between 1812 and 1817 when the house was being restyled. New 'American Clumps' were planted near the house and the drives much improved. However, after this much of the park was broken up into agricultural holdings to increase the rent roll, and by 1839 the 5th Earl retained only about a quarter of the park as plantations, ponds, and the gardens around the mansion.

The park is now bounded all around by roads, a distance of about 6 miles today. Leaving the village and going north past the church, New Road skirts Church Close and the churchyard, and leads to the main entrance to the park at Broom's Lodge. Here there are pillared entrance gates topped with stone pineapples. This was formed about 1766 when the park was enlarged and a new road built replacing the old road through the village. To the right of the gates was the site of the village horse pond. The wall was built over it and may be seen leaning at an angle because of subsidence over the pond area. According to Frederick James, close by, beyond the Lodge where he once lived, was the burial ground of the Poulett family horses. When they reached the end of their lives, or were injured and had to be put down, they were not fed to the dogs, but were interred in a trench under the wall within the park.

Broom's Lodge itself is an attractive little stone and slate bungalow of about the same date as the gates, situated behind the wall just inside the park. To the left of the gates a tree was planted by the late Countess Poulett in 1953 to commemorate the Coronation of Queen Elizabeth II.

About half a mile along the road to Dinnington is another entrance at Pit Gate, its name taken from the now vanished hamlet of Pit which was close by. This was the entrance for the successive army camps established here during the last war. To the right of the gates stood Pit Cottage, a picturesque though insanitary little building of chalk and thatch which was demolished soon after the war ended.

The road continues to Dinnington and then turns left up the lane by Dinnington Church. Climbing steeply the road forks up Fisher's Lane to North Lodge which lies at the north-east corner of the park. The Lodge is thought to have derived its name from its location as the northerly of two lodges originally built here. North Lodge, now beautifully restored, is traditionally said to be the site of the White Lodge where the 'junket' was held for the Duke of Monmouth, when he was touched by Elizabeth Parcet for the 'King's Evil'. The road here is the route from Ilminster to Crewkerne and the park boundary runs from North Lodge to Warren Hill. About half a mile further on is Clamour Gate where a footpath from Pit Gate emerges. This path was the subject of the dispute between the late Earl Poulett and the villagers of Hinton over the right of way.

About a mile further along, the south-west corner of the park is reached at its highest point at Warren Hill. Here, some 700 ft above sea-level, stands another lodge, Warren House, originally a listed building, which has now been rebuilt. The name Warren may derive from old woodland recorded here in 1360 and named Warener. The road now joins the main A30 from Chard to Crewkerne at St Raynes Hill. Nearby was a fifteen-century hermitage and in later years a lime kiln. Warren Hill is clothed in trees and the woods continue along the boundary road as it turns left into Liddon Hill, where it drops down along the eastern side of the park with Castle Hill on the right. Here on the left is now the main gate for the farms in the park. This entrance is comparatively new, as originally all traffic came in at Brooms Lodge. The road now leads southwards to Harford Lodge. This stretch up to the main A30 road was built about 1770 and replaced a medieval road across the park through the old hamlet of Craft, which was then closed to traffic. The extensive woodland of Harvant Wood now stretches into the park and runs along the road to pass Harford Lodge. Possibly 200 years old, the last of the park lodges is built of red brick and slate. Harvant Wood merges into Stockbridge Wood, and where the road bends sharply just before Stockbridge Brook, are the white gates leading to the carriage drive or promenade through Old Gardens Plantation and Terrace Wood to Hinton House. A short way up the hill the road reaches Hinton St George at the junction of South Street and Gas or Back Lane. Here the park boundary passes along Gas Lane where a door in the wall once led to a golf course now long since disappeared. Passing the almshouses and Phoenix House the village entrance to Hinton House is now reached, closed off by wooden gates. Vine Cottage stands on the right, at one time housing the village telephone exchange and for many years the home of the Estate Bailiff, while opposite stood Gas House with its workshops producing the gas supply for the village.

A visitor going into the park in 1895, describes it in the following way. His somewhat lyrical descriptions may be excused when it is remembered he was writing with a view to selling the Estate.

The park extends over 1,258 acres of rich grass lands, and the gigantic timber testifies to the fertility and depth of its soil. It has long ranges of level slopes, undulations and hills, well interspersed with plantations and fringed with belts. It is green all the year round, for the large number of fir trees and ivy-clad trees mingled with the general timber, gives a freshness of appearance all through the winter. We reach a shelving road, between two pretty bits of woodland which lie high on either side, and where in the autumn, pheasant shooting presents some remarkable rocketings. A little beyond this we reach the 'Lady's Bath', a dell in a jungle, where silver firs of prodigious size, reminding us of California or Vancouver, stand with their clean straight columns, surrounded by immense yew trees and general forest timber. The dell is resonant with the music of song birds and is made lively by the gambols of game, squirrels, and other creatures of the woods. Here is the 'rivershead' a gushing spring protected in a small brick enclosure, which, when open from the top, reveals the flowing crystal liquid which supplies the reservoir, and thence the mansion and the village. There are springs at other parts of the park, one chalybeate in character emptying itself into a stone trough for the cattle; another spring turns a wheel and by its own natural force fills a reservoir. The spring runs in summer and winter. A venerable oak can look back on nine centuries of years, while splendid beeches, limes, sycamores and other foliaged monuments of natural beauty bear evidence of antiquity. Near the Old Lodge Farm are four weird-looking cedars that have seen many generations of their lordly masters pass away; they are of enormous size, and in standing at the base of one of them and looking up through it, its stately form resembles a cathedral pile. Various parts of the park have different designations, thus we find 'Old Park', the 'Great Deer Park', the 'Little Deer Park', where herds of the antlered ruminants formerly existed. A monument of Diana stands in the park, and is a conspicuous object from the mansion. At Nettlebed Copse and Warren Copse there is a grassy slope, affording a choice site for a gallop; it is bounded by a row of ancient forest beeches and a belt of timber and plantations. The three farm homesteads of Pond Hayes, Lodge Farm, and Croft Farm stand in the park, but the contour of the land and placement of the plantations and timber hide them from the mansion and grounds, from which, however, they are at long distances, as the park itself forms a considerable estate in size. The park also contains an enclosure of buildings, which were used as dog kennels by the present Earl Poulett (the 6th Earl) when he kept a pack of hounds there. The reservoir is in the park.'

That somewhat poetical description of Hinton Park may be said to have held good until the sale in 1968. Then, on entering the park at Brooms Lodge, the landscape presented a well wooded appearance, with many oak and horse-chestnut trees skirting the drive. Passing the mansion on the left is Old Gardens Plantation with its carriage drive, surrounded by ornamental shrubs, trees and flower beds. Near here was the mansion's golf course. To the west can be seen the statue of Diana the Huntress on her tall pedestal. Copied from an old Greek original, in 1968 she was in a sad state of repair. An old story in Hinton says that when Diana hears the bell ringing at Hinton House she gets down from her pedestal and drinks from the water in the park. Surrounding the statue is a double ring of large lime trees.

Traces of ha-has can be seen on either side of the road, built to serve as a fence to keep back the deer but to be invisible from the mansion. The ha-has are twice the normal distance from the house, so the lawns are extremely grand. A path leads away to the right to North Lodge and Clamour Gate, passing the nearest visible piece of woodland quaintly known as Drake's Ground Clump. Now our path divides into three, the track to the east leading to the former kennels, with a little cottage and kennel buildings topped with a fine weather vane bearing the figure of a fox. Successive earls maintained their own packs of hounds, but the last to be housed there was the Seavington Hunt pack. The original pack of harriers was started here in 1863 by one Tom Nash. No hunting has taken place in Hinton Park for many years and the cottage and kennels are derelict. Behind the kennels is another belt of woodland known as Harvant Wood which is linked to Old Gardens Plantation by Stockbridge Wood.

Returning to the main path and taking the right-hand fork, the buildings of Croft Farm are reached. The farmhouse (now known as Oakland House) is a handsome building with a recently tiled roof. It has a projecting porch with the upper storey supported on pillars similar to Brown's Farm in Hinton, and dates from the seventeenth century. The house is possibly all that remains of the hamlet which had existed hereabouts since about 1260, named Craft or Hintonscraft (hence 'Croft') and which still appeared on maps as late as 1850. Close by is Oakland Cottage which was converted in 1964 from two smaller cottages. The wooded plantation close to the farm is known as Paddocks. Due south of Croft Farm and on rising ground can be seen the buildings of Lodge Farm (now known as Hinton Park Farm). The farmhouse is a large building of stone and slate with its farm buildings clustered about it. This was the site of another medieval hamlet known as Upcraft. Further south again the land rises steeply to the woods skirting the main road. Here are Warren Copse, with grass-capped Warren Hill in its midst, Nettlebed Copse and Daniel's Hole. Little Springbottom Copse lies to the south-east of Lodge Farm while Withybed Goil almost encircles it to the west. Castle Hill, outside the park, may be seen to the east above the trees of Shippen Lea Goil. The southern part of the park is in West Crewkerne parish.

Retracing our steps back to the footpath past Drakes Ground Clump (which contains two ponds, the haunt of various water birds) the track leads due west. On the right is Diana and her encircling trees. The path lies between areas of woodland known as Cobbles Plantation to the south, and Thorny Clump. Close by is a pond known as Diana's Pond. This was the site of the statue in 1704, at the centre of radiating avenues cut through the woods and shown on an estate map dated 1795. Also shown are clumps of trees arranged scenically while nearer the mansion is a large lake 'planned by Mr Kent', but there is no record that it was ever completed. Diana and her plinth were moved to the present hilltop position when Diana's Pond was created as part of the waterworks in the last half of the eighteenth century. Our path would appear to be the 'shelving road, between two pretty bits of woodland' mentioned in the 1895 description. It is indeed a charming spot with the sloping grassland and trees and woods all around. The path continues through a narrow strip of woodland and crosses a stream whose spring rises close by. On the right is the large wood known as Keeper's Quarry Plantation, the site of the old quarry for Hinton stone. Here now is a series of ponds, waterworks and a pumping house which supplied the water to Hinton St George. In a clearing on the other side is a very old house, possibly the 'banqueting room' first mentioned in 1650 and now the Keeper's Lodge. Traces may still be seen of the four pavilions at each corner of the enclosure. The name derives from occupancy by the Estate Game Keeper, and the construction of a game-larder there after the lodge ceased its original use. Our path leads up to the gate at North Lodge. To the left are two small areas of woodland known as Ratlett's Clumps, while to the right is Butt's Plantation wherein rises the spring known as the Lady's Bath. This part of the park lies in the parish of Dinnington where beyond Butt's Plantation lies Pondhayes Farm.

Crossing now to Keeper's Lodge a path here leads back towards Hinton. The woods beyond the Lodge are known as Beech Copse. Just before the path passes Diana on her plinth to the right, the mound of the modern reservoir is seen on the left. During the Second World War this part of the park was the temporary home of successive army regiments. There were Irish troops, followed by Czechoslovakians, English troops and finally Americans. The US forces did things in grand style. As well as tents under the trees, there were many huts and other buildings, and a hard surfaced road led into the camp from the Dinnington Road. At Pit Gate flew the Stars and Stripes and a notice board proclaimed 'Camp Hinton St George'. After D-Day when the site was vacated, work began to convert it to a prisoner of war camp, but the war ended before the scheme was completed. Very little evidence of the army occupation remains today. From Pit Gate the modern plantation of Brooms Drive follows the line of the road back to Brooms Lodge.

While the park remained closed to public and huntsmen alike, it became a great sanctuary for wild life of all sorts. Jackdaws nested in the old trees in their hundreds; coots, moorhens, and dabchicks haunted the ponds. Rabbits, hares, foxes and badgers could be seen in most places, while the occasional deer ventured out from the denser woodland. Kestrels, sparrowhawks and even buzzards nested there, while partridges and pheasants were left to breed undisturbed. Bats roosted in the old decayed lodges, while white barn owls could be seen swooping about at twilight.

DIANA – HINTON PARK

CHAPTER 12

The Church of St George and the Poulett Monuments

To see the high tower, so stately and tall
Above all the houses, looking so small.
William Barnes

There has been a church at Hinton St George since at least the twelfth century. In 1220 Jocelin, the Bishop of Bath, Glastonbury and Wells granted on 1 August to the Master and Brethren of St Bartholomew's Hospital (founded by Rahere in 1123) various tithes of the sheaves of the church land in Hinton, and also tithes of other sheaves and hay; and two acres suitable for the making of barns; Robert de Barnville having already granted in 1193 'as far as a lay person could' the church to the Hospital for maintenance of priests. The master acknowledged the bishop's jurisdiction by granting him the advowson, and in return was confirmed in all that Robert had given. (About forty years ago a descendent of Robert de Barneville, the late F. Lowry Barnwell lived in the parish at Hinton Place.)

Later there were disputes about the grant. Robert, Prior of Bath, and the Dean and Chapter of Wells, disallowed Jocelin's grant, and about 100 years later, in 1334, Pope John XII had to appoint a commission to settle the question of tithes at Hinton between Bath and Wells and St Bartholomew's Hospital. The Rector of Hinton, Richard de la Hegh was called as one of the witnesses, but the matter was decided in favour of the Hospital. Another Rector, Ralph de Botyler, had already, in gratitude for the good works of the Brethren, given up his lifetime of payments due from them to his church from 6 June 1280. A few years later, in 1341, one named Nicholas-of-the-Yard of Crewkerne, and John and Robert his sons, gave up to the Hospital all their right to a messuage and three acres of land in Hinton, some of which lay next to the land of Thomas Denebaud, one of the lay owners.

It is possible that part of Hinton was included in Henry II's gift to the Abbey of St Stephen at Caen of the church at Crewkerne, which was afterwards exchanged for Burton, and reverted to the Crown from whence it came eventually to the Earls of Devon.

All these early grants were confirmed under a charter of Henry VIII in about 1540 when the church and all tithes, glebes, and houses with their rights were granted to the Hospital of St Bartholomew as well as the patronage of the living. In 1578 a lease, which St Bartholomew's intended to grant, was checked by Queen Elizabeth I in the interest of Sir Amias Paulet, and the matter was held over until he returned from the Embassy in France. St Bartholomew's Hospital still owned land in Hinton until 1860 when their remaining 9 acres and some buildings were sold to Earl Poulett.

The present church building, constructed of local ham-stone and with a fine leaded roof, is a good example of the Perpendicular period of the fifteenth century. It has an exceptionally well-cared for appearance both inside and out.

The Exterior

The main entrance is by the south porch which has an embattled parapet and a niche over the arch, which contains a modern statue of St George. The outer arch has two orders of ogee moulding supported by shafts with moulded caps and bases. The inner doorway also has a moulded pointed arch, and the original timber door and ironwork are still in position. The ceiling is a barrel vault of five bays with ribs and panelling. The walls are faced inside with rubble masonry in thin courses, and there are stone seats on each side. Outside above the buttresses, carved beasts project from the corners but do not serve as water-spouts. The water stoup by the door was discovered under layers of plaster in 1887. The embattled parapet continues around the south-west corner of the church, while the rest of the building has a plain parapet, made to match the alterations of 1814.

The west tower is the glory of the church and was completed about 1495, under the auspices of the first Sir Amias Paulet (d. 1537). It is recorded that the rector of the time, Thomas Marsh, left £4 towards its building in 1494. The tower is in four stages with set-back buttresses continued in shafts set diagonally, and ending in subsidiary pinnacles set in the

St George's Church

middle of the sides. The embattled parapet is decorated with pierced quatrefoil panels and shield centres, and has a moulded cornice. At the south-east corner is a hexagonal staircase turret with its parapet similar to that of the rest of the tower though on a smaller scale, and with pinnacles rising from carved heads. Surmounting the turret is a gilded iron weather-cock, 3 ft 6 in in height and length and dated 1756. The main cornice of the tower, some 5 in below the top of the parapet, is carried around the turret and there are large gargoyles with water-spouts at the corners and centres of each side.

On each side of the tower are beautifully proportioned bell-openings, each of two lights with a transom. All have the original chequer-pattern stone lattice above and below the transom. In the third stage of the south side is an empty statue niche similar to that on the porch. On the west side is a four-centred door contained within a square head with tracery. Above it is a four-light pointed window. On the north side, high up in the second course is a small window to light the bell-ringers' chamber. On the east side is the clock face, painted blue with gilded figures, and below it is another statue niche.

The north wall of the church close to the tower is of uncoursed rubble and is all that remains of the earlier church. Here there was a doorway and the disturbance to the old walling can be seen in the bond to the tower. The north side of the church was originally similar to the south side, but was altered in the early nineteenth century by Jeffrey Wyatville for the 4th Earl Poulett to form the present Poulett pew and memorial chapel. Surrounded by iron railings in the angle of the pew wall and the nave wall is the entrance to the Poulett family vault, enlarged and altered at the same time.

A door surmounted by the family arms leads into the Poulett pew and chapel which together form the north transept. In the angle on the other side of the transept is the rector's vestry bearing the date 1814, which replaced an earlier vestry at the east end of the church.

The great east window is of five lights, altered from the original three lights in 1883. The buttresses on either side were also rebuilt at that time. The east window of the south aisle has five lights with rich tracery and a four-centred arch, and retains its original saddle-bars and stanchions. Between the two windows on the south side may be seen the old priests' door, now blocked, and which has a pointed arch and two orders of moulding.

There are three scratch dials, the ancient clocks, on the exterior of the building. One is on the buttress to the east of the old priests' door; the second is on the west wall of the south aisle and the third is on the south-west buttress of the tower. This last has no visible lines but merely the centre hole for the rod of the sundial.

The Interior

On entering the church by the south door the visitor is immediately impressed by the lightness and airiness of the interior. The fabric has been well cared for over the ages due no doubt to the benevolence of the lords of the manor, and it thus escaped the often unnecessary 'restorations' of the Victorian era which so drastically changed the appearance of many of our ancient churches.

The building today consists of a nave and chancel, north transept, south aisle, south porch and western tower. The south aisle extends westwards and forms a chapel of one bay. Before 1814 there was a similar chapel to the east of the north transept. At that time the north transept was remodelled to form the Poulett family pew, while the chapel to the north-east was altered to form the Poulett memorial chapel. A new vestry was built next to the chapel replacing the old vestry at the east end of the church. Apart from these alterations the main fabric remains much the same as it was in the fifteenth century.

St George's Church – Interior

The Nave

The nave is divided from the south aisle by an arcade of three wide bays and a narrower one at the east end which is splayed to meet the chancel arch. The piers have four roll shafts and the pointed arches are four-centred. At the west end the inner member of the arch is carried on a single short shaft with a pear-shaped base against the wall. The chancel arch is of similar design to the south arcade, as is also the arch of the north transept. The tower arch, however, which is carried to the full height of the nave, is panelled.

The roof of the nave is of particular interest. The fifteenth-century work is intact and is of daring construction in that it has no abutment or support on the north side except for the transept, and none on the south except the lean-to roof of the south aisle, which conveys the thrust of the roof to the outer wall, which itself has no buttressing but the south porch. A.K. Wickham calls it: 'An unusual type . . . the double-framed couple roof of Hinton St George, whose dangerous thrust is only counteracted by the strength of its aisles.' It is divided into six bays by principals without cross-tie in any form, on the undersides of which are thin cusped braces which are purely decorative with no constructional value. Each brace has at its foot a sham hammer-beam of the same thickness, with the end covered by an angel holding a shield, and each pair of braces meet in a short pendant under the ridge piece, thus forming six panels on each side. Each panel is subdivided into four by a lesser rib running each way, thus forming 288 panels in all. At the intersections of the purlins and principals there are bosses and crowsfeet, and smaller bosses at the intersections of the lesser ribs and the cusps of the braces. All the timbers are well moulded. Early this century the roof was light coloured with the angels picked out in bright colours. A plaster cornice was added in 1814 but has since been removed.

The earliest part of the church remaining is the northern part of the north wall of the nave where the uncoursed rubble was visible outside. The north doorway existed behind the present monument to Rebecca Poulett. In the west wall is a glass panel through which can be seen the original stonework of the west wall before the tower was added about 1490. The church was reseated in 1924 when the old box pews were replaced.

The South Aisle

The roof here is of lean-to form and is of the same date and similar construction to the roof of the nave. The roof rests on a moulded stone course. There were formerly sixteen bays having moulded principals and two purlins, forming panels which were sub-divided again. However, the timbers of the seven western bays were renewed in plain form probably in the eighteenth century and many of the remaining timbers were mutilated or renewed. To stop the roof sagging a row of deal struts was inserted which sprang from some distance down the wall and met the roof about a third of its width across. All the timbers were concealed beneath a layer of plaster. Happily all this was removed in the repair work of 1916–17. The missing timbers were re-instated and the principals strengthened. Dating from that time is a boss above the south window of the chapel which was carved in the likeness of Earl Kitchener who was drowned in June 1916 in the sinking of HMS *Hampshire*. The south aisle and its continuation east as a wider chapel are the work of one period although differences may be seen in various details. The east and south windows in the chapel are more richly moulded than those in the aisle, having two orders of moulding while the aisle windows have only one. The east window has five lights with rich tracery and a four-centred arch, and as has already been noted, retains the old saddle-bars and stanchions. The south window is of four lights with the arch two-centred and pointed and with the original bars. This chapel would have been used by former rectors entering by the old priests' door. Here now stands the font recently moved from beside the south door, where it had stood since an earlier move in 1924 from the centre of the church when new seating was installed. The font is one of the links with the original old church and was probably carved during the first half of the thirteenth century. It consists of a circular bowl with an interior depth of 1 ft 3½ in and a diameter of 1 ft 10½ in, and has a sculptured chamfer, a circular pedestal and a base of five rolls placed on a chamfered plinth. The chamfer under the bowl consists of a design of cones placed one against the other like a row of small trumpets with the wide ends forming a band round the lower part of the bowl; while on top of each cone is sculpted a spray of foliage which is characteristic of early English architecture. The design is beautifully executed and the branch bearing the leaves is entwined around each cone so as to present the appearance of a continuous scroll, forming a most effective and pleasing pattern. The whole font would have been painted originally and be rich in colour and gilding. In the fifteenth century, probably when the new church was completed, the bowl of the font was recut and it was adorned with twelve panels decorated with quatrefoils having centres of small shields alternatively charged with the armorial bearings of the Poulett family (sable, three swords in pile argent, pommels and hilts or) and the armorial ensign of St George (argent a cross gules). At the same time the early English circular shaft was ornamented with ten trefoil-headed panels, and the whole of the new work with the tinctures on the shields would have been painted in colour. The work was probably carried out at the behest of Sir Amias Paulet, whose mother was the heiress of the Denebauds. The carved oak font cover was made in 1915 by Wippel's of Exeter.

The Chancel and Sanctuary

On the north and south sides of the chancel, Perpendicular arches open into the Poulett memorial chapel and the south chapel respectively. The arches have only one order of moulding on both edges, and like the tower arch, the soffit is sunk panelled, with the panels arched and cusped at the ends from top to bottom.

The original roof of the chancel has been replaced by a pointed barrel vault of three bays with longitudinal ribs, in plaster to imitate stone.

The great east window was enlarged from three to five lights when the stained glass was inserted in 1883. The old mouldings were followed in the new. The south window is an old pointed one of two lights and retains its ancient saddle-bars. On the north side the window sill has been removed and the jambs carried down to form the doorway into the rector's vestry. On the south side is a piscina with a quatrefoil bowl under a trefoil head. It is low down on the wall which is a reminder that the floors of the nave and sanctuary were originally on one level before the present step was built in 1881. The woodwork in the sanctuary – reredos, panelling, door and altar rails – were installed in 1933 in memory of a former rector, the Reverend Frank Shelmerdine. Before then the sanctuary had been hung with curtaining since 1911. The stone floors were relaid in 1937, replacing a parquet floor of oak and walnut laid in the sanctuary in 1903. The oak choir stalls were installed in 1903 also but originally had heavy ornamental carved decorations at each end. These were removed when the church was reseated in 1924. Before 1814 a vestry was situated behind a screen across the east end of the chancel with entrance doors on either side of the altar.

The North Transept (Poulett Pew, Memorial Chapel) Vestry and Vault

The north transept was rebuilt in 1814 by Jeffrey Wyatville for the 4th Earl Poulett, who was completing work at Hinton House after the accidental death of James Wyatt in September 1813. It is possible that Wyatt produced the original plans for the alterations in the church, to form the Poulett Pew and the memorial chapel. The original old walls appear to have been retained in the pew, and also the fine four-light pointed window of fifteenth-century date. The roof was renewed with a plaster ceiling while the floor is raised above the level of the nave affording the family a good view of the congregation during services. A wooden screen divides the pew from the body of the church with a door and steps down to permit access to the nave. The pew was furnished with purple lining and curtains, and purple upholstered furniture.

The memorial chapel, reached by a door in the east wall of the pew, originally formed a chapel similar to that on the south side of the church. The north wall has been built out to the line of the pew wall and the old three-light square-headed window re-set in it. The east wall remains but its gable end was cased on the outside and the old pointed window filled in. Traces of this window can be seen outside above the vestry. The vestry was built in the angle of the sanctuary and the memorial chapel and bears the date 1814. The chapel also has a plaster ceiling and the roof outside was finished off with a new plain parapet which runs round most of the church. The Poulett monuments were then re-arranged in the new chapel.

As well as the work on the pew and chapel, the 4th Earl commissioned Wyatville to enlarge and improve the family burial vault. The original vault dates from the late sixteenth century and was probably built for Sir Amias Paulet or Sir Anthony Paulet. It is situated under the memorial chapel and is constructed of rendered brick, measuring some 15 ft west to east, by 10 ft north to south, with a barrel-vaulted roof 10 ft high. To the west there is a later seventeenth-century entrance of brick, also with a vaulted roof. Wyatville's new extension is situated under the Poulett pew which was built after the vault was completed. It is of plain brick construction with an arched vaulted roof, giving the pew above its raised floor. The vault is some 20 ft west to east and 15 ft north to south, and 12 ft high. When the extension was built the old vault was sealed off by a brick wall. There is room in here for twenty-four coffins resting on two shelves on each side of the chamber.

The entrance to the vault is built against the external west wall of the Poulett pew, and is formed by a ham-stone porch with a stone parapet, and enclosed in a paved and railed courtyard. A flight of fourteen stone steps leads down from the oak west door which is painted blue with black iron studs. At the foot of the steps an arched opening leads directly into the vault to a passage 2 ft 9 in wide between the shelves and ending at the blocked wall of the old vault.

A recent survey revealed that the old vault contains twenty-two coffins in the entrance area. As far as can be ascertained these contain the remains of Sir Amias Paulet and his wife, Sir Anthony and his wife, the three Barons and their wives, the 1st Earl, his wife and children, the 2nd and 3rd Earls, and one son of the 4th Earl who appears to have been left behind when his mother, brothers and sisters were moved into the new vault in 1814. Also interred here are Bernard Hutchings, a servant and close friend of the family, and Nathaniel Lloyd, the uncle of the 3rd Countess Poulett. Several of the coffins are richly decorated and that of the 1st Earl bears an earl's coronet in applique.

In the new extension there are now seventeen lead-lined coffins on the shelves, containing the remains of the 4th, 5th, 6th and 8th Earls, their wives and some of their children. These coffins were originally covered in red or black velvet, and that of Rosa, Countess Poulett bears a large open coronet. Outside, close by, a rainwater head bears the date 1814.

The Tower

On the ground floor behind the oak screen, dating from 1917, is the present choir vestry. From here a narrow spiral stone staircase leads up first to the organ loft. The Gothic front of the loft was built in about 1814, probably by Wyatt or Wyatville, while the Royal Arms are those of King George III, dated 1812. It is made of Coade stone and is by Coade and Sealey of London. The present organ, by Speechly of London, was installed in 1904 and replaced an earlier one of 1876 which had been a gift of the Reverend James Ratcliffe Dolling, a former rector. The present organ was electrified in 1945, when electric lighting was also installed in the church replacing the old gas system. Before this the organ was blown by hand. The handle of the pump can still be seen on the north side of the organ.

Higher up the staircase is the bell-ringers' chamber and the works of the clock. The present clock and time system, installed in 1948, is by Gent & Co. of Leicester. The chimes were restored in 1903 in commemoration of the Coronation of King Edward VII after a silence of twenty-five years.

The six bells can be seen from a door even higher up the tower. They were rehung in 1930 and are dated and inscribed as follows:

1. 1922 by Taylor of Loughborough. Lt Col W.D. Lowe, D.S.O., M.C., Litt D. 'A verray parfit gentil Knight.'

2. 1828 by Kingston of Bridgwater.
3. 1756 by Bayley, Street & Co. of Bridgwater.
4. 1624 by Wiseman of Montacute. 'All that hath breath praise the Lord.'
5. 1783 by Davis.
6. 1624 by Wiseman of Montacute.
'I sound the sick to bed: Repent,
I sound to bed the sick: Repent.
In hope of life when breath is spent.'

A door at the top of the staircase leads out on to the roof of the tower. A magnificent view of the surrounding countryside is obtained from here and a closer look may be had at the gilded weather-cock made by Thomas Bayley of Bridgwater. The tower roof, like the roof of the nave, is covered in lead.

Memorials to the Poulett Family

Hinton St George church naturally contains a large number of memorials to the first family of the village, in the form of plaques, monuments and stained-glass windows.

In chronological order they may be viewed as follows:

The oldest monument in the church lies beneath the screen of the Poulett pew and is an effigy of a knight in armour on a tomb chest. Traditionally it is thought to represent Sir John Denebaud whose daughter Elizabeth married Sir William Paulet in the fifteenth century and brought the Hinton Estates to the Poulett family. Sir John, however, died in 1429 and the figure is in plate armour of about 1475 with the head and feet resting on lions. The front of the tomb is ornamented with three panels with cusped heads, divided by two quatre-foil panels with shields in the centre. The figure was once brightly coloured and traces of this can be seen still.

Close by on the floor near the pulpit is a very interesting brass. It depicts a Knight and his Lady with a shield of arms and an inscription plate. This reads:-

Hic jacent Johes Thudderle Armig Fili et Heres Johes Thudderle et Alicia Ux eius Quonda Ux Johis Juyn Militis Filia Willm By the More.
(Here lies John Chudleigh Esquire, son and heir of John Chudleigh, and Alice his wife, formerly the wife of Sir John Juyn, daughter of William by the More.)

No date is given but from the style of the armour and the lady's dress it is from about 1475. The knight wears plate armour with a fluted helmet, from which his long hair protrudes. He wears his sword suspended behind him, and a dagger. His lady wears a butterfly headdress with a close fitting gown cut low in front, with fur edging and cuffs, and a sash round her waist. The shield bears the arms of Chudleigh of Silverton, Devon, showing acorns and oak trees, and birds' heads. The brass was placed in its present position in 1948 having been away from the church for many years. It was formerly on the floor on the south side of the chancel. It was re-discovered in an outbuilding at Grove Park, Warwickshire in 1924 but how or when it got there is unknown. For some time its origin was a mystery, but it was finally traced to Hinton St George through a reference in *The Gentleman's Magazine* of 1812, which described the brass in its original position. By the kindness of Lady Dormer of Grove Park the brass finally found its way home. John Chudleigh was the half-brother of William Paulet who married Elizabeth Denebaud. Their mother was Margaret de Burton who married three times, first about 1400 to John Dorchester; second about 1404 to Thomas Paulet (7) the father of William; and third about 1410 to John Chudleigh, the father of John who is commemorated on the brass.

To the north of the chancel is the Poulett memorial chapel with its collection of monuments almost without equal in Somerset. In here are the next group of memorials in date order.

Against the north wall are two similar monuments made of beer-stone on ham-stone bases. They commemorate (to the right) Sir Amias Paulet and (to the left) his son Sir Hugh Paulet, together with their wives. They appear to have been made at the same time, probably by Sir Hugh for himself and his father. The decoration is ornate with Gothic and Renaissance detail. A figure of Sir Amias lies dressed in plate armour and a helmet with a raised visor. By his side is his second wife Lora Kellaway, in a veiled headdress. Along the front of the tomb are the kneeling figures of their three sons and one daughter, at desks with open books. Above are the arms of the Paulets impaling those of Kellaway. Over the canopy is the inscription: *Hic jacet Amicius Poulet Miles, Qui obiit Decimo Die Aprilis 1537* (Here lies Amias Paulet Knight who died the tenth day of April 1537).

The tomb of Sir Hugh is very similar. He lies here with his wife Philippa Pollard and there are figures of their three sons and two daughters. The inscription above reads: *Hic jacet Hugo Poulet, Miles, Qui obiit Die Decembris Anno Dni.* (No date is given.) (Here lies Hugh Paulet, Knight, who died December Anno Domini. . .)

On the west wall of the chapel is the tomb of Sir Amias Paulet, the Keeper of Mary, Queen of Scots, the son of Sir Hugh. He died in 1588 and was originally buried in the old church of St Martin in the Fields. When that church was rebuilt in 1728, the first Earl Poulett removed the body and most of the monument to Hinton. Apparently the parishioners of St Martin's refused to re-erect the monument in their new church.

The figure of Sir Amias is in alabaster and is thought to have been made about 1610. Francis Bacon is said to have erected a monument to his friend Sir Amias in St Martin's and it may well be that this effigy is Bacon's tribute to his old chief made over twenty years after his death. The figure lies on a mat which is rolled up under the head and turned up under the feet. Sir Amias wears plate armour with a ruff, and his head is bare. He lies on an altar tomb which was probably remade when it was set up at Hinton. This is flanked by two marble columns with bases and voluted capitals supporting the overhead canopy. There are no less than seven separate inscriptions on the monument. On the entablature:

Honoratissimo Patri D'Amicio Pouleto Aquite Aurato Insulae Prefecto Apud Christianissimum Regem Quandam Legato Nobilissime Ordinis Garterii Cancellario et Serenissima principis Elizabetha Consiliario Antonius Monumentum posuit.
(To his most honoured father Amias Paulet, Knight and Captain of the Island [Jersey]. To the most Christian King at one time most noble Envoy, Chancellor of the Order of the Garter, and Counsellor to the most serene Princess Elizabeth, Anthony has raised this monument of filial devotion.)[1]

Beneath this are the words:

St Martin's Church in Westminster Being Pulled Down And it Being Refused to Place This Monument in the New Church There, It was removed with the Body to this Place,

---

1. Translations of inscriptions on the tomb of Sir Amias Paulet are by Dom John Stephan, O.S.B., of Buckfast Abbey.

In respect to the Memory of Sir Amos Poulett By The First Earl Poulett, Knight
Companion of the Most Noble Order of the Garter Anno 1728.
Two more inscriptions flank the Poulett armorial bearings over the effigy. The left one reads:

GARD LA FOY

Quod verbo Servare Fidem (Poulete) Solebas
Quam bene conveniunt haec Tria verba tibi
Quod gestis Servare Fidem (Poulete) solebas
Quam bene conveniunt Haec tria Signa tibi
patria te Sensit, Sensit Regina Fidelem,
Sic Fidus Civis Sicque. Senator eras.
Te Fidum Christus Te fidum Ecclesia Sensit
Sic Servas inter multa pericla Fidem
Ergo Quod servo Princeps Ecclesia nato
Patria quod fido cive sit orna dolet,
Interea Christus defuncti facta Coronat
Aquo Servatam viderat esse Fidem
Margareta Poulet hoc Epitaphium moeroris simul
Et amoria in perpetuum testem Amicio Conjugi
Sua Charissimo Clarissimo Dicavit.

(KEEP THE FAITH

Since by word thou was wont to 'Keep the Faith'
How well these three words become thee, Paulet
As by deeds thou was wont to 'Keep the Faith'
How well these signs become thee.
Thy country and thy queen knew thee as true,
And so was thou as citizen and Senator.
Christ in His Church relied on thy loyalty
As thou didst prove it amid many dangers.
Hence while a Queen mourns over a subject,
The Church over a son and country over a citizen,
Meanwhile Christ His dead servant's deeds crowns,
Margaret Paulet has raised this monument of grief
And of Love, as a perpetual memorial to Amias her spouse
Most dear and most renowned.)

The right hand inscription reads:

Conjugis est (testante Deo) pars altera Conjux
Vir Caput est, unum corpus uterque refert.
Uno Caro, mens una, thoro sociata jugati.
Solamen Vitae praesidium que suae;
Ergo me luctus quis par queat esse dolori
Cui vitae pars est altera dempia meae,
Sed quid flere juvat non sic revocabere, conjux

Namque tibi pietas stravit ad astra viam
Haec Spes Sola juvat qui nos conjunxit in Unum
Hinc sibi postremo jungere velle die.

(God's word declares the wife is her husband's counterpart;
He is the head, but with her one body he makes,
One flesh, one spirit, united intimately.
He is the comfort and guardian of her life.
Whence no one can grieve as I do
For the loss of half my life;
Weeping availeth little, it will not restore thee to me;
For thee hath piety prepared the way to heaven,
This hope alone helps, that He who united us here
Will re-unite us on the last day.)

Beneath the effigy is the following inscription in old French:

Passant Arreste, Icy, Voy L'honneur D'Angleterre
La Foy, La Piete, La Bonte, La Valeur,
Bref, Des Autres Virtus, Le Plus Beau Le Meilleur
Que Ce Petit Tombeau Dedans La Terre Enserre
Non Non Iene Croy pas qu'un si petit De Terre
Couvres Tant virtus, Ait Esteint tant Honneur
Que ce preux Chevalier, ce Renomme Seigneur
Avoit Acquis En paix avoit acquis En Guerre
Ce Nestoit que Douceur, Savoir, Integrite,
Prudence et Bon Conseil, Constance et Gravite
Dont le Ciel Honoroit ce Coeur cette ame Belle
La Vertue ne meurt point; Son los est Eternell;
Ce Tombeau au tient Ses os; sa Belle ame est au ciel
Sa Lovange Icy Bas est Grande est Immortelle.

(Pilgrim, stay here and behold England's honour
For Faith and Piety, Goodness and Valour,
In brief, the best and comeliest model of all virtues
Which this tomb enshrines in its bosom.
No, no, I can't believe that a pinch of earth
Covers so much virtue or ends so much glory
As this noble Knight, this renowned Lord
Had won in peace as well as in war.
There was naught but Sweetness, Learning, Integrity,
Prudence and Wisdom, Constance and Gravity
With which Heaven had honoured this great heart and soul.
Virtue dieth not; its reward is everlasting.
This tomb his bones retain, his soul is acclaimed by heaven.
His praise here is great and immortal.)

There are two more inscriptions on the base of each column. That on the left reads:

The former age ceast not their praise to sound
In whom one special virtue might be found
All virtues in this noble Knight did dwell
What age might then suffice his praise to tell.

On the right:

E.R.
Never shall cease to spread wise Paulet's Fame
These shall speak, and men shall blush for shame
Without offence to speak what I do know,
Great is the debt England to him doth owe.

The letters 'E.R.' above this last inscription are thought to stand for Elizabeth Regina and may thus indicate that these two verses are personal tributes to a faithful servant by his sovereign.

On the south side of the chapel, beneath the chancel arch, is the large monument to Sir Anthony Paulet, son of Sir Amias, and his wife Katherine Norris. It is made of Bath

Monument to Sir Anthony Paulet

freestone. The two effigies lie on a table tomb, the lady on the right as the daughter of a peer. The bearded Sir Anthony wears plate armour and is bare-headed. Katherine has a ruff and a jewelled headdress. Small figures of their five sons and five daughters appear on each side of the monument. Each daughter has a shield with the Paulet arms impaling a blank half-shield signifying that they were unmarried at the death of their father. Two, however, have the Paulet arms impaled on the opposite side to the other three, signifying that they had already died unmarried. The monument is entirely Renaissance work with a four-centred coffered arch over the figures, supported on columns on each side. The top of the monument is decorated with carved heraldic achievements, obelisks, helmets and crests. An inscription on the north side reads:

Hic jacet Antonius Poulet Miles et Dux Insulae Jersey, Qui obiit 22 Die Julii Anno Dni, 1600.
(Here lies Anthony Paulet, Knight and Lord of the Isle of Jersey, who died 22nd July 1600.)

On the south side an inscription reads:

Hic jacet Dna Katherina Poulet Uxor Antonii Poulet Militis Filia Unica Henrici Dni Norreis Baronis de Rycot qui obiit 24 Die Martii Anno Dni 1601.
(Here lies Lady Katherine Paulet, wife of Anthony Paulet, Knight, only daughter of Henry Norris, Baron Rycot, who died 24th March 1601.)

The remaining monument in the chapel is against the east wall and is surely the most remarkable in the church. It is a memorial to John, 1st Baron Poulett (d. 1649), the son of Sir Anthony. It is built of plaster in a richly decorated Baroque style. Sir Nikolaus Pevsner suggests that it dates from the early eighteenth century and could be the work of an itinerant foreigner, possibly a Portugese. Katherine Esdaile in her book *English Church Monuments* in which it is also illustrated, refers to it thus: '. . . the most amazing being the astounding work at Hinton St George showing the soul chained to mortality but rising on outspread wings towards immortality'.

There is a richly decorated sarcophagus resting on a sphinx and two lions. This is flanked by two wild figures, presumably the male and female Poulett supporters. The top of the sarcophagus rises in the middle amid thick acanthus foliage where a winged figure with two trumpets stands on skulls. Above this figure is a thick garland of flowers hanging from the looped-up corners of a raised curtain. The entablature is encrusted with decoration and surmounted with a coat of arms, while above it all sit two cherubs holding a wreath of leaves. At the sides are two over-sized Ionic columns surmounted by urns. An inscription beneath reads:

John Lord Poulet first Baron of Hinton St George married Elizabeth daughter and Heire of Christopher Kenn Esq of Kenn in this County, by whom he had three sons and vii daughters. He died March ye 29 Ann Dom 1649.

On a side panel is what appears to be the remains of another inscription which reads:

Anne one of the Daughters & Coheirs of Sr Thomas Brown of Wallcot in Northamptonsheer Baronet by whom hee had two sons & foure Daughters hee dyed the 15 of September 1665.

Monument to 1st Baron Poulett

This seems to be all that remains of a memorial inscription to the 2nd Baron Poulett and refers to his second wife Anne Brown.

The next monuments chronologically are in the Poulett pew. Against the east wall is a handsome bust by the sculptor John Michael Rysbrack of John, 1st Earl Poulett. It stands on a plinth above a large classical base inscribed as follows:

John Earl Poulett born April 26 1675 succeeded his Father as Baron Poulett the 20 of June 1679. Soon after the Accession of Queen Anne became a Privy Councillor and having been one of the Commissioners for the Treaty of Union Anno 1706 was the same year on the 29 December created Viscount of Hinton St George and Earl Poulett. Having declined accepting for some years several places of great Distinction he consented to be appointed on the 8 August 1710 First Commissioner of the Treasury in which station he continued till the year 1711 when on 12 June he was declared Lord Steward of her Majesty's Household, on 26 of October 1712 was elected Knight Companion of the Most Noble Order of the Garter at which time he was likewise Lord Lieutenant and Custos Rotulorum of Sommersetshire. He married Bridgett Daughter and Coheiress of Peregrine Bertie Brother of Robert Earl of Lindsey by whom he left 4 sons and 4 daughters dying the 29 May 1743.

This is only the Monument of a Friend's Grief – the Earl Poulett –
His monument is that Fame which he has left in the world.

Nova Dignitatis Insignia domui suae intulisse, nomen suum novis adauxisse. Titulis minima erat pars laudum Illius, qui Virtute morum Elegantia, Animiq Vi Humano etiam generi honorem addidit.

(He conferred new distinctions of rank upon his house, and with these distinctions increased the importance of his name. His titles were only the smallest part of his renown, for by his virtuous conduct he brought elegance, and by his forceful personality he brought honour to humanity as a whole.)
Erected at the Expense of the widow.

On the opposite wall is a memorial to the 1st Earl's widow which takes the form of a sculptured bust with a blue marble obelisk background, and with a large classical inscribed base which reads, in Latin:

Verus, Comes Poulettus
Amore, et Pietate, erga Parentum
Praeditus
Bridgettae Comitessae Poulett
Quae obiit anno 1747
Hoc monumentum excitavit
Ah Matrum Optima
Vale
Te Honos, te virtus, te Beneficentia
Te incorrupta Fides, te Amicitia
Deplorat

(Vere, Earl Poulett possessed with love and dutiful affection for his parent erected this monument to Bridgett Countess Poulett, who died in the year 1747. Ah, Best of Mothers, farewell. You are lamented for your honour, your virtue, your generosity, your unswerving loyalty and your friendship.)

There are no memorials in the church to John, the 2nd Earl or his twin brother Peregrine. To the left of the 1st Earl's monument is a large marble plaque to the memory of Vere, 3rd Earl Poulett, the former's third son. It reads:

Near this place are deposited the mortal remains of Vere Earl Poulett who adorned the high station in which he was placed with many excellent endowments and eminent virtues. In public life conspicuous for unquestionable loyalty and duty to the king and a sincere regard for his country. Steadfast in his attachments to both he preserved in all his conduct an integrity unsullied and an independence unshaken. Though he accepted no lucrative office yet actuated by true patriotism he spared no thought nor pains to promote the interest of the state. Zealous on all occasions to aid by his counsel and advice every measure that tended to its welfare and prosperity.
In private life distinguished by a peculiar urbanity of manners, a transcendent courtesy and affability and a prompt disposition to acts of kindness and benevolence. Blessed with an ample fortune the enjoyment of which was neither spoiled by miserable

avarice nor disgraceful prodigality he maintained the ancient dignified character of nobility by a generous hospitality. Studious of letters and elegant arts which he had cultivated from his youth he continued the pursuit and experienced the consolation and delight which was offered to a liberal mind in every period of life fulfilling all relative and social duties. He secured the esteem and love of all who knew him and will be recorded in their memories as an indulgent husband, an affectionate father and a sincere friend. Afflicted with a long and painful disorder under which he expressed no murmur of impatience he at length closed a virtuous life with the same tranquillity and composure in which he had led it on the 14th day of April 1788 aged 78 years. As a last tribute to so eminent a character and more especially in grateful remembrance of the constancy of his affection during a happy conjugal union of 34 years this monument is erected by the express order of his faithful and affectionate widow who served her Lord 31 years, dying on the 26th day of April 1819 in the 87th year of her age. Dignified yet affable in her manner, kind and condescending in her acquaintance and affectionate and undeviating in her friendship, she closed a long and useful life in the same and steadfast hope of a glorious and blessed immortality.

The plaque is flanked by two classical female figures, one holding a baby and the other with a child at her side. Draperies below bear the Poulett arms in colour. The memorial was designed by Sir Richard Westmacott, RA.

Memorials to two more of the children of the 1st Earl may be seen to the west of the Poulett pew on the north wall of the nave. There are three monuments here and the centre one is an elaborate memorial to the Honourable Anne Poulett. The white marble plaque on a blue marble base is surmounted by an obelisk of pink marble with two classical figures by an urn. One has an owl and the other has a dog at her feet. Above them is a medallion with a portrait of the deceased. The Poulett Arms appear below the inscription which reads:

Sacred to the memory of the Honourable Anne Poulett son of the 1st Earl Poulett Knight of the Garter etc., and a member for Bridgewater in four Parliaments. Whose sedate fortitude and steady resolution in everything which was just. Whose sincerity of friendship, and propriety of judgement and universal knowledge could not avert that death which tore him from his afflicted family and friends on the Xth of July MDCCLXXXV to receive the reward of a well spent and virtuous life.

In grateful memory of the many years she knew thy worth accept a sister's tears. Thy spotless truth and love fraternal, claim this sad last tribute to thy hallowed name to guard thy ashes has she rear'd this stone, T'express thy friendship and record her own.

This sister was Lady Susan Poulett who had earlier put up the next monument to their sister, Lady Rebecca. This is a large marble plaque sumounted by a pink obelisk with a flying cherub holding a portrait medallion. The inscription reads:

Rebecca Poulett youngest daughter of John Earl Poulett of Hinton St George by Bridgett his wife, daughter and coheiress of Peregrine Bertie son of ye Earl of Lindsey, died March the Second MDCCLXV.

Many daughters have done virtuously but thou excellest them all. This monument is erected to her memory by her sister, Susan Poulett.

Above the pulpit are two plaques, the topmost is of marble surmounted by a blue obelisk with a garlanded urn and a portrait of the deceased. The inscription reads:

Here lies Nathaniel Lloyd Esq. Uncle of the present Countess Poulett whom he bred up and educated almost from her early youth leaving her at his Death, The greatest share of his Thoughts and his residuary legatee who, in gratitude of such his tender attention made it her request that he might have burial in or near the place where she herself intends to be interred whenever it should please God to call on her to resign that life which he gave. He was early engaged in mercantile business in which he acquired no less reputation than Wealth; he was a man of letters and much admired for his cheerful disposition and that which still more charmed people's estimation of him, his great honour and punctuality. His loss could not avoid being severely felt by the poor on whom he conferred many acts of charity both living and dying. His philosophic turn of mind only appears by his declining business at a time when he might have doubled his fortune but may be read in these lines in which he made his last request to have inscribed on the monument – Nor love thy life nor bale but what thou livst. Live well how long or short permit to heaven – He departed this life 21st Feb 1711 in the 80th year of his life.

The first memorial of the three on the north wall of the nave commemorates the 4th Earl. Also designed by Sir Richard Westmacott, this is a large marble plaque decorated with draperies and acanthus leaves. Underneath is a medallion with the Poulett and Pocock coats of arms. The inscription reads:

Near this place are deposited the mortal remains of the Rt. Honourable John, 4th Earl Poulett and Viscount Hinton and 8th Baron Poulett[2] of Hinton St George. Lord Lieutenant and Custos Rotulorum of Somerset. Colonel of the 1st Regiment of Somerset Militia and of the Eastern Regiment of Yeomanry Cavalry. One of the Lords of His Majesty's Bedchamber, Recorder of Bridgewater and a Knight Companion of the Most Ancient Order of the Thistle. Who died on the 14th January 1819 in the 63rd Year of his age.

To a Kind and placid disposition he united the most perfect suavity of manners and was beloved and respected by all who knew him. In the despatch of the duties of his public station he acted with the strictest honour and fidelity. His loss will therefore be sensibly felt both in public and private life and his liberality to the poor will long be remembered with gratitude.

He married first Sophia, Daughter of Admiral Sir George Pocock, Knight of the Bath by whom he had ten children. He married secondly, Margaret Lady Smith Burges, Relict of Sir John Smith Burges Bart of Thorpe Hall in the County of Essex, and only daughter and heiress of Ynyr Burges Esq. of East Ham in the same County who in testimony of her affection has caused this monument to be erected.

A second memorial to the 4th Earl and his family is the great east window. The stained-glass by Clayton and Bell was inserted in 1883 and the window was enlarged from three lights to the present five. The work was commissioned by the 4th Earl's youngest daughter, Lady Augusta Poulett. The main theme of the window is the Ascension of Our Lord into

---

2. The 4th Earl is believed to be the 7th Baron Poulett. Although it raises the question of an unrecognized Baron, the inscription is apparently in error.

Heaven with the kneeling disciples around Him. Below are five small scenes depicting from left to right: Mary Magdalene and Jesus in the Garden of Gethsemane; The Road to Emmaus; The Last Supper; Jesus and Doubting Thomas; and Jesus appearing to the Disciples. An inscription beneath reads:

This window is erected to the Glory of God and in memory of John 4th Earl Poulett and Sophia his wife and their 10 children, by Augusta Mary their youngest daughter.

At the opposite end of the church, on the west wall is a white marble plaque with a black surround, surmounted by the arms in colour of the Poulett and Beaufort families, inscribed:

Sacred to the Memory of Mary, second daughter of John 4th Earl Poulett K.G. and widow of the Lord Charles Henry Somerset, second son of Henry 5th Duke of Beaufort, K.G. Born February 24th 1788 Died June 11 1860. Her remains rest in one of the catacombs in the Brompton Cemetery and by permission of her brother John 5th Earl Poulett, this tablet is placed here. (It being the home of her youth and one which she so much loved.) In grateful remembrance of the most beloved of mothers by her only son Colonel Poulett G.H. Somerset, C.B. and M.P. for the County of Monmouth.

Lady Mary's sister is commemorated by the stained-glass in the centre window of the south wall. The glass depicts the Annunciation of the Virgin Mary and was inserted in 1888. The brass plaque beneath records that:

This window was erected by Rosa, widow of William Henry 6th Earl Poulett in affectionate memory of Augusta youngest daughter of John 4th Earl Poulett.

The remaining memorials in the Poulett pew are the next to be considered. To the left of Lady Poulett's monument is one to the tragic family of the 5th Earl. Above a large inscribed marble plaque stands a mourning female figure, against a dark marble obelisk, with a dove in a cloud above. She leans on a draped column with the names of the four children commemorated:

John, Vere, Margaret and Amias – The Lord gave and the Lord hath taken away. Blessed be the name of the Lord. Not my will but Thine be done.

The inscription below reads:

In Remembrance of John Rolle, Viscount Hinton born the 8th of June 1821, died the 18th August 1843 aged 22 years. He was an officer in the Grenadier Guards.
    Vere, 2nd Viscount Hinton, born the 20th August 1822, died the 29th August 1857 aged 35 years. He was an officer in the 68th Light Infantry and afterwards Colonel of the 1st Somerset Militia.
    The Lady Margaret Charlotte Poulett was born on the 16th of July 1830, died on the 31st May 1834 aged 3 years and 9 months.
    The Honble Amias Poulett was born on the 6th February 1835. He was a captain in the Grenadier Guards, served with his regiment in the Crimea, was at the memorable siege and taking of Sevastopol in the years 1855–6 and died on the 20th of February 1857 aged 22 years.
    These four dearly loved children of John 5th Earl Poulett and of Charlotte his wife it

pleased the Almighty to take unto himself in the bloom of youth leaving their afflicted parents childless. This monument is erected to their loving memory in deep sorrow for their irreparable loss, though in humble resignation to the Divine Will, by their disconsolate mother Charlotte Fanny Poulett.

The monument was designed by Edward James Physick of London.

The window here is also in memory of these four. It shows scenes from the life of David. Much of the glass is in deep shades of purple, blue and red. From left to right the scenes depict: Saul anointing David; David the shepherd boy; David with the head of Goliath; and the crowning of David. Beneath is a brass plaque which reads:

To the Glory of God and in memory of John, Vere, Margaret and Amias. The four children of John 5th Earl Poulett and Charlotte his wife. They were of this world where the youngest and the loveliest die the soonest. They are Gone! and their Mother erects this window as a memento of her grief and affection.

The memorial by the pulpit is a white marble plaque on a blue base and was erected by the 6th Earl Poulett in memory of his family:

In memory of Vice-Admiral the Hon. George Poulett, R.N. (2nd son of John 4th Earl Poulett) who departed this life suddenly, February 10th 1854, and his wife Catherine Sophia (eldest daughter of Sir George Dallas, Bart) who departed this life April 11th 1831. And their daughter Augusta Margaret who died 11th September 1836 aged 16 years, also of their sons, George a Captain in H.M. 54th Regiment who died October 5th 1850 aged 30 years. Henry Ashton Vane a Lieutenant in the Native Infantry of Bengal who died August 26th 1846 aged 24 years. John Powell who died in infancy April 2nd 1829. This tablet is inscribed with the names of his parents, sister and brothers by the only survivor of his family William Henry 6th Earl Poulett.

Too early lost! In life's unfolding scene. All that I loved like shadows passed away. So bright and fair their future might have been, to realms where sorrow comes not nor decay. They sleep in hope and let not grief repine that far apart their kindred ashes rest for memory keeps them in her inmost shrine and faith awaits the union of the blest.

Above the south door is a monument in the form of a marble obelisk with a cross on a rock and bears the following inscription:

Sacred to the Memory of Emma Sophia The Gentle, Affectionate and truly loved wife of William Henry 6th Earl Poulett. Her Kindness of Heart Amiable Benevolent and Charitable Disposition Caused her to be beloved and esteemed by all who knew her. She departed this life the 16th September 1876 aged 38 years.

Emma was the second wife of the 6th Earl. A memorial to his third wife may be seen in the east window of the south aisle. The stained-glass by Clayton and Bell depicts the Crucifixion. A brass plaque beneath reads:

To the Glory of God and the dear memory of Rosa, Countess Poulett this window is dedicated by her loving children.

She rests in hope – Jesu mercy 1916

The memorial to the 6th Earl can be seen to the east of the south door. A large white marble plaque on a black marble surround is hung with drapery on one side. In the pediment is a book, a chalice and a thorny crown, while at the apex is the all-seeing eye. Beneath are the Poulett arms surrounded by bows and swags. In the centre is a handsome portrait in a roundel and an inscription which reads:

To the Glory of God and in ever loving memory of William Henry 6th Earl Poulett born 22nd September 1827 died 22nd January 1899.
    Father in Thy Gracious Keeping
    Leave we now Thy Servant Sleeping.

The eagle lectern made of oak was also given in memory of the 6th Earl in 1911.

A memorial to the 7th Earl, William John Lydston, takes the form of the screen beneath the organ loft, erected in 1918. An oak tablet reads:

To the Glory of God and in Memory of William John Lydston Seventh Earl Poulett. This Screen was erected in token of a Lifelong Friendship by Harry Weller Richards.

The grave of the earl marked by a large table-top monument in an enclosure, may be seen outside the church to the north of the tower. It is adorned with the Poulett arms and the crest of the Royal Artillery. An inscription reads:

In loving Memory of My Husband William John Lydston 7th Earl Poulett born September 11th 1883 – Died July 11th 1918.

His wife Sylvia lies by his side, but her grave is unmarked and has no memorial. Her son the 8th Earl felt unable to pay this last tribute to his wayward mother.

A little way to the east may be seen a simple cross marking the grave of the 8th Earl's half-sister and erected by him after his mother's death. The inscription reads:

Phoebe Amie Sybil Poulett
Born – 25.10.22
Died – 10.5.48

A more recent memorial to a member of the Poulett family is the window at the east end of the south wall, which contains a very beautiful and fine example of modern stained-glass. It was dedicated in 1962 in memory of Countess Poulett, the second wife of the late 8th Earl. The artist was A.E. Buss and he has depicted St Francis of Assisi surrounded by birds and animals to be seen in Hinton Park. In the top lights are swallows, while below can be seen pheasants, a barn owl, a nuthatch, a duck, a heron, a hawk, a sparrow, a pigeon, a woodpecker and a jay. There are butterflies, a squirrel and a young deer. Beneath St Francis are the household pets of Lady Poulett: the Alsatian, the white cat, and the two Dachshunds. Above one of the little dogs are perched the white canary and the budgerigar. The central design, in which may be found the Poulett arms, is surrounded by a garland of leaves and flowers. An inscription reads:

Erected by the VIII Earl Poulett in memory of Olga Lorraine Countess Poulett his devoted and most loyal wife.

The last earl himself is remembered by a memorial dedicated in 1987. It may be seen in the Poulett pew on the north wall over the door. An inscription in gold lettering on a marble plaque reads as follows:

SACRED
To the Memory of
GEORGE AMIAS
FITZWARRINE
The VIII and Last
EARL POULETT
June 23rd 1909 – March 1st 1973
Erected by His Loving Wife
Christine Countess Poulett

The plaque is surmounted by the Poulett armorial bearings in colour.

Also in the church are monuments to four faithful servants of the Poulett family which should be considered. The earliest is situated in the Poulett memorial chapel, high up on the west wall. It consists of a black marble or stone sarcophagus flanked by coupled pilasters and with a pediment above. An inscription reads:

Incorrupta fides nadaq vertias Quando ullum invenient parem BERNARD HUTCHINGS ESQ. By real merit and great industry with perfect honesty made a considerable Fortune by his good nature and prudence, with a quick genius, sound judgement and plain truth raised himself in the esteem of all men from the lowest to the highest. He served his Country faithfully in several publick employments and wherever he professed any kindness was the finest and most generous friend, having the gentlest manners with the bravest mind and for these and other noble virtues is buried in this place amongst the NOBLES of the POULETT FAMILY; having ever been a true friend to the present Earl Poulett and his children who in gratitude erected this Monument to his memory. He was aged sixty five years and died the seventh of October one Thousand Seven Hundred and thirty three.

This is the only monument in the chapel which is not to one of the Poulett family. Bernard Hutchings was a servant and close friend to the 1st Earl Poulett and his family, so close that in his will he left the property he had leased from the estate to members of the family. He is the only person to be interred in the Poulett vault with no immediate family connection.

A monument to a bailiff may be seen on the south wall of the nave. It consists of a marble plaque with a moulded cornice on which stands a brown and grey obelisk supporting an urn. In the centre is a smaller plaque with the following inscribed:

This plate is erected to perpetuate the Memory of John Hellier Esq sometime Lieutenant Colonel of the Somerset Militia and one of his Majesty's Justices of the Peace for this County and son of John and Elizabeth Hellier. He departed this life the 11th day of July 1792 aged 85. He served the Earl Poulett as Bailiff in the year 1730 and continued in friendship with the family to the day of his Death. He gave a piece of Ground in Meriot called Nidons containing five acres to the poor of this parish for the remainder of a term of three thousand years the rent of it to be laid out on St Thomas's Day every year by the Minister and Churchwardens for the time being, in the purchase of Shoes and Stockings.

The third memorial is situated on the west wall on the nave. This comprises a grey marble plaque with a cornice supporting a draped urn. On a scroll is the following inscription:

In the humble yet fervent hope of a blessed immortality through the Atonement of his Merciful Redeemer departed this life THOMAS BEAGLY in his 70th Year on the 14 Day of April 1825 whose long attachment and faithful Services during a space of nearly Fifty Years stands recorded in the last Will and Testament of the fourth Earl Poulett. Ye of all Ages who with Reverence tread, Or lightly roam the Mansions of the Dead; stop and contemplate at this hallowed shrine The awful Change from Mortal to Divine; 'Fight the good Fight', the paths of truth explore, Uprightly walk with Man and God adore.

A further tribute to Thomas Beagly may be seen outside the church on the wall under the east window.

The last memorial to a Poulett servant is the window at the west end of the south wall of the nave. The stained-glass by Clayton and Bell depicts three saints, Dunstan, George and Alphege. It was inserted in memory of Charles Farnham Irish who was bailiff to the Poulett family and connected with the Hinton St George Estate for over fifty-eight years. He was a highly respected and much loved member of the community. He was a churchwarden, chairman of the Parish Council for seventeen years, and acted as a manager and treasurer to the village school for some twenty-one years. He was succeeded by his son, the late Mr Charles Irish, as the last bailiff to Earl Poulett. Their home was the bailiff's house at Vine Cottage near the gates of Hinton House. The family now live at Fords Croft Farm behind Castle Hill.

A brass plaque beneath the window reads:

This window was erected by William Seventh Earl Poulett to the glory of God and in memory of Charles Irish the trusted and faithful servant of the Poulett family for 58 years. 1915.

In the churchyard may be seen other table-top tombs and gravestones commemorating more Pouletts and their servants.

MONUMENT TO SIR AMIAS PAULET – HINTON CHURCH

CHAPTER 13

Poulett Family Portraits and Other Works of Art at Hinton House

The story of the Pouletts whilst alive has been told, and the monuments to the memory of many of those now departed have been looked at. To conclude with, mention must be made of another family collection, the portraits of the Pouletts which hung in Hinton House until the sales in 1968.

Hinton House was always renowned for its collection of paintings and other works of art. In 1812 Horace Walpole visited Hinton House and listed some 100 family portraits which he called 'capital and interesting'. The inventory of 1895 lists no less than 590 separate items of oil paintings, water colours, crayon drawings, etchings and prints. Among them were eight oils by Van Dyck, and the collection included works by Holbein, Murillo, Reubens, Watteau, Rembrandt, Romney and Hogarth. The 1st Earl Poulett (d. 1743) was obliged to petition the sons of Lord Chancellor Clarendon for permission to copy the portraits of his grandparents – full length studies by Van Dyck, which appear to have been plundered from Hinton House during the Civil War and acquired by Clarendon. Permission was only obtained with great difficulty as it was thought the copies would detract from the value of the originals.

The collection has been reduced over the years but in 1968 there was still a large number of family portraits and other notable works of art in the mansion.

Most of the principal paintings are of the seventeenth century with some earlier works of the fifteenth and sixteenth centuries, and there are later paintings of the eighteenth and nineteenth centuries. The collection comprised works of the English, Dutch, Flemish, Italian, Spanish and French Schools.

Family portraits of the Pouletts comprise the greater part of the collection and are of the most interest to this present work.

In 1968 most of the contents of Hinton House, including the pictures and works of art, were consigned to Sotheby's of London to be auctioned. However, after inspection the experts rejected a large amount as being of 'insufficient commercial value' to be sold at their London Gallery. The discarded furnishings and some sixty-six paintings were later sold at Hinton House by the firm of T.R.G. Lawrence & Son. Over half of these paintings eventually went to Georgia, U.S.A. Here they were later studied by an art expert,[1] over a period of nine years. The result of his work has been the discovery of several important works of art among the paintings originally discarded as worthless by the experts in England. They include a work by Van Dyck, others by Sir Peter Lely and Sir Godfrey Kneller. All these have found homes in America. The rest of the Poulett collection is no doubt now scattered around the world.

1. Mr Sammy J. Hardman.

186

The following then is a record of the family portraits and some other paintings offered for sale at Sotheby's and at Hinton House.

Perhaps the most familiar portrait in the house is that of Sir Amias Paulet, the Keeper of Mary, Queen of Scots. It was reputedly painted by Federigo Zucchero, the sixteenth-century Italian artist, who came to England in 1574. He is also said to have painted Queen Elizabeth, and there is a portrait of Mary, Queen of Scots at Chatsworth House, also said to be his work. However, it has been thought doubtful if she actually posed for him as she was under close confinement at that time, but perhaps both the captive queen and her keeper may have sat for Zucchero at some period during her long imprisonment. The painting of Sir Amias is also famous for its colossal carved frame already described.

Three other paintings of the sixteenth century are attributed to the Flemish artist Marc Gheeraedts. One is a portrait of the two elder daughters of Sir Amias Paulet, Joan and Sarah, showing them as children in green dresses with white ruffs. The other two are of George Paulet, the second son of Sir Amias, and George's wife, Elizabeth. She wears a red skirt with a lace overskirt and bodice, and is holding a macaw. Her husband wears a brown and black doublet and hose.

Another well known painting in the house is the large scene entitled 'The Return of the Poulett family from the Wars'; painted during the seventeenth century by an unknown artist (Walpole attributes this painting to Van Dyck), it shows the 1st Baron Poulett reunited with his family after the Civil War, and has already been described in an earlier chapter.

The family of the 1st Baron is represented by several portraits. There are two paintings of his two younger sons, Amias and Francis, both in military dress, and two paintings of his daughters, Elizabeth and Helena, both in white satin dresses, all painted in the style of John Hayls, the English painter famous for his talent for copying Van Dyck. Another painting of Elizabeth by the English School shows her full length and holding a holy picture. Portraits of the third daughter, Susanna, with her negro servant; and her husband, Michael Warton, are painted in the style of the great artist Van Dyck. Portraits of two other daughters – Florence, in gold and pink, holding a dog; and Margaret, in black, and with a dog on a cushion – are attributed to John Hayls. Florence's father-in-law, Sir Hugh Smyth is represented by a half-length portrait attributed to William Dobson, an English painter much influenced by Van Dyck but with a quite different style.

The family of the 2nd Baron Poulett is represented by two portraits of his wife, Catherine Vere, in a head and shoulders study and a full length painting attributed to the prolific English painter Thomas Gibson, though these are probably copies of earlier works since Catherine died while Gibson was still a child. The painting of the 2nd Baron's daughter, Vere, is attributed to Mrs Mary Beale, a distinguished English portrait painter of the seventeenth century, who was employed by many of the most eminent persons of her time. A portrait of Francis Fulford, together with one of his wife, Margaret, another of the 2nd Baron's daughters, have been found to be by Sir Peter Lely. Lely was another prolific portrait painter and at the Restoration he was made principal artist to King Charles II who made him a baronet. There are a great many of his works in private hands.

Yet another daughter, Catherine, and her husband, James Johnston, Secretary for Scotland, have portraits in the style of Mrs Beale. There are portraits of the 2nd Lady Poulett's parents, Horace, Lord Vere and his wife, painted after the Scottish artist J.M. Wright. Their relation John Vere, 16th Earl of Oxford has a portrait attributed to Gibson. Their daughter Mary is portrayed in a green gown in a painting by John Riley, another distinguished artist who painted Charles II, James II, and King William and Queen Mary.

John the 3rd Baron Poulett was painted twice in armour, in the style of Sir Godfrey Kneller of whose work there are attributed some dozen examples in the mansion. Kneller had an unrivalled reputation as a portrait painter and there was hardly a person of note of his time that he did not paint, including Queen Anne, Peter the Great and Louis XIV of France. There is also a head and shoulders portrait of Lord Poulett after the style of William Dobson. John's wife, Essex Popham, is seen posing with a vase of flowers in a painting in the style of the Dutch artist Simon Verelst, famous for his portraits with floral surrounds. There are three paintings of their daughter Letitia, two full length and a head and shoulders study, all attributed to Gibson. Letitia's husband, Sir William Monson, sat for John Riley. There is a portrait of Lady Monson by the Dutch artist Josef Bokshoorn, who had an extensive practice in England.

The 3rd Baron's second wife, Susan or Susanna Herbert is shown in three portraits, two after Kneller, one in a blue dress, and another after Mrs Beale. Susanna was the daughter of the 5th Earl of Pembroke, and there are several portraits here of her family. Philip, 4th Earl of Pembroke was painted by the school of Henry Stone (known as Old Stone) who also painted in the style of Van Dyck. Herbert, a son of the 4th Earl is in the style of Lely. Philip, the 5th Earl of Pembroke was painted in the style of Stone, and the portrait of his wife, Catherine, is attributed to Gibson. Their son, the 8th Earl of Pembroke, was painted in the style of Michael Dahl, a Swedish artist who rivalled Kneller, and both Queen Anne and her husband Prince George were painted by him. A portrait of Charlotte, the daughter of the 7th Earl of Pembroke, is attributed to Gibson. There is also a group of the earl and his family painted by the school of Van Dyck.

John, the 1st Earl Poulett and his family are well represented. The earl himself was painted by Thomas Gibson shown full length in peers' robes of red and ermine. Another painting attributed to Lely depicts him as a young man standing full length with his gun and dog. Yet another shows him with a staff and wearing a blue cloak, and is attributed to Gibson.

A portrait of his wife, Bridgett Bertie, shows her three-quarter length in a gold brocaded gown with a robe of crimson velvet and is by Thomas Gibson. A further portrait of her (recognized in America as being by Sir Godfrey Kneller) shows her as St Catherine in green and purple robes, sitting by a broken wheel and holding a palm branch.

The pictures of their children are all by (or are attributed to) Thomas Gibson. There are two of John, the 2nd Earl, a full length portrait in a red coat with his spaniel, and a half-length study showing him wearing a red coat with a blue cloak. There is a matching picture of his twin brother, Peregrine, in blue and wearing a tricorne hat. Another of Peregrine shows him full length with a garland of flowers and his pet deer. Their brother Vere, who became the 3rd Earl, is represented in two portraits, one as a child in Roman dress feeding a parrot, and another, half-length and again in Roman costume. The earl's fourth son, Anne, is shown in two pictures as a child, one by a fountain, and another, with a matching study of his sister Susan. There are three other paintings of Susan as a child, one three-quarter length with a basket of flowers, and one with a tame squirrel. Another daughter, Bridgett, is shown in a charming study, full length in a green and gold gown with a blue wrap, standing with her pet lamb. (This has been confirmed in America as being by Gibson.) A third daughter, who became Lady Catherine Parker, is shown with her infant son. There appears to be no portrait of the remaining daughter of the 1st Earl, Lady Rebecca. Lady Bridgett's husband, Pollexfen Bastard, was painted by Elizabeth Creed and is shown half-length in a blue coat and a white cravat. Two boys, Edward Bastard and George Parker, are depicted in a pair of portraits attributed to Elizabeth Creed. Miss Creed painted several altar pieces and painted portraits of her friends.

The 1st Countess Poulett's parents, the Honourable Peregrine Bertie and Mrs Bertie, both have portraits painted after Beale. Mrs Bertie, shown holding a spray of citrus blossom, was also painted by Sir Godfrey Kneller. Peregrine is seen again in armour in a painting after Dobson. Henry Bertie, son of Robert, Earl of Lindsey has a portrait by John Hayls.

John, the 4th Earl Poulett was painted by Thomas Stewardson, in military uniform with the Order of the Thistle, and again in a military uniform with a green sash, by James Northcote, R.A., an artist who worked in the studio of Sir Joshua Reynolds for five years before branching out on his own. There are two portraits of Margaret, the 4th Earl's second wife, painted by the artist George Romney, a fashionable portrait painter much influenced by Reynolds and Gainsborough. There are also two silhouette studies of John and his first wife, Sophia.

There appears to be only one portrait of the 5th Earl Poulett, by an unidentified artist, showing him in a black high buttoned coat. There is a portrait of a boy with a pet spaniel which is thought to be his son, Vere, later Viscount Hinton, born in 1822; it is attributed to James Northcote.

The next member of the family represented is Vice-Admiral George Poulett, the father of the 6th Earl. His portrait, signed and dated 1797 by the artist Northcote, shows George as a boy dressed in midshipman's uniform standing on a beach. An unknown artist painted his wife, Katherine Sophia, in a cream dress with a turquoise sash and lace bonnet. Their son, William Henry, the 6th Earl Poulett is shown in his portrait as Master of the Hambledon Foxhounds. He is mounted on a fine horse with his hounds around him. The picture is signed by the artist Harry Hall and dated 1867.

The 6th Earl's son and two daughters, William John Lydston, Eleanor Augusta Rose and Violet Nita, were painted as children in 1887. The picture bears the date and the signature of the artist Sydney Hall.

The last members of the Poulett family to be painted were the 7th Earl, William John Lydston and his wife Sylvia. Their two portraits, now restored to the Gallery in Hinton House, show them in peer and peeresses robes for the Coronation of King George V in 1911. They are signed by the artist Wood.

There are two portraits of the mysterious Elizabeth, Countess of Essex at Hinton House. Both show her dressed in black widow's weeds. In one, a copy by Gibson after the artist William Wissing, she is accompanied by her son in a crimson cloak and her daughter in a blue and white gown. In the other, by the Dutch artist Daniel Mytens, she is alone. Various stories have been told about her but history relates that she was the daughter of William Paulet of Edington, Wiltshire, and a granddaughter of the 3rd Marquess of Winchester. She married Robert Devereux, the 3rd Earl of Essex, but the marriage did not turn out well. A child was born who died in infancy and the mother was accused of adultery. The couple were separated although Elizabeth affirmed that the charges against her were the result of a conspiracy amongst her husband's attendants. Lady Essex is said to haunt Hinton House, appearing in black as in her portraits, shortly before the death of a Poulett. She appeared twice to the late Earl Poulett, then a child of nine, before the death of his father, the 7th Earl. The apparition was also reported to have been seen before the death of his grandfather. It is not known why Lady Essex should be haunting the home of distant relatives.

Mention must be made also of a painting by the Bolognese artist Benedetto Gennari the Younger, who worked at the courts of Charles II and James II between 1672 and 1688. The painting 'The Holy Family' is thought to have been acquired in Rome about 1767, probably by the 3rd Earl Poulett or his brother, the Honourable Anne Poulett. It has an interesting history which has been traced since it left Hinton House. The painting was commissioned by the wife of King James II, Mary of Modena, for her private chapel at St James's Palace. When James was deposed and left the country, Gennari followed to France. The painting was then among many weeded out of the Royal collection as being too blatantly Roman Catholic, although it was the subject of the picture rather than the artist that was disapproved of, since there are still several of Gennari's works at Hampton Court. Gennari returned to Bologna and in a volume written in his own hand entitled *Racolta di Memorie* he described the paintings he had done for Charles and James during his time in England. This memoir is preserved in the *Bibliotheca Communale* at Bologna and from this the origins of the painting have been rediscovered and the date 1682 on it confirms this. It is not known how the painting got to Rome from England.

Among the paintings that reached America are a pair first thought to be pictures of the 3rd Earl Poulett and his wife. These have now been confirmed as portraits of Viscount and Viscountess Torrington by Jeremiah Davidson, who had a large practice in England and Scotland. Another painting depicts the two celebrated dwarfs Richard and Anne Gibson by Sir Peter Lely. Richard was a page to Charles I and was married at court to Anne. They were both only 3 ft 10 in high. This painting had no name or description in the Hinton sale catalogue.

Perhaps the greatest find among the paintings in America is that of Lady Villiers, Duchess of Richmond and Lennox, by Sir Anthony Van Dyck. She is shown in a satin gown with a wide fur collar, and is wearing pearl earrings and a pearl necklace. Mary was an aunt by marriage to Susan Herbert, who married the 3rd Baron Poulett. The painting was sold at Hinton House, described as 'A Stuart Lady' by a seventeenth-century artist. It fetched £80.

Epilogue

And oh! what changes we all know
Long years can bring in one small place
In names and shapes from face to face,
As souls will come and souls will go.

                                William Barnes

In conclusion I would like to bring readers up to date with what has befallen Hinton House and Hinton St George since the Poulett family left in August 1968.

As previously mentioned, the sale of Hinton House and 1,298 acres realized a total of £225,000 and was all over in three minutes. A syndicate bought the whole property and then sold the mansion and its grounds to a business man. The timber went to a property company, while the four farms were bought by sitting tenants. The furniture and paintings realized a further £175,000 in a sale on the premises and several sales by Sotheby's in London. The value of many of the treasures was poorly appreciated, such as the Van Dyck painting which sold for £80.

As soon as the sale was completed, the rumours started to fly regarding the future of the mansion. Hinton House was to be converted to a country club; it was to become another wild life park similar to nearby Cricket St Thomas; it was to be converted to flats, at one time even a Borstal or open prison was rumoured. However, all the proposals were apparently turned down by the local planning authorities and the frustrated owner put the mansion up for sale again.

Hinton House changed hands once more in October 1969 for £20,000. The new owner and his wife had very definite ideas on the future of the house. The stable courtyard was to be converted into craft and antique shops and the rest of the mansion would be restored and opened to the public as a stately home, which would provide a market for the kind of items available in the stable shops. They embarked on a crash programme of restoration. This was very necessary as parts of the house had been badly neglected for years. A large part of the cost of restoration was raised by selling the lead from the roof of the state-rooms and replacing it with corrugated asbestos and roll roofing. The Grand Entrance Hall was given a new ceiling and the walls re-lined. The state-rooms and the Chinese suite were repaired and redecorated, and the main staircase and the Grand Saloon also received immediate attention. A large quantity of Jacobean furniture was purchased to fill the empty rooms, and panelling from demolished Arley Hall in Cheshire was fitted to the walls in the State Drawing Room. Paintings are a necessity in a stately home, and there were gaping holes in the panelling where the Earl had sold his portraits and tapestries. Two artist, Barry Leighton-Jones and Keith English, were commissioned to supply them and moved into some vacant rooms with a friend to carry out the work. After acquainting themselves with the history of the house, a series of portraits of everyone remotely connected with the house from Nell Gwynn to Mary Queen of Scots was produced and installed in the empty rooms. A new version of 'The Return of the Pouletts' showing, rather oddly, Cavaliers riding up to the nineteenth-century

George and Crown Inn

George and Crown Inn – After the fire

west front of the mansion, was placed in the position of the original in the State Dining Room. A special series of paintings (rather inappropriate for their surroundings) and featuring Greek gods and goddesses, was hung in the Grand Saloon in the spaces vacated by the tapestries. Then in June 1970 an announcement in the local press, coupled with a timely appearance of the Ghost of the Gray Lady on the Grand Staircase, heralded the opening of the doors of Hinton House to the general public. The venture was apparently a great success with some 1,000 visitors a week. Teas were served in the old cellars, and there was a pets corner and amusements for children in the grounds. Unhappily the local planning authorities had not been consulted. The narrow lanes leading into Hinton were considered unsuitable for the increased traffic and the numerous signs directing intended visitors which sprouted up on the roads around and in Hinton were not approved by the Historic House Committee of the British Tourist Authority. The result was the closure of Hinton House for good as a stately home after only three months.

After this, planning permission was obtained to convert the whole house into separate units of living accommodation and to sell them privately. The south wing containing the state rooms became one and later two units, very successfully, in that the rooms have not been altered to any great extent. Several of the new paintings may be seen there, but the poorer ones have disappeared to make room for a few Poulett portraits that have returned. The rest of the mansion, while virtually unchanged on the outside, other than the unfortunate loss of the medieval kitchen building, has been drastically altered inside so that hardly any of the original room layout now remains. Much of the interior fittings have also been removed either by the sale or the developer, including the Wyatt bookcases from the library, along with fireplaces, doors and stained-glass. The Grand Entrance Hall has been split up, while the immediate entrance area, together with the Wyatville porch, clocktower and gatehouse form one living unit, the entrance porch having been closed in to make a room. The stable courtyard has been named Brettingham Court and now has some eighteen units around a lawn where the pond used to be. The kitchen yard is now known as Wyatt Court and has eight units, each with a cottage garden inappropriately defining their piece of the mansion. The basement area which led to the old kitchen entrance and storage rooms was filled with rubble and garages were built along the north wall of the courtyard. The old saw-mill became another unit and the saw-mill yard became garages and carports for Brettingham Court. Also gone is the ornamental bridge that formed an underpass beneath the drive from the village for the earl and his guests to pass from one garden to another uninterrupted. During the conversions there were two fires. The first, not very serious as it happened, occurred in the old stables which were being gutted for rebuilding. The second broke out in the south-west wing, destroying several rooms which were almost ready for occupation, including the former family drawing room with its ornate fireplace, the boudoir, and the small dining room, together with all the rooms above on the first floor. For a while it appeared that the entire mansion would be lost, as there was a severe shortage of water which had to be hauled in tankers, while a hose-pipe was run several hundred feet to a stream. The rooms were eventually rebuilt, but not without considerable problems as the developer had been using the proceeds of the sale of each unit to pay for the completion of the next!

So Hinton House has been converted from a huge, nearly empty liability, occupied by only two people part-time, into a series of self-contained homes with all modern conveniences for a large number of mostly retired couples and families. While we may sigh for the old order of things, we can rejoice that the historic mansion for the most part has been saved and is now in the hands of caring private owners for whom it is playing a useful role.

In Hinton Park, unfortunately, thousands of trees have been cut down, including the double row around Diana, and in Broom's Drive Plantation, Terrace Wood, the old Gardens Plantation and many of the rest of the copses and woods. As the trees that supplied the view from the mansion gradually disappear, logs are being hauled into the sawmill that has been established in the park, and huge timber trucks grind along the narrow lanes. Deer, fox, badger, rabbit and hare can still be seen occasionally in the park and even on the mansion lawns, but the clearance and even burning of the decorative shrubs that once abounded in Old Gardens Plantation, has caused a serious reduction in wild life. Harford Lodge, North Lodge and Keeper's Lodge have been restored and occupied. New houses have been built from the remnants at Warren House and Kennel Cottage, now called Harvant House. The old ha-ha has been almost totally filled in.

The statue of Diana – about to fall off her plinth which had been split by a tree growing from the top of it – has been rescued, beautifully restored and reinstated on her plinth in the grounds close to Hinton House. The ancient trees around the house have had care to preserve them for the first time in anyone's memory, and new oaks, limes and cedars have been planted for future generations to enjoy. The lawns at Hinton House are manicured again by owners who can afford – and are dedicated – to maintain the property as it was at the best of times.

As already mentioned in the Prologue, the mansion is playing its part once again with the opening of the Grand Saloon for village activities, re-establishing the traditional relationship between the village and Hinton House. Many lament that Hinton has become a village for the retired and weekenders from London, and that the village is dying for lack of children. This happily was not borne out recently when crowds of children thronged the lawns of the mansion to see three hot-air balloons take off from the grounds!

Hinton St George too, has undergone more changes in the last few years than in the whole of its history. The vacant site of the old George and Crown Inn has been filled with attractive houses which do their best to blend in with the village architecture. The departure of the Pouletts has meant that former building restrictions have gone also. The old kitchen gardens of the mansion at the end of West Street have now been filled with a close of new houses, as has a vacant area off The Green. The wall along Gas Lane opposite the almshouses has been breached, and several modern bungalows built into the park in a most attractive setting. Other bungalows have been built opposite here at the rear of the houses in High Street. New dwellings may be found on the site of Old Farm and on the village outskirts.

Continued advances in the mechanization of agricultural production has cut agricultural employment in Hinton as drastically as anywhere in the nation. Only one working farm remains today where there were six in the village fifty years ago. However, after centuries with a population which had little mobility or choice but agriculture or service on His Lordship's estate, Hinton has found stability and prosperity with incoming residents who came there because they thought it the best village in which to live, in contrast to the villagers and their ancestors, who over the past centuries had had little choice but to remain where they were.

In the village church the Poulett pew and memorial chapel have now been beautifully restored and may be viewed by the public. Regrettably, however, the rich purple upholstery and hangings have been removed from the pew and replaced by a rather dull green.

Since the death of the 8th and last Earl in 1973, his sister Lady Bridgett Poulett-Robledo paid her last visit to Hinton in May 1978. She died two months later on 31 July at her home in Bogota, Colombia, having suffered many years of poor health and several miscarriages. The death was also reported in 1984 of her ex-husband, Luis Robledo, a distinguished Colombian diplomat. It was revealed that they had divorced and he had later re-married. He left a son. Sadly too must be mentioned the death in Ireland of the late earl's only cousin, Major Edward Rhys Wingfield, also in 1984, the last grandson of the 6th Earl Poulett. Another link with the family was severed at the end of 1993 by the death of Frederick James at the age of 90, the lifetime friend of the last earl and his sister.

Christine, Countess Poulett returned to the village from Jersey in September 1987 to attend a service for the dedication of a memorial to her late husband the 8th Earl, and to commemorate the restoration of the church roof, to which Her Ladyship had generously contributed.

So life in Hinton St George continues without its former landlords. Like other attractive places it underwent a boom in house prices over the last few years. Cottages that were exchanged for a few hundred pounds in the 1950s at the time of the sale by the University Estate, have lately realized close to a hundred thousand pounds. The church livings of Hinton, Merriott, Lopen and Dinnington have been amalgamated. The Rectory has been sold and Hinton St George no longer has a resident rector. The present rector lives in Merriott and looks after all four churches and their parishes. The life of the church in the village continues, but with fewer services, while the Brethren Chapel closed several years ago and is now a private house. The village post office in West Street, after operating there for some eighty years, has also closed, the postal business having been transferred to the sole remaining village shop. The Women's Institute has ended after nearly seventy years of monthly meetings and the singing of 'Jerusalem'. It was replaced by the Thursday Club and the Women's Fellowship.

After being one of the first villages in England to have gas, and then losing it many years ago when the earl's gas plant closed down, Hinton now has mains gas again. In some places British Gas found and removed old pipes and installed new ones in the same place.

The modern world has indeed caught up with Hinton St George, nevertheless the old traditions continue. The Men's Institute still meets in the old Reading Room, and despite threats of closure, the village still has its school although the older children travel into Crewkerne. The ancient custom of Punky Night is still observed at the end of October, commemorating, it is said, the search with mangold lanterns by the wives of Hinton for their menfolk who stayed overlong at Chiselborough Fair.

So with a picture in our minds of the darkened streets of the village, with the flickering eerie lights from the 'punkys' wending their way from house to house, we know that Hinton remains basically the same, as we hear the children chant as they have done for longer than living memory:

> It's Punky Night tonight
> It's Punky Night tonight
> Give us a candle, give us a light
> It's Punky Night tonight
> Adam and Eve wouldn't believe
> It's Punky Night tonight.

Postscript 1995 – Some Unsolved Mysteries and Queries

The publication of the first edition of this book in 1976 gave rise to a number of queries from around the world. These came in letters from a variety of Paulets, Pollets, Powlets, Hintons, etc., enquiring if they were related to the family from Hinton St George. They came from America, Australia, France and elsewhere as well as England. It would take half a lifetime to unravel all the complicated relationships to prove their origins. While some without doubt would certainly turn out to be related to our Pouletts, others could have descended from the family of the Marquess of Winchester or others bearing the same name. I have also been told of previously unrecorded illegitimate births in letters from descendants of children of the 4th Earl; the son of the 5th Earl; and a daughter of the 6th Earl (who I have since learned had the reputation of claiming something akin to his '*droit de seigneur*' at every opportunity!).

The Poulett family after the 1st Earl is not on the whole very well documented, and there are several unsubstantiated stories of unknown members of the family. Even the family portraits present a problem. Neglected for so long, the identification of many of the sitters became almost impossible to verify. Artists ascribed to some of the pictures were either dead or unborn when their subjects were supposed to have sat for them! Obviously a number of the paintings were copies of earlier works. I also received many requests for identification of such pictures from their new owners.

Although I have been able to correct some of the stories and legends concerning the Pouletts and their home, several mysteries do still persist. One that constantly crops up is the tale of the untimely death of a son or daughter of one of the earls. The statue of Diana which stood in the middle of the park is frequently said to have been placed there as a memorial to such a lost child who had died of an accident whilst out hunting or riding there. Fred James heard one such story of an earl's son, said to be slightly mad, who met such a fate. A similarly ill-fated daughter is told of in a story recalled by the Reverend Alan Holt.[1] She was supposed to have eloped with her lover against the wishes of her father the earl who disapproved of her choice. When the fugitives were discovered the earl shot the young man dead, causing the girl to die of a broken heart. The story says it is she who appears as a ghost on the Grand Staircase. However, I have discovered no written records or evidence to prove that any of these events ever occurred.

Perhaps the strangest story is that of the late Mr Edward Ryall. He claimed to have lived a previous life in Somerset as one John Fletcher in the seventeenth century. In his book *Second time Around* he tells of his existence then as a farmer, and recalls the Monmouth Rebellion and the Battle of Sedgemoor. Strangest of all he tells of his ill-fated love affair with the beautiful Melanie, the daughter of the 2nd Lord Poulett. Because of her wayward behaviour

---

1. See *East Somerset* – Revd Alan Holt (1986).

her family banished her to Old Basing in Hampshire, where she died of the plague in 1665. The book is full of fascinating historic and topographical detail, much of which has been verified, and of which a relatively uneducated man as Mr Ryall would be unlikely to have been aware. An American psychiatrist, Dr Ian Stevenson, who specializes in these cases, wrote to see if I had any record of Melanie Poulett. Unfortunately we have been unable to verify her existence. It is odd that another of the ghosts said to haunt Hinton House, and who appeared before the death of a Poulett, is that of the Countess of Essex, who came from the Paulet family of Old Basing.

I will close by saying that I have it on good authority that the ghosts of Hinton House have not gone to rest. Mysterious happenings are still experienced in the cellars and elsewhere in the old mansion. Perhaps after all the Pouletts have not left their home and are still very much in residence!

Bibliography

Chapter 1   *The Oxford Dictionary of English Place-Names*
                 The Domesday Geography of South-West England – ed. H.C. Darby and R. Welldon
                 Finn –1967
                 The Fifteenth Century – E.F. Jacobs – 1961 (*Oxford History of England*)
                 The Earlier Tudors – J.D. Mackie – 1964 (*Oxford History of England*)
                 Constitutional History of Jersey – LeQuesne
                 Biographical History of Jersey – G.R. Balleine

Chapter 2   *The Reign of Elizabeth* – J.B. Black – 1959 (*Oxford History of England*)
                 The Letter Books of Sir Amias Paulet – ed. John Morris – 1874
                 The Queen of Scots – Stefan Zweig – 1941
                 Mary, Queen of Scots – Lady Antonia Fraser – 1969
                 Raleigh and the Throckmortons – A.L. Rowse – 1962

Chapter 3   *The Early Stuarts* – C. Davies – 1959 (*Oxford History of England*)
                 History of the Civil War – Clarendon
                 The Addled Parliament of 1614 – T.L. Moir
                 Sir Ralph Hopton – F.T.R. Edgar – 1968
                 Somerset 1625–1640 – Thomas Garden Barnes – 1961
                 Worthy Doctor Fuller – William Addison – 1951
                 The Great Civil War in Dorset 1642–60 – A.R. Bayley – 1910
                 The Earlier Smyths of Ashton Court from their Letters – Anton Bantock 1982.
                 Somerset in the Civil War and Interregnum – David Underdown – 1973

Chapter 4   *Marlborough, His Life and Times* – Winston Churchill – 1933–8
                 The Peace and the Protestant Succession – G.M. Trevelyan – 1934
                 British Politics in the Reign of Queen Anne – Geoffrey Holmes – 1967
                 The King of Hearts – Dorothy E. Somerville – 1962
                 Robert Harley – Angus McInnes – 1970
                 The Backstairs Dragon – Elizabeth Hamilton – 1970
                 Queen Anne – David Green – 1970

Chapter 5   *The Political Journal of George Bubb Dodington* – ed. John Carswell and Lewis A.
                 Dralle – 1965

Chapter 6   *Correspondence of George, Prince of Wales* – ed. A. Aspinall

Chapter 7   *The Winter Kings* – Ivor Herbert and Patricia Smyly – 1968
                 A Race Apart – Reg Green

Chapter 10   *Smile, Bow and Pass On* – Grace W. Phillips – 1980

Chapter 11   *The Age of Inigo Jones* – James Lees Milne – 1953
                 Buildings of South and West Somerset – Nikolaus Pevsner – 1958
                 Memoirs of a Professional Architect – Sir John Soane

Country Houses of Dorset – Arthur Oswald – 1959 edition
Biographical Dictionary of Architects 1660–1840 – H.M. Colvin – 1954

Chapter 12   *Churches of Somerset* – A.K. Wickham – 1965
The English Way of Death – Julian Litton – 1991
Dictionary of British Sculptors 1660–1851 – Rupert Gunnis
English Church Monuments – Katherine A. Esdaile – 1946

Chapter 13   *Bryan's Dictionary of Artists and Engravers* – ed. George C. Williamson – 1918
Lord Poulett's Paintings in America – Sammy J. Hardman – 1978

General   *Dictionary of National Biography*
Burke's Peerage
Debrett's Peerage
The Complete Peerage – ed. H.A. Doubleday – 1945 edition
History of Somerset – Collinson – 1791
A Genealogical History of the Families of Paulet, Berewe, Lawrence and Parker – Charles A.H. Franklyn – 1963

Other Printed Sources consulted

Hinton House, Hinton St George – An Architectural Study – John and Jane Penoyre – 1989
Report on Poulett Burial Vaults – J.W.S. Litton – 1981 and 1986–7
Notes on Hinton St George – collected by Dorothy Lowe and Lauretta Martineau, and subsequent edited edition by W.G.C. Gundry – 1951
Poulett Manuscripts – at County Record Office, Taunton
The Poulet Family in Jersey – A.C. Sarre (Societe Jersiaise)
Notes and Queries of Somerset Archaeological and Historic Society – at Taunton Castle
Matthias Lock – J.F. Hayward – *Connoisseur* – December 1960
Art at Auction 1968–69 – ed. Philip Wilson
Sir Amice Poulet's Monument at Hinton St George – Earl Poulett – in *Baconiana* – January 1948
Saltram – Nigel Neatby – 1971 (The National Trust)
The Saltram Collection – 1967 (The National Trust)
The Victoria County History of Somerset – ed. R.W. Dunning
A History of Somerset (1978 and 1983) – R.W. Dunning
Paulet Pedigree – compiled by Arthur H. Holman
Report of the Committee of Privileges of the House of Lords – The Poulett Peerage – The British Museum
The Land Roll – January and February 1895
Catalogues of Sale of Hinton St George Estate, 1968 – Messrs. Knight, Frank and Rutley
Catalogue of Sale at Hinton House, 1968 – Messr. T.G.R. Lawrence & Son, Crewkerne
Catalogues of Sales, 1968–9, Messrs. Sotheby & Co. London
Files of *The Western Gazette,* Yeovil
Various national newspapers and magazines
Letters from Lady Bridgett Poulett-Robledo and Sir Nikolaus Pevsner
Letters and Memoirs of Frederick James, Salisbury

Index of Names

Index of Places